Why India Ne

D0489915

Presidential System

Bhanu Dhamija is the founder and chairman of the Divya Himachal Group, the largest newspaper publishing company in Himachal Pradesh, India. Earlier, in America, Dhamija founded a media company that published trade journals and organized conferences for the magazine publishing industry, becoming in effect a 'publishers' publisher'.

He was born in Bulandshehar (UP) in 1959, but has lived almost half his life in the United States. After attending Punjab University in Chandigarh, he acquired a postgraduate degree from the Stern School of Business at New York University. He has worked in the financial, computer and media industries in the US and India. While in the US, Dhamija married an American and soon after they moved with their three children to Dharamshala in Himachal Pradesh.

Why India Needs the Presidential System

BHANU DHAMIJA

HarperCollins *Publishers* India

First published in India in hardback in 2015 by
HarperCollins *Publishers* India

Copyright © Bhanu Dhamija 2015

P-ISBN: 978-93-5136-346-0
E-ISBN: 978-93-5136-347-7

2 4 6 8 10 9 7 5 3 1

Bhanu Dhamija asserts the moral right
to be identified as the author of this work.

The views and opinions expressed in this book are the author's own and the facts are as
reported by him, and the publishers are not in any way liable for the same.

HarperCollins *Publishers*
A-75, Sector 57, Noida, Uttar Pradesh 201301, India
1 London Bridge Street, London, SE1 9GF, United Kingdom
Hazelton Lanes, 55 Avenue Road, Suite 2900, Toronto, Ontario M5R 3L2
and 1995 Markham Road, Scarborough, Ontario M1B 5M8, Canada
25 Ryde Road, Pymble, Sydney, NSW 2073, Australia
195 Broadway, New York, NY 10007, USA

Typeset in 10.5/14.5 Aldine401 BT
By Saanvi Graphics Noida

Printed and bound at
Thomson Press (India) Ltd.

To all those who care for India

Contents

Preface

A great society is languishing. The citizens of India have access to a pathetic quality of life and discredited institutions. The result is a morally weak populace. Rather than lament or just comment, I decided to do something concrete. I moved back to India after living in the US for nearly two decades and launched a daily newspaper for the community in which I was going to live. The thinking was that the ideas and exposure that my newspaper brought would change public opinion. It probably did. But the rot, I realized, was much deeper than just a lack of awareness. This hardened my resolve and the result of that process of churning is this book. India is my only cause. I have no political, ideological or party affiliations.

This book is an attempt to save India. With each passing day, the current system of government in India is doing irreparable harm by killing people's initiative and destroying their moral fibre. The book offers a prescription, not just a diagnosis. It is no lecture, but a heartfelt effort to heal India of its ailments. That the treatment is not a new invention is reassuring. I do not ask the reader to follow me, but the much wiser founders of the American system. Whatever else ails that society, my study convinces me of the efficacy of their system of government.

I am thankful to HarperCollins for publishing this controversial book, and to its highly professional yet kind-hearted editors. For bringing me to them, I am forever grateful to Kanishka Gupta, a literary agent with a divine eye. As I was about to lose faith in the face of many rejections, Kanishka was a godsend. The doyen of India's political analysts, Kuldip Nayar, gave me invaluable advice; and the political rising star Shashi Tharoor provided tremendous words of encouragement. I am indebted to both. I also thank my newspaper colleagues – chief editor Anil Soni and columnist and editorial advisor, Prof. N.K. Singh, for their suggestions and encouragement. My deepest gratitude is owed to my wife, Lisa, who read through shoddy first drafts without showing any loss of respect or love for me.

Bhanu Dhamija

Dharamshala
March 2014

1

The System of Government Matters

Confucius came upon a woman who was weeping bitterly by a grave. 'Your wailing,' said the Master, 'is that of one who has suffered sorrow on sorrow.'

'O Master that is so,' she replied, 'once my husband's father was killed here by a tiger, my husband was also killed and now my son has died in the same way.'

The Master said, 'Why do you not leave the place?'

She paused. 'There is no oppressive government here,' she answered.

'Remember this, my children,' the Master said, 'oppressive government is more terrible than even tigers.'[1]

All history has shown that governments can indeed be horrific. Countless many have lost their lives in resisting or escaping oppressive governments. Behind every revolution there is tyranny of one form or another. And behind every violent protest lies an injustice left unaddressed by government.

The system of government under which man lives is fundamental to his being. It affects man more than anything else. From his material well-being to his spiritual development, the state touches everything. What he eats, how large his family is, what information he gets, what he thinks, how he expresses himself, the kind of work he does, the type of entertainment he enjoys, whether he prays, how he worships – government impacts everything. Government is behind every evil in society, and every virtue. It shapes a society's character. A good

1

government allows individuals to become honest and virtuous; a bad one makes them wicked and corrupt. A system of government, therefore, isn't simply a matter of man's prosperity or liberty, it is also a matter of his morality.

'The Constitution of the United States,' said Thomas Jefferson in 1801, 'has committed to us the important task of proving that a government ... can be so free as to restrain [man] in no moral right, and so firm as to protect him from every moral wrong.'[2] The system they invented was mindful of man's dignity and decency; it strived to provide an impetus for right actions but protection from wrong ones.

In the more than 200 years since its adoption, and the many successes of the nation, the American system has shown that the vision of its founders was not only moral but also practical. The Americans are no better or worse than any other people. They have made their share of mistakes and have faced many of the same ordeals as the rest of the world: a bloody war for independence, a brutal civil war, two world wars, a great depression, a cold war, and several regional conflicts and recessions. This small nation of thirteen colonies that went up against the mighty British Empire wasn't born with a silver spoon in its mouth. Contrary to what many believe, it wasn't rich, or homogenous, or literate, or anything special. It acquired its wealth and power through centuries of hard work.

The only thing unique about the United States of America is its system of government. This system is the secret behind America's success. In order to understand that assertion let us consider what a good political system ought to be.

WHAT'S IN A SYSTEM?

A nation's political system must foster a national vision, ensure fairness and encourage participation. When a nation has vision, when its citizens' efforts are fairly rewarded and when there are opportunities for participation, the nation rises.

A people need to see where they are going and why. When there is no national vision, the society remains unmoved. It is never sure what the government's agenda is and for what reasons. The process of developing a national agenda is crucial for both its quality and its implementation. If it emerges from the masses, after openly debating competing proposals across the entire nation, it becomes the people's agenda, not something that is of interest to politicians.

Similarly, without fairness in the political system there is no hope for building strong character in people. Political fairness must precede social and economic fairness. It is not possible for a society to be fair if a faction cannot have fair representation in government. By the same token, it is not possible for the economy to be impartial if groups or individuals are barred from public contracts or licences. Once a system becomes politically unfair, it destroys any chance of social and economic equality.

The nation's political system must also provide a genuinely participatory democracy. Not just one where people simply vote, but one in which they feel they have equal opportunity. Otherwise, every area – sciences, arts, sports, business, etc. – becomes mired in politics. Those who are politically connected receive opportunities, others shrivel. If one needs a godfather to enter politics, or to run for office one has to make back-room deals with party bosses, or to get the government's attention one has to become partisan, these factors act as a strong disincentive for society-wide participation. Limited avenues for political participation only help the haves become more and more powerful. Without equality of opportunity, a society's drive and creativity fades.

India's current system fails to deliver any of these three ingredients. The failure of India's system is more profound than it appears because it does its biggest harm in not fostering a national vision. Without a nationwide election for the topmost government official, a national agenda doesn't emerge from the bottom up. The oligarchs at the top render the entire system in the hands of a few. The people don't participate, beyond just voting in frustration. No vision, no character and no true participation.

Churchill once said, 'It's a wicked thing to take away a man's hope.' What's most worrisome about India's system is that it has killed hope. Today, a common man in India doesn't believe that this system can ever change. It is sapping people's energy and killing their initiative. In 2002, when the National Commission to Review the Working of the Constitution reported that 'maladministration has paralyzed the creative energies of the people,'[3] it was only half right. Because the chief failing of India's Constitution was that it created hopelessness.

Within the binary of the Presidential vs Parliamentary systems of governance, it must be asked: how does the US system deal with these issues?

FOUR LAWS OF POWER

History has shown that the taming of power is behind every good government. When powers are unfettered, governments become abusive. When they are too restrained, governments become timid. And when powers are poorly assigned, governments tend to be ineffective.

Power can be said to have four laws. First, as expressed by Lord Acton, 'power tends to corrupt, and absolute power corrupts absolutely'. Second, power consolidates when it is more than essential. Third, power dissipates when it is less than sufficient. And fourth, power cooperates only when it can be encroached. If the powers are properly assigned, government serves the people; otherwise, it becomes useless, or worse, it becomes their master.

About how power corrupts, it turns out that Lord Acton was right, but not because, as he said, 'great men are almost always bad men.'[4] Power corrupts only when the system allows it. In a column entitled 'The Psychology of Power',[5] two university researchers recently concluded that 'power corrupts, but it corrupts only those who think they deserve it.' The researchers were investigating whether power corrupts, or whether it merely attracts the corruptible. They discovered that not only do people with power tend to think they can get away with it, but also 'they feel at some intuitive level that they are entitled to take what they want'. In other words, people in high office are not innately corrupt; they become so because the system gives them an elevated sense of their worth, and an opportunity. It is therefore not the politicians, but the system that is to blame.

The other three laws of power were first confirmed by James Madison, the Father of the US Constitution. He had undertaken an exhaustive analysis of confederacies that existed in the three thousand years preceding. 'It is a melancholy reflection,' he had noted at the end of his study, 'that liberty should be equally exposed to danger whether the government have too much or too little power.'[6] What Madison had found was that governments failed to serve not only when they were too powerful, but also when they were too weak. A strong government was as necessary as a non-oppressive government. And the trick was to balance the powers just so.

As for the fourth law, which states that two powers cooperate only when each can encroach upon the other, there were two further conditions. One, the encroachment must be limited. In other words, a power must not be able to completely overwhelm the other. And two, the limits of infringement must be precisely defined. When Madison and his colleagues began to think about their system of government, they concluded that simply separating or unifying their government's departments was not going to work. Madison declared that 'unless these departments be so far connected and blended as to give to each a constitutional control over the others, the degree of separation … essential to a free government, can never in practice be duly maintained'.[7] In short, separation of powers in government works only when its departments are also given powers to infringe.

Methodically, the American Constitution makers addressed all four power-related problems. To deal with power's tendency to corrupt, they separated powers. As Jefferson declared, 'the way to have a good and safe government is not to trust it all to one, but to divide it among the many'.[8] For the basic problem that their national government was too weak, they did the opposite. They bolstered its powers. Then, to ensure that it didn't become too strong and tyrannical, they set up a system of powerful state governments. Each government, national and state, was assigned only limited and essential powers. And finally, to solve the problem of cooperation, they created a system of 'coordinated' departments through checks and balances. This gave each department certain constitutional rights over the others.

No other framers of a nation's Constitution ever had more experience than the fifty-five men who gathered in Philadelphia in 1787 to make the US Constitution. They already had first-hand experience with fifteen different Constitutions – the British; their own decade-old first Constitution, the Articles of Confederation; and the thirteen different Constitutions of the colonies that were joining together to form the United States.

As for India's system of government, this book shows how its powers are severely and irreversibly out of balance (Chapter 7). And why a US-type system will deliver better governance and a healthier polity if applied to India (Chapter 11). The Indian system began to break down almost immediately after Independence, because the powers of its two topmost officials were poorly defined.

When it came to prescribing powers, the Indian system got almost everything wrong. It concentrated powers at the Centre, farthest away from the people. It centralized them in one institution, Parliament, giving it supremacy. Since power consolidates when more than essential, this created an oligarchy. On the other hand, the Indian system diminished the powers of state governments, the organ closest to the people. Here, since power dissipates when it is less than sufficient, governance on the ground suffered. What made matters worse was that the parliamentary system's design was ill-suited to separate powers to begin with, because it didn't have separate institutions. With no separation of institutions, the question of giving one power of encroachment over any other, in order to check or balance it, had no meaning.

BRITISH SYSTEM IS DECEPTIVELY ATTRACTIVE

The Indian Constitution makers did not really understand the subtle power play of the British parliamentary system. This was most evident in the Indians' view of the monarchy. The framers of India's Constitution felt that a king wasn't essential to the system and that they could do with an 'elective monarch'. They were wrong on both counts. A non-partisan institution in whom were reposed all powers was a crucial part of the system. The system of a constitutional monarchy didn't fit in with a pure republic. And as Walter Bagehot, Britain's famous constitutional scholar had cautioned, 'you might as well adopt a father as make a monarchy'.[9]

In fact, the entire British system was deceptively attractive. Almost every one of its constitutional principles was something different on the inside than its appearance. It wasn't a system controlled by the legislature as it was made out to be. In reality, the hegemony of the king in this system had been replaced by the hegemony of the Cabinet. The government controlled the legislature. As Sir Ivor Jennings had noted, 'The theory is that the House controls the Government. ... The truth is, though, that a member of the Government's majority does not want to defeat the Government.'[10] The British system promised 'responsible' government, but in reality government under this system worked in secret. It spoke of 'popular' government, but a parliamentary government could be run only by a faction. It professed 'collective' responsibility of ministers, but it was impractical since it was up to the Cabinet to own a minister's decision. It boasted coalition governments, but the system fell apart when the number of parties was any greater than two. In the name of efficiency, it created an oligarchy. Sir Sidney Low, also a renowned British constitutional authority, had described these and other similar features of his nation's system as its 'fantastic attributes'. In the same vein, Bagehot had said of his nation's Constitution: 'An observer who looks at the living reality will wonder at the contrast to the paper description.'[11]

To make matters worse, India was an unsuitable nation for the British system. It had none of the ingredients necessary for the parliamentary system's success. By definition, the parliamentary system was a sectarian government, while India's severest problem was a sectarian divide. This system needed no more than two non-sectarian parties. It needed a polity in which there was no permanent majority. It needed a society that was deferential. As stated earlier, it needed a monarch. It needed a small homogeneous nation with no religious controversy. It was a system fit for a unitary state, not a federation. And it required a bureaucracy that was apolitical. As early as 1934, after a review of the factors necessary for the success of parliamentary government, the British themselves declared: 'In India none of these factors can be said to exist today.'[12]

SYSTEM ADOPTED FOR POOR REASONS

The truth is that the Indians adopted the British parliamentary system for poor and unsubstantiated reasons. Vallabhbhai Patel, the first leader to attempt a justification of this system in India's Constituent Assembly, could come up with only one reason: familiarity. 'It would suit the conditions of this country better to adopt the parliamentary system ... with which we are familiar,' he said.[13] Nehru, who almost single-handedly picked this system of government, never really bothered to explain his choice in the Assembly. The only clue to his thinking came when he was compelled to respond to the members' demand that the topmost official of the country, the president, be directly elected. Refusing to accept their request, he said, 'We want to emphasize the ministerial character of the Government that power really resided in the Ministry and in the Legislature and not in the President as such.'[14]

Ambedkar was the chief defender of the parliamentary system, but he came on the scene only after the decision to adopt this system was already taken, and he lacked credibility. For years, and to the moment he was appointed chairman of the Drafting Committee, he had always opposed this system. Only seven months before his stint with the

Assembly, Ambedkar had declared that 'there is no doubt that the British type of executive is entirely unsuited to India'.[15] To one of the subcommittees of the Assembly he had proposed forming a 'United States of India', with some features similar to a US-type presidential system of government. Ambedkar's justifications of the parliamentary system were all made *after* the Assembly had voted in its favour.

In return for his support in the Assembly, Ambedkar drew many benefits. He was appointed law minister in Nehru's interim government. As a known Gandhi hater, he was able to play a role in denying Gandhi any say in the making of India's Constitution. He was also able to obtain reservations for his constituents, the scheduled castes. Scheduled castes were the only group granted reservations in the original Constitution. As law minister, he was able to push the Hindu Code Bill, an omnibus measure to reform personal and property laws, but only for Hindus. And, of course, he was appointed chairman of the Drafting Committee.

But Ambedkar's love for the parliamentary system quickly disappeared. Within three years after the adoption of the Constitution, he would become the first framer to disown this system. During a debate in the Rajya Sabha in 1953, he said: 'My friends tell me that I have made the Constitution. But I am quite prepared to say that I shall be the first person to burn it out. I do not want it. It does not suit anybody.'[16]

In the Constituent Assembly, Ambedkar had alluded to two main benefits of this system, that it provided 'more responsible' governments and a 'strong centre'.

This book exposes how these benefits were more than just unrealistic, they were impracticable. More importantly, the Constituent Assembly did not examine or adequately debate how concentration of powers in a Central government created a 'strong' government. What made a national government 'strong' in a large diverse nation, a union based on willing participation of units or one based on force?

ONE MAN'S DECISION

These and other similar questions were never really debated in the Constituent Assembly. The decisions were made by a coterie of the Congress party. In fact, it turns out that they were really made by one man – Jawaharlal Nehru.

The choice for the parliamentary system was a fait accompli a decade before India's independence. It seems Nehru had made up his mind in 1937. It was then that the British had allowed the first Indian-only governments in the provinces. The Congress party under Nehru's leadership had won an overwhelming majority and formed Congress-only governments. Nehru refused to share powers with Jinnah and his Muslim League followers because this system of government allowed one faction to rule. Jinnah declared that he was 'irrevocably opposed to … a majority-community rule … under the guise of democracy and a parliamentary system of government'.[17] But Nehru did not relent. Within three years, the movement for a separate state of Pakistan went from a mere academic thesis to an irreversible political demand.

Nehru was the chairman of two all-powerful committees – Experts Committee of the Congress party and the Union Constitution Committee of the Constituent Assembly – that put India firmly on the path of adopting the parliamentary system. Once these two committees had decided, the selection became immutable; not that powerful leaders didn't try to change Nehru's mind.

One of the astonishing stories about the making of India's Constitution is that in a joint meeting of Nehru's Union Constitution Committee and Patel's Provincial Constitution Committee on 11 June 1947, Nehru was asked by a resolution to reconsider his decision to have the president elected by the legislature, instead of directly by the people, but he refused to do so.[18] Years later, one of those in attendance in the joint committee meeting, K.M. Munshi, would write that 'when the protagonists' [of direct election of the president] view gained their point, those who were opposed raised a protest that the Joint Committee had no power to bind the Union Committee by its decision.'[19]

Nehru's refusal to reconsider led to a major split between Patel and Nehru. Patel's committee had approved that the chief executive of state governments, the governor, be elected directly by the people. Patel's adoption of this hallmark principle of the presidential system was even approved by the full house. But the Assembly would later be compelled to drop this feature because it didn't fit in with the Union Constitution. This was the Assembly's only major reversal. When it came, Patel wasn't in attendance.

Patel, Ambedkar and Jinnah were not the only ones who recommended a different system of government. The Father of the Nation, Gandhi, did too. Instead of the parliamentary system, Gandhi wished for a system based on village panchayats. He wanted to develop a Constitution of India that was entirely its own rather than a copy of the British. 'If India copies England, it is my firm conviction that she will be ruined,' he had written. In 1930 Gandhi had noted that it was 'very difficult to get rid of our fondness for Parliament'[20] But he was totally ignored. This was a telling difference between the framing of India's and the United States of America's constitutions. While India's framers ignored the father of their nation, the US framers cajoled theirs to ensure that he participated in their Constitutional Convention. George Washington had retired after long service to his nation, but not only was he invited back to sit in the Convention, he was also elected the first president of the United States under the new Constitution. America would have had a very different Constitution, if not for Washington's presence during its making.

Nehru and his men could ignore everyone else because India's Constituent Assembly was an unabashedly packed house. It was owned by the Congress party and Nehru was its unquestioned leader. The Congress controlled more than two-thirds of the seats. Ambedkar was the first to declare that it 'holds this House in its possession'.[21] But that wasn't all. The framing of India's Constitution occurred in a blatantly partisan fashion. Decisions were made in party meetings outside the Assembly and then whips were issued to Congressmen to vote along party lines. If any member tried to push unauthorized amendments, he was compelled to withdraw. Many acknowledged in the Assembly that they were not free to speak or vote their mind. If a member so much as raised the issue that the Congress party was issuing whips, he was heckled. 'This august House has a total of 303 members at present,' said a member, '...the Congress party controls 275 votes and if members of the party are to follow the ukase, there is no chance for any other opinion to prevail.'[22] This was an astonishing way to make a Constitution, unprecedented in any republic in the history of mankind.

As India's Constitution was being adopted, it was quite evident that it had failed to inspire. Nearly a third of the members rose to criticize it in the Constituent Assembly itself, but no one rose in praise of the parliamentary system. Members used words like 'farce', 'deception', 'façade', 'queer', 'unwholesome', 'futile', 'misfortune', and 'lifeless' to describe the document. One said, 'Democracy of this country has yet to be realized, and certainly not in this Constitution.'[23] Another said, 'According to me, parliamentary democracy is not democracy at all.'[24] Another commented, 'If the present Constitution can be described in a nutshell it is one intended to fit in with the present administration.'[25] Even a member of the Drafting Committee came forward to criticize the Constitution's 'over-centralization', calling it 'entirely repugnant to a free democratic Constitution'. He also revealed how the Drafting Committee was 'only asked to dress the baby'.[26]

When some members praised the Constitution's adoption of adult suffrage, its abolition of untouchability and its ending of princely India, one member couldn't hold it back: 'After all, what have we done so as to deserve this self-praise and mutual congratulations,' he asked. Kamalapati Tiwari, a Congressman, went on to chastise the Assembly: 'If you had not included these broad features in the Constitution, what else would you have included in it? We shall have reason for self-gratification only when the nation praises us,' he said.[27]

It was the parliamentary system that had received the Assembly's most scathing criticism. And to the surprise of many, it was delivered by a Congressman. Ramnarayan Singh, a member of the Bihar Legislative Assembly, had come forward to speak his mind regardless of the consequences. 'This parliamentary system of government must go,' he had screamed. 'It has failed in the West and it will create hell in this country.'[28] As a man of experience, he argued that 'it will develop surely into the party system of government' and that 'strikes at the very root of democracy'. 'In the presidential system of government it is easy to find one honest president,' he said, 'but it is not so easy to find an army of honest ministers.' In a similar vein, another member had thrown Ambedkar's own words back at him, that 'it is wiser not to trust the legislature to prescribe the forms of administration'.[29]

WORSE THAN THE BRITISH

The Indian version of the parliamentary system was worse than even the British. Its extreme centralization of power had most in the Constituent Assembly deeply worried. Speaker after speaker scorned this aspect of India's system, even as they voted to adopt the Constitution. Many worried that it had the makings of a dictatorship; some even likened it to the situation in Germany that gave rise to Hitler. 'Not that I do not want a strong central government,' said one, 'but just contemplate for a moment what is likely to happen if another Hitler were to arise and take charge.'[30] Others worried that the concentration of power would cause corruption and kill people's initiative. A senior Congress leader and a member of the House Committee, H.V. Kamath, said that this system was nothing but 'a centralized federation with a façade of parliamentary democracy.'[31]

Even in its original form the British system was elitist. It was designed for oligarchs to rule, not for multitudes to self-govern. In the guise of creating a government that was strong, it created one that was autocratic. As Bagehot once said, in the British system a government could 'despotically and finally resolve'.[32]

One would expect the Indians to know better than anyone else the true nature of the British system. It was evident as early as the 1700s. In 1783, an India Bill, which would have completely reorganized the British East India Company, as it was found guilty of incompetence and mismanagement in handling the affairs of India, was passed in the

House of Commons by a two-to-one margin. The Bill provided for a seven-member governing board responsible to Parliament. But it was rejected by the House of Lords because King George III declared that he would regard anyone voting in its favour as his enemy.[33] Such examples had continued to the days of Nehru. Twice during the early 1900s, the British people had voted in a government of the Labour Party, due largely to its platform of 'Dominion status for India'. Both times the government was brought down by the Conservative Party, which held a permanent majority in the House of Lords. If the 1924 government of Prime Minister Ramsay MacDonald had been allowed a full term, India's partition might have been avoided. His bill to create a Commonwealth of India was introduced in the Commons – it only went through one reading before his government fell – a decade before the idea of Pakistan was even born.

Gandhi was the one Indian leader who clearly understood how arbitrary the British system really was. 'Your democracy is a superficial circumscribed thing,' he had told the British Secretary of State in 1932. 'My whole being rebels against the idea that in a system called democratic one man should have the unfettered power … To me this is a negation of democracy,' he said of the British system.[34] But in the making of India's Constitution he was completely sidelined.

Not only did Nehru and his men adopt this system of arbitrary rule, in their version they made the centralization of powers even worse. A promised Instrument of Instructions which would have delineated powers between the president and the prime minister was purposefully dropped from the Constitution. This left the president at the mercy of a more popularly elected prime minister. As such, arbitrary use of power by the latter quickly became a matter of routine. Although skirmishes between Prime Minister Jawaharlal Nehru and President Rajendra Prasad never became public, the one-man rule, that of the prime minister, began within days of the Constitution's adoption. A system with two elected top officials – Sir Ivor Jennings had called it a 'hazardous experiment'[35] – failed almost immediately. Within the first year, Nehru would threaten to resign three times, and each time he acquired more powers. By late 1951, the concentration of powers was complete. Nehru was prime minister as well as the president of the Congress party, and Prasad a mere figurehead president.

Subhash Kashyap, a constitutional scholar wrote recently of how completely Nehru controlled the system: 'I believe that if Jawaharlal Nehru had been India's first president and Rajendra Prasad its first prime minister, our political system would today be more presidential than parliamentary without any change in the Constitution.'[36] Although inaccurate – the structure of the Indian system is entirely different from that of the United States – Kashyap's comment illustrates how the Indian system was open to power grabbing by an individual.

Nehru believed that he knew what was best for the nation. As such, he felt that his views deserved to reign supreme. He was attracted to this system because it offered all the trappings of aggrandizement. It provided the wherewithal for one man to prevail.

ABSOLUTE FAILURE

But no single man, or even faction, can always know what is best for the whole nation. A good system of government must ensure that even the minority views have teeth. Each view must not only have the opportunity to be aired, it must also have a chance of being adopted as policy. In this, India's system was a total failure. In the end, it failed even Nehru. His China policy was a one-man show. When it led to war and brought India a humiliating defeat, Nehru was exclusively responsible. And the frequently touted parliamentary benefits of 'responsible government' and 'collective responsibility' were nowhere to be seen. Nehru remained in office, and his defence minister, Krishna Menon, faced only a small demotion. But it was clearly ominous that the system had failed in the making of vital national security policies for the nation.

This inherently arbitrary system continued to fail the Indian people. Within twenty-five years of its adoption, and as many in the Constituent Assembly had warned, the system turned into a brazen dictatorship. In the mid-1970s, Prime Minister Indira Gandhi all but extinguished India's democracy with her Emergency. India's system allowed a leader of the political party, who came to power with less than 44 per cent of the votes, to rule the entire nation single-handedly from her residence. She had a puppet president issue a proclamation within hours. Cabinet wasn't even informed, making a mockery of 'collective responsibility'. She put thousands in jail, razed homes, allowed torture, imposed censorship, curtailed liberties and denied fundamental rights. 'Repression would be piled upon repression,'[37] as Granville Austin, the famous constitutional historian, would write. She had already replaced the Chief Justice of India with a pliant judge, superseding three others who were senior. She passed laws for personal benefit. She amended the Constitution with retroactive effect. She decided on her own what Constitution the nation was to have, pushing through amendments that removed every semblance of separation of powers. Nani Palkhivala, a famous constitutional scholar, could only beg the Indians to awaken 'before the light goes out of the Constitution'.[38]

Indira Gandhi's reign exposed in no unmistakable terms that in the parliamentary system it was impossible to hold the Constitution supreme, or have a truly independent judiciary, or practise genuine federalism. Parliamentary supremacy trumped them all. The government controlled the president, the legislature, the governors and the justices of the Supreme Court. It had unlimited powers to amend the Constitution. The Supreme Court ruled one way or another depending on the political winds, on whether or not the Constitution had an untouchable basic structure. In 1951 (Sankari Prasad) and 1965 (Sajjan Singh), the court held that there were no restrictions on the amending power of Parliament, but in 1967 (Golaknath), in 1973 (Kesavananda) and again in 1980 (Minerva Mills), it declared the opposite. Today, the Constitution is presumed to have an immutable basic structure, but no one can say with authority what it is. The Constitution, however, still stands with Indira Gandhi's forty-second amendment that there shall be no limitation whatever on the constituent power of Parliament.

The two most fundamental changes in the balance of power made by Indira Gandhi – the president compelled to act as advised and removal of the judiciary's power to safeguard the Constitution's basic structure – still remain. Succeeding governments retained these features, in the name of parliamentary supremacy.

A single centre of power, however, was not this system's most menacing failing. There were two others that were even more so: it fragmented Indian society and it produced inadequate leaders.

The system rewarded fragmentation of political parties because it handed power to party bosses. Factions began to form their own political parties almost from the very beginning. But the practice mushroomed after 1969 when Indira Gandhi split the Congress party for the first time in its eighty-four-year history. Then, when she delinked the holding of national and state elections in 1971, even small-time state leaders started brandishing their own outfits. The number of parties in India grew from roughly seventy in the first general election in 1952 to 900 in 2007. This had two terrible outcomes: the nation's legislature became utterly unrepresentative since members got elected by only a small fraction of the voters (some as few as 17 per cent); and the governments became progressively weaker because in this system, as Arun Shourie, the famed political analyst has pointed out, 'every puny "leader" is king'.[39] Blackmailing and corruption to gain support in parliament became rampant. Unsurprisingly, governments would be horribly unstable. Of the thirteen prime ministers since Independence, six would last for less than a year.

As for the quality of leaders, the picture was clear from the very beginning. Nehru noted that 'third-rate individuals were being chosen on grounds of caste and sub-caste'[40] as he prepared for the first general elections in 1951. This system is incapable of producing visionaries who can move people to do big things, because they are elected by winning small elections. All representatives are chosen in small constituencies where elections are won by caste or other small-picture considerations, or by corruption. They are hardly the type of leaders needed to inspire more than a billion diverse people. This system can even plant an individual at the topmost seat of power who has never won a popular election, not even a small one. Such was the case with India's former prime minister.

High-handed, questionable practices didn't end with Indira Gandhi's Emergency; they continue to this day. The Parliamentary system still installs puppets as president. It still allows the majority to amend the Constitution to suit its needs. Governments continue to pass laws without considering minority views and without much debate. They still have a free-for-all in launching populist measures, at times right before elections in a blatant effort to buy votes. Due to a lack of oversight, this system is still fraught with corruption. Prime Minister Rajiv Gandhi declared almost three decades ago that 'the fence has started eating the crop'.[41] Corruption scandals have rocked almost every single parliament.

This unicentric system is also the main culprit behind India's awful judicial system. Until 1993, the prime minister continued to have an exclusive control over the appointments of judges, but since then India has a system of judges appointing and promoting themselves. Either way, there was no accountability.[42] The combination of a centralized system of courts and only one master accountable to no one, created one of the world's most irresponsive and corrupt systems of justice. Today, it has more than 30 million cases pending in its high courts and subordinate courts.

The most troubling failure of India's system is this: 'More lives have been lost due to internal insecurity than in the five wars India has fought since independence.' This was reported in 2010 by Ashok Mehta, a retired major general of the Indian Army.[43] Far from settling violent insurgencies that existed at the time of Independence, like Kashmir and Assam, India has only managed to begin several new ones. A Maoist insurgency, in one form or another, is now reported to have 'presence in 20 of the 28 states' according to *The Wall Street Journal*. Punjab, West Bengal (Gorkha), Andhra, Telangana, and Rajasthan

(Maru), are some of the other states where armed rebellions continue to fester.

India's system has failed to provide people with basic security also because the politicians and criminals have become indistinguishable. More than 20 per cent of India's legislators have a criminal background. In 2007, the Central government actually pleaded in the Supreme Court that convicted criminals be allowed to stay in the legislature, or the government could fall. Recently the Indian government even attempted to shield political allies from criminal prosecution by issuing a mere ordinance.

Poor governance and lack of internal security prove more than anything else that India's system is an utter failure in its federal structure. India has pseudo-federalism. The state governments are irresponsible because they are not independent. In making and enforcing laws, in delivering justice, in managing their finances and in exercising internal security, they have enough dependence on the Central government to provide them with excuses.

Genuine federalism has eluded India because the parliamentary system is unfit for a federal set-up. For two good reasons: it has no institution like the US Senate that provides equal representation to state governments; and it allows the Centre to dissolve state governments. The latter is contrary to a basic principle of federalism: that an independently elected state government is responsible only to the people. As for the Rajya Sabha, the parliamentary system was unsuitable, by definition, to have two equally powerful elected assemblies. Since the entire basis of this system was that a popularly elected legislature controlled the executive, it was unviable to have two assemblies appoint the same executive. One had to be dominant. In England, the House of Lords worked only as long as it had the monarch's backing. After the democratic reforms of the 1800s, and especially the Parliamentary Act of 1911, it was defenceless against the House of Commons. In India, the Rajya Sabha is no bulwark of states, also because now the members no longer need to be residents of the state they represent. But what really makes a travesty of federalism in India is that governors are 'agents of the Central government', according to a former governor himself. [44]

This forceful centralization of the system has created a fundamental problem for a diverse nation. It has denied Indians recognition of their deep-seated regionalism. Gandhi once said: 'As the basis of my pride as an Indian, I must have pride in myself as a Gujarati ... Otherwise, we shall be left without any moorings.'[45] Federalism is not only necessary to nurture regional diversity, it is also essential for good governance. For, it is amazing what man can do to a place, if he considers it as his. While giving people autonomy, all a system in India needed to ensure was that no region or sect could infringe on the rights of others or its minorities. Even the British Cabinet Mission Plan of 1946 had suggested such a system.

And since more than the essential powers were granted to the Centre, following the second law of power, they consolidated. India turned into a brazen oligarchy of political party bosses. As this book shows, and as A.G. Noorani, one of India's most respected constitutional scholars, noted: 'They control everything.'[46]

WILL MODI FIX THIS FAILED SYSTEM?

It is ironic that Narendra Modi came to power by running a presidential-type campaign. Months before campaigning for the 2014 election actually began, Arun Jaitley, a Modi confidant, had declared that the 'next year's election will be somewhat like a Presidential election'. It was 'because people want a better leadership,' he had said.[47]

During the campaign, and beyond, Modi didn't just copy the style of American presidential elections, he also imitated the messages of some US presidents. President Ronald Reagan's famous quip 'government is not the solution to our problem; government is the problem,' probably gave Modi his leading slogan, 'minimum government, maximum governance'. Similarly, President John Kennedy's great line, 'Ask not what your country can do for you, ask what you can do for your country,' perhaps influenced one of Modi's main messages: 'mera kya, mujhe kya (what about me, what do I get), this attitude has ruined our nation'.

As we go to press Modi has been in power for about seven months but people's misconception that he is governing the nation in a presidential style continues. Of course, nothing could be farther from the truth. He has inherited a system of government that allows him to be all powerful and that is in line with most Indians' false impression of the US presidency.

It is too early to say whether Modi will do anything to fix India's system. But the signs are not promising. First of all, there are good reasons why Modi wouldn't even bother. The existing system permits him to amass powers to his heart's content, and the current circumstances only encourage him to do so. Then there are the day-to-day pressures of meeting ultra-high expectations – which Modi himself raised – allowing him no room in his packed agenda.

Once again the people of India have placed all their hopes in one man. They were in such a state of despair after the utter failure of the previous government that at the first ray of hope they became frantic Modi supporters. They saw a competent and incorruptible leader with good experience and quickly decided to give him carte blanche. His presidential style, nation-wide campaign on the message of good governance made supporting Modi a no-brainer. The people readily reposed their trust in Modi, thinking, as they have done before, that the nation can only be saved by a 'strong' leader.

Of course, one man cannot consistently deliver wise governance. We have seen this happen throughout history, in small nations and large, that monocracies become corrupt, complacent and bereft of good ideas. Yet in India, this fallacious reliance on a 'strong' leader continues. When recently a leading Indian commentator, Tavleen Singh,was ridiculed for criticizing some of Modi government's initial actions, she quickly corrected the 'wrong impression', by calling Modi 'India's only hope for a better tomorrow'.[48]

It is not advisable to leave the fate of 1.2 billion people in the hands of one man. Nor is it practical that one person alone, no matter how good, can run a diverse and large nation like India. There is a world of difference between running a state – which was Modi's entire experience – and leading a union of states that are led by fiercely independent parties. But since no one has shown the people of India a better alternative, they continue with this erroneous thinking that 'strong' leadership means a government that can act autocratically.

Thus far, Modi is running a monocracy. He makes all major decisions himself, sometimes overruling even his cabinet colleagues. Even worse, almost all decisions have been taken through executive actions or ordinances, bypassing parliament. Without public debate or opposition's involvement, Modi has granted himself more and more powers. He diluted the opposition's role in selecting the chief of CBI, India's investigative agency already notorious for its political control; he abolished the Planning Commission, a sixty-year-old institution heavily involved in central fiscal controls and replaced it with a mere think tank; he increased limits on foreign investments in the insurance industry; he seriously enhanced government's powers to acquire private land, and so on. Only one major decision – changing the method of appointing judges – has been sanctioned by parliament. But this too only enhances the government's role. Modi's use of ordinances has exceeded more than one a month; his government has been labelled the 'Ordinance Raj.'[49]

People are applauding this skirting of parliament because India's system is so broken that in their view it is not allowing Modi to fulfil his promises. Modi has majority control only in the Lok Sabha, so the Rajya Sabha is not cooperating. And as usual in both Houses, the opposition is more interested in disruption than dialogue. Also, the system is no longer suitable for a single-party majority. For decades India's central governments were made up of coalitions of smaller regional parties; they are not easy to dislodge from power. Then there is this constant campaigning in state elections, in which Modi is the only draw; that doesn't leave him any time to devote to parliament.

Because the system is incapable of delivering, Indians are relying on Modi to make good decisions. That is faith, not wisdom. His decisions maybe good, for a while and in some areas. Having more representative control over the appointment of judges, or more government control over fiscal policy, or less politics in the selection of the director of CBI, or a more investment friendly climate, or faster implementation of land based projects, etc., are perhaps smart decisions. But there can't be any doubt that had these decisions emerged out of a good system, they would be smarter and easier to implement, for they will be based on a wider consensus.

India, as well as Modi, needs a better system. One that is based on decentralized institutions under the direct control of the people. Changing the man at the helm doesn't change the system. Unfortunately, due to the reasons cited above, Modi is unlikely to make changing the system his priority. It came as no surprise when a leading newspaper columnist, Pratap Bhanu Mehta, recently reported, 'There has not been a single major gesture by the government to restore institutional credibility.'[50]

The irony is Modi himself would benefit from a better system, especially if it was based on presidential type institutions. If he held the office of the presidency he would be better able to set a national agenda rather than get bogged down in states' politics. He could then focus on all important matters like international relations, national security and investment climate. He would become more effective in changing cultural attitudes, for example towards women or cleanliness. He would be able to speak for all Indians with respect to communal harmony. Sheltering some of his party's MPs who have a Hindu agenda is hurting his credibility. Modi will be free to choose for his cabinet people with experience and credibility, rather than politicians.

A presidential-type, federal structure will also help Modi deliver good governance on the ground. Independent state governments empowered by direct elections and taxing authority would behave more responsibly. They would become accountable for governance in areas that affects people the most – law and order, education, health, public records, welfare schemes, etc. Modi wouldn't have to control state governments through funds, or through stooges in the form of governors; each state's people would do so themselves. This will fulfil Modi's own promise of true federalism.

Also, a presidential-type legislature would behave, because the members can be kicked out every two years. They can be held more accountable for delivering on a legislative agenda. Since the opposition would have a say, the laws would be better. Coming out of a wider consensus, they would be more acceptable to a greater percentage of the population. The judiciary would also improve because people's representatives would have a say in selecting judges.

All this would produce better leaders for the present, and for tomorrow. More cooperative centres of power – in states, cabinet, legislature and judiciary – give more people a chance to show their mettle. Party bosses, and political dynasties, would disappear because candidates would be chosen through primary elections.

And this perhaps is the overarching reason why Modi would be reluctant to change the system, especially to the presidential type. That form of government empowers the opposition; Modi is known for decimating it. There is a telling story about how effective Modi is in eliminating all opposition. In 2011 when I had a chance to discuss with L.K. Advani his feelings about India adopting the presidential system (see chapter 13 for more) one of his remarks was, 'It is not necessary to have the presidential system, you can deliver even in the existing system; look at Modi in Gujarat.' That was of course before Advani was deposed, by Modi, as the next in line to become a BJP prime minister.

I shudder to think what India's fate would be if Modi, the nation's last best hope, doesn't alter the system for the better. Let us assume he succeeds in providing good governance for a very long time, but if in the process he further centralizes the system and destroys all opposition, where would India find the next Modi?

FAILED IN PRINCIPLE

It is astonishing that the Indian system actually negates the parliamentary system's most sacred principle, that of legislative control of the executive. In India, the government's control over the legislature is absolute. And the party bosses control the government. As a result, this system continues to make bad laws. Since lawmakers are the same as law enforcers, they make or implement laws to suit themselves. No one is interested in the quality of laws because in this system legislators are not allowed to legislate. Only laws introduced by government have any chance of passing; those in majority must vote in favour and those in opposition must vote against, especially after the anti-defection laws of the 1980s.

Since there is no oversight over government, it runs amok. The opposition has no teeth. It can make speeches in parliament but it has no powers to stop a government action or to investigate. Governments can pass harsh or unfair laws, make them effective retroactively, or launch fiscally irresponsible programmes, or abuse police and investigative agencies with impunity. The brazen abuses of authority with preventive detention laws or with CBI investigations by the Central government, and of police and state vigilance authorities by states, have become commonplace.

The Indian system brandishes the fusion of executive and legislative as an efficient mechanism. In India's history, only one government had to resign because it lost a no-confidence motion. Without separate institutions to check each other and without oversight powers, there can be no responsible government.

Similarly, 'collective responsibility' has become meaningless since a government in a comfortable majority cannot be taken down, and one in a coalition can always disown a minister's decision. The idea behind 'efficient government' was to deliver to the executive a quick response, in support or against, from people's representatives, not, as they have become in India, a rubber stamp. This is the chief reason behind the ineffectiveness of Indian governments. The parliamentary principle of debating the opposition, designed to make an informed decision on governmental action, has also become meaningless, since decisions are already made before they are brought to vote. Since the opposition has no powers, every legislative fight is nothing but politicking. Also, the principle of 'popular government' is not so in reality, because an

Indian government is a factional government representing only about half the people. Even in the 2014 elections, the Bharatiya Janata Party won 31 per cent of the vote share and the National Democratic Alliance together won 38.2 per cent. With that it formed the largest majority government in two decades. That this unprincipled system has failed should come as no surprise to anyone.

'Has the Constitution failed?' Palkhivala asked this question in 1979.[51] The answer was as clear then as it is today: yes. We have only to remove its 'sacred' veneer and our nationalistic pride, and look at the bare facts. As Palkhivala said, 'The peacock must not be replaced as the national bird by the ostrich.'

In 2009, a justice declared in India's Supreme Court that 'the whole government machinery is corrupt, whether at the Centre or in the States'.[52] 'Even God will not be able to help this country,' he said. Two years later, Rahul Gandhi, the Congress party's youthful leader called the Indian system 'rotten'.[53] In 2013, as soon as he was elevated to the number two position in his party, he declared: 'The answer is not to run the system in a better way, but the answer is to completely transform the system.'[54] Arun Shourie has already declared that 'for 15-20 years now, we have been attending the elongated funeral rites of the parliamentary system'.[55] Similarly, another political commentator, Pratap Bhanu Mehta, has recently written, on behalf of India's Parliament: 'Dear Citizens, I write to you, my creators, to put me out of my prolonged agony.'[56]

AMERICAN SYSTEM IS A SOUND MODEL

When at the height of the recent global financial turmoil a television interviewer asked Warren Buffet, America's well-known billionaire, if he was worried about his country's revival, he immediately replied, 'No, because we have a great system that works.' Two years later, in 2011, in his famous annual report to his company's shareholders, Buffet wrote: 'The prophets of doom have overlooked the all-important factor that *is* certain: Human potential is far from exhausted, and the American system for unleashing that potential – a system that has worked wonders for over two centuries despite frequent interruptions for recessions and even a Civil War – remains alive and effective.'[57]

Americans have such confidence in their system[58] not just because it has passed the test of time – it has been in operation for 225 years – but because it is just. America's founders devised their system on the principle that 'a coalition of a majority of the whole society could seldom take place on any other principles than those of justice and the general good', in the words of Madison.[59] They ensured that this system was *not* run by a faction.

'In the American model of constitutionalism, everything that could lead to concentration of power was avoided,' Klaus Von Beyme, director of Political Science Institute at the University of Heidelberg, wrote in his 1987 book *America as a Model*. 'The American system was seen as a variation on the British,' he noted, 'that had set itself the target of ironing out the supposed degenerations of the Westminster model, such as the Cabinet system and the type of political parties.'[60]

The Americans came within a hair's breadth of adopting a British-style system. In six different votes in their Constitutional Convention, they voted in favour of a president controlled by the legislature; once even unanimously. But in the end, they rejected the British system so completely that they ended up inventing one that was starkly different. Their biggest rejection was with regard to legislative supremacy. They had seen first-hand its ineffectiveness, but more importantly, its corruption. Madison agreed with the French political scientist Montesquieu that 'there can be no liberty where the legislative and executive powers are united in the same person, or body of magistrates'.[61] They also rejected the British model because, as Beyme noted, 'They did not believe that a "republican" imitation of England's monarchist Constitution was possible.'[62] The Americans were similarly unequivocal about their rejection of the idea of a Cabinet. They wanted their president to be completely responsible; 'leave no screen of a council behind which to skulk from responsibility', said Jefferson.[63]

The Americans' most consequential rejection of the British system was with respect to majority rule. 'When a majority is included in a faction,' Madison wrote, 'the form of popular government … enables it to sacrifice to its ruling passion or interest both the public good and the rights of other citizens.'[64]

When the fifty-five men set out to frame the US Constitution, they were given the nation's approval on one condition: the independence of state governments must be maintained. This became the basis of their federalism as well as their entire system of government. The other key principle that these men followed was that the national government must be limited. It must have only those powers that are necessary. Their aim was to create a 'strong' but 'safe' national government with an underlying principle that less government is better. They took very seriously their belief that individuals have 'inalienable rights' upon which no government can infringe.

Just as important was the significance of good executive distilled from the American experience with fifteen different Constitutions. Government, after all, was what touched the people, and that was the executive, not the legislature. As governor of his state of Virginia, Jefferson noted that 'if … the legislature assumes executive and judiciary powers, no opposition is likely to be made; nor, if made, can it be effectual'.[65] He had also experienced (not just as the head of his state government but as the US ambassador to France) that the size of the executive mattered. He wanted one man responsible. Any form of a 'plurality, however promising in theory, is impracticable with men constituted with the ordinary passions', he wrote.[66]

The Americans' chief accomplishment was to devise a system that stopped a majority from taking hold of the entire system. Madison knew that 'causes of faction are … sown in the nature of man' and that the system must involve the 'spirit of party and faction in the necessary and ordinary operations of the government'.[67] But he also knew that the system must safeguard against 'mischiefs of faction' and their 'schemes of oppression'. To do this the makers of the US Constitution not only divided powers among the various government institutions, they also divided the people's representatives in government. That meant having a greater number of representatives per citizen, selected from constituencies of varying sizes and divided among the various branches of government. And all of them directly elected, so that they were accountable to the people, not to each other.

What is most instructive for India in this scheme is that it avoids the pitfalls of small elections. The definition of constituency varies for each representative. A city council legislator is elected by a portion of the city, a mayor by the entire city, a state legislator by a few counties and the state's governor by the entire state. Similarly, for the national legislature, Americans directly elect a member for the House of Representatives from a portion of the state, but the entire state selects its two senators. And then, of course, the president is elected directly by the entire nation. This avoids the formation of easy factions, but more importantly, it safeguards against 'the vicious arts by which elections are too often carried', as Madison noted.[68] The US system *is* strikingly different. It has many unique features: its approach to limiting the role and size of government, the famous separation of institutions and powers, coordination of departments through checks and balances, federalism, direct elections, usage of people's representatives directly in each branch of government, bi-level judiciary, the concept of judicial review, the usage of political parties as policy factions rather than ruling factions, the concept of responsible government utilizing both daily institutional and electoral checks, its mid-term elections every two years, two equally powerful legislatures, stable governments, its independent bureaus to manage the economy and internal security ... the list goes on.

In the following pages I have endeavoured to show how the presidential system removes almost every defect of the Indian system and polity. How it delivers better governance and a healthier polity. Since it relies more on local governments, it provides more responsive and accountable administration and better laws. Even in the areas of the parliamentary system's most touted benefits, responsibility and efficiency in government, the presidential system prevails. An American government aims to serve people, not rule them.

This is not to say that the American system doesn't have problems. This book also addresses its main criticisms. They mainly fall into two areas: responsibility and deadlock.

Deadlock is, in fact, the most repeated criticism. However, both assertions – that deadlocks are bad and that US governments are prone to paralysis – are erroneous. For governments have no right to act when there is no consensus of the people. Instead of locking separate institutions into paralysis, the US system really provides a constitutional mechanism to break deadlocks, rather than creating a constitutional crisis like the Indian system.

This commonly held myth that US governments become paralysed due to its separation of powers between the legislative and executive wings was debunked once and for all in 1991. In his famous work *Divided We Govern*[69] published that year, David Mayhew, a professor of government at Yale University, showed that in a forty-five-year period various US governments passed 'landmark acts about as frequently per year in "divided" as in "unified" times.' The same was true for Congress's launching of investigations of the executive. Mayhew did so again in his 2011 book, *Partisan Balance*[70], by showing that over the last sixty years the US system produced largely majoritarian outcomes without any bias towards any party. Still, every once in a while, new voices are raised in America expressing their frustration with the system's seeming inability to act quickly. A recent book, entitled *It's Even Worse Than It Looks*, blames one party, the Republicans, for America's recent explosion in partisanship. The authors, Thomas Mann and Norman Ornstein, argue that there is a mismatch in the US between 'political parties which have become as vehemently adversarial as parliamentary parties, and a governing system that, unlike a parliamentary democracy, makes it extremely difficult for majorities to act.'[71] However, he argued that this is precisely the strength of the US system. As Beyme noted, 'the presidential system offers better protection against arbitrary acts by the majority'.[72] A majority in this system cannot act alone for long; they must hold back until there is a broader consensus among the people. This invariably produces better decisions.

Usually the performance of the American system depends on the quality of leadership of the president. When a president can articulate a vision well and act in a non-partisan fashion, when he is a master of the art of campaigning as well as the art of governing, he accomplishes big things. A president of the United States must have the ability to inspire people, the astuteness to make compromises and the skills to be a good administrator. That is a tall order. But since this system produces worthy leaders, through gruelling nationwide direct elections, America has had many such presidents.

The all-important US presidency has created the wrong impression that the American system is prone to authoritarianism. The US president is powerful, but not because of his office. It is due to his nation. His office, in fact, is one of great responsibility. The Americans didn't select a system of a single chief executive to grant him all authority; they did so to assign him all responsibility. As we shall see, the presidential system cannot turn authoritarian. Unlike India with its history of the Emergency, in more than 200 years of its history, the US system has never even been accused of showing authoritarian tendencies.

A question is often raised: What about a semi-presidential system like that of France? There is the usual admonition that it hasn't met the test of time. France is already on its so-called Fifth Republic since its Revolution, which was roughly at the same time as the American Revolution. Charles de Gaulle pushed through the current Constitution of France in 1958 replacing the one that had been in operation for only a decade.

But there is a more cogent answer as to why hybrid systems don't work. Professor Douglas Verney, who studied the world's systems of government in the 1950s, explained: 'There has been an attempt to introduce something of the "responsibility" common to parliamentary systems,' he wrote, '[but] the President may be unaffected by such a procedure and it then becomes an ineffective weapon in the hands of the Assembly. If he *is* affected, then the system becomes parliamentary and the attempt to create a separate Executive has failed.'[73]

WE THE PEOPLE MUST ACT

The presidential system was best suited to India at the time of Independence. The Indian people were desperate for genuine self-rule, and also to forge a nation. After the prolonged but highly moral nature of their freedom struggle, they had a profound feeling of nationhood. For the first time in their long history, deeply divided Indians were feeling united. As the constitutional historian Granville Austin noted, 'the forces for unity operating in the country were stronger and more numerous than the forces against unity'.[74]

It would have been an ideal time to establish a federal system; especially because India was coming together as a large and diverse nation. India could only be governed properly by local administrators who were directly accountable to the people. Various communities wanted recognition. They wanted control over their governance. It was a perfect opportunity to give local governments the responsibility for day-to-day administration, while keeping national issues such as defence, foreign affairs, communications, money supply, etc., at the federal level. This is exactly what the US system does. This was also what the British had suggested in their Cabinet Mission Plan. But in the guise of building a strong government, Indian leaders chose a centralized, unrepresentative version of the parliamentary system. They forgot that the strength of a nation comes not from a forceful government, but from a willing people, willing to behave as one.

Wisdom is in admitting mistakes. That also is the necessary first step towards fixing them. We can fix our rotten political system. There is no doubt now, even in the minds of the so-called common men, that our existing Constitution has failed us. In a recent online survey asking whether or not India's Constitution has failed (conducted by the author's Divya Himachal newspaper group on its website divyahimachal.com) respondents said 'Yes' by a two-to-one margin.

India's Constitution is not sacred. In fact, no book or document ever is, no matter how fanatical the following. 'I may point out that the Constitution which we frame is not an end by itself,' Nehru said in the opening days of the Constituent Assembly, 'but it would be only the basis for further work.'[75] Patel categorically declared that 'this Constitution is for a period of ten years'.[76] At the end, facing an Assembly less than inspired by the Constitution, Nehru noted: 'A Constitution, if it is out of touch with the people's life aims and aspirations, becomes rather empty. If it falls behind those aims, it drags the people down ... there is no permanence in Constitutions ...'[77] Two centuries ago, Jefferson asked, 'Can one generation bind another, and all others, in succession forever?' 'I think not. The Creator has made the earth for the living, not the dead.'[78]

The Indian Constitution is completely out of touch with our aims and aspirations. It is stunting our growth. It is making us corrupt and impotent. Let us change this faulty system. Consider these words from America's Declaration of Independence: 'Whenever any form of government becomes destructive to these ends – life, liberty, and the pursuit of happiness – it is the right of the people to alter or to abolish it.'

Our nation is in peril. And it is We the People who must come forward to change this system, because our leaders have a vested interest in the status quo. We the People must come forward, because we must leave our children a brighter future and a greater nation.

NOTES

1   'The Taming of Power,' Russell, B. (1961), *The Basic Writings of Bertrand Russell*, New York: Simon & Schuster, p. 664.

2   Padover, S.K. (1939), *Thomas Jefferson on Democracy*, New York: Mentor Book, New American Library, Hawthorn Books, p. 66.

3   Kashyap, S.C. (2004), *Constitution Making Since 1950*, Delhi: Universal Law Publishing Co., Vol. 6, p. 299.

4   http://www.acton.org/research/lord-acton-quote-archive, accessed 8 March 2014.

5   *The Economist*, 21 January 2010.

6   Madison to Jefferson, 10 October 1788, Madison, J. (1900),*The Writings of James Madison, comprising his Public Papers and his Private Correspondence, including his numerous letters and documents now for the first time printed,*Gaillard Hunt (ed.) New York: G.P.

Putnam's Sons, Vol. 5, accessed from http://oll.libertyfund.org/ title/1937/118854/2400578 on 8 March 2014.

7   Madison, J., Alexander Hamilton and John Jay, (1787-88), *The Federalist Papers*, No. 48, retrieved 13 February 2011, from The Avalon Project, Yale Law School: http://avalon.law. yale.edu/ subject_menus/fed.asp

8   Padover, op. cit., p. 62.

9   Bagehot, W. (2007), *The English Constitution*, Charleston, SC, USA: BiblioBazaar, p. 50.

10   Jennings, I.W. (1961), *The British Constitution*, London: Cambridge University Press, p. 78.

11   Bagehot, op. cit., p. 49.

12   Report of the Joint Committee on Indian Constitutional Reform, cited in Noorani, A.G., 'Constitution Today,' *Frontline*, 13 February 2010.

13   *Constituent Assembly Debates*, 15 July 1947.

14   Ibid., 21 July 1947.

15   'Memorandum to the Subcommittee on Fundamental Rights', 24 March 1947; Rao, B. S. (2006), *The Framing of India's Constitution*, Vol. 2, Delhi: Universal Law Publishing, pp. 84–104.

16   Shourie, A. (2009), *Worshipping False Gods: Ambedkar, and the Facts Which Have Been Erased*, New Delhi: Rupa & Co., p. 386

17   Rao, Op. cit., Vol. 5, p. 28.

18   Minutes of Joint Committee Meeting of the Union and Provincial Committees, 11 June 1945; Rao, ibid., Vol. 2, p. 612.

19   Munshi, K.M. (1997), *The President Under the Indian Constitution*, Mumbai: Bharatiya Vidya Bhavan, p. 24.

20   Chatterjee, D.K. (1984), *Gandhi and Constitution Making in India*, New Delhi: Associated Publishing House, p. 71.

21   *Constituent Assembly Debates,* 17 December 1946.

22   Ibid., 31 May 1949.

23   K.T. Shah in Constituent Assembly, 17 November 1949.

24   Mahboob Ali Baig Sahib Bahadur in Constituent Assembly, 30 December 1948.

25   P.S. Deshmukh in Constituent Assembly, 5 November 1948.

26   Syed Muhammad Sa'adulla in Constituent Assembly, 21 November 1949.

27   *Constituent Assembly Debates,* 23 November 1949.

28   Ibid., 5 November 1948.

29   Z.H. Lari in Constituent Assembly, 8 November 1948.

30   N.G. Ranga in Constituent Assembly, 17 November 1949.

31   *Constituent Assembly Debates,* 19 November 1949.

32   Bagehot, op. cit., p. 197.

33   Carey, George W., and James McClellan (eds) (2001), *The Federalist (The Gideon Edition),* Indianapolis: Liberty Fund, accessed from http://oll.libertyfund.org/title/788/108729/2275182 on 11-09-2011.

34   To Sir Samuel Hoare, 11 March 1932; cited in Shourie, A. (2009), *Worshipping False Gods,* p. 236.

35   Pandit, H.N. (1974), *The PM's President: A New Concept on Trial,* New Delhi: S. Chand & Co, p. 74.

36   'Clash of Titans that Strengthened India,' *The Times of India,* 23 January 2010.

37   Austin, G. (1999), *Working a Democratic Constitution: A History of the Indian Experience,* New Delhi: Oxford University Press, p. 309.

38   'The Light of the Constitution,' 22 October 1976, in Palkhivala, N. A. (2009), *We, The People,* New Delhi: UBS Publishers, p. 201.

39   Shourie, A. (2007), *The Parliamentary System: What We Have Made of It, What We Can Make of It,* (henceforth PS) New Delhi: ASA Publications, Rupa & Co, pp. 29, 36.

40   Malhotra, Inder, 'The First Vote Cast,' *The Indian Express,* 20 March 2009.

41   Austin, op. cit., p. 645.

42   A recent government effort to establish a National Judicial Appointments Commission is mired in a tug of war with the judiciary. The proposed commission is an attempt to bring some balance to the process of appointments.

43   'Standing Up to India's Enemy Within,' *The Wall Street Journal,* 25 February 2010.

44   L.P. Singh, cited in Austin, op. cit., p. 574.

45   Quoted in Chandra, Bipan, M. Mukherjee and A. Mukherjee (2008), *India Since Independence*, New Delhi: Penguin Books, p. 151.

46   Noorani, A.G. (2010), *Constitutional Questions & Citizens' Rights*, New Delhi: Oxford University Press, p. lxii.

47   In a lecture on 'India 2020 - Challenges Ahead' in New Delhi, 24 August 2013; http://www.dnaindia.com/india/report-next-election-will-be-like-presidential-contest-arun-jaitley-1879376

48   'A Misconception,' *The Indian Express*, 4 January 2015

49   *The Indian Express*, 8 January 2015

50   'The Centre We Need', *The Indian Express*, 1 January 2015

51   Palkhivala (2009), op.cit. pp. 41–43.

52   Justice B.N. Agarwal. See, Noorani, A.G., 'Talking Judges', *Frontline*, 25 February 2011.

53   *The Indian Express*, 17 April 2011.

54   Ibid., 20 January 2013.

55   Ibid., 18 September 2012.

56   Ibid., 29 November 2012.

57   Berkshire Hathaway Annual Report 2011.

58   Rise of movements such as Occupy Wall Street or We Are the 99 Percent are demonstrations of how Americans continue to have faith in their system. As Ezra Klein of the *Washington Post* reported, 'These are not rants against the system… It's not that 99 percent of Americans are really struggling… It's that 99 percent of Americans sense that the fundamental bargain of [their] economy - work hard, play by the rules, get ahead - has been broken, and they want to see it restored.' ['Who Are the 99 Percent?', *Washington Post*, 4 October 2011]

      The movement made its impact. In the 2012 presidential election fixing income inequality became a top campaign issue. It was a stellar example of how a grass-root campaign can suddenly emerge in this system, without any organization or a leader, and change the national agenda.

59   *The New York Times,* 19 June 2011.

60   Beyme, K.V. (1987), *America as a Model,* New York: St Martin's Press, p. 15.

61   Madison, J. et al, *The Federalist, No. 47*.

62   Beyme, op. cit., p. 36.

63   Padover, op. cit., p. 35.

64   Madison, J. et al, *The Federalist No. 10*.

65   'Notes on Virginia', Jefferson, T. (1904), *The Works of Thomas Jefferson*, Putnam's Sons (libertyfund. org), Vol. 4.

66   Padover, op cit., p. 59.

67   Madison, J. et al, *The Federalist No. 10*.

68   Ibid.

69   Mayhew, D.R. (1991), *Divided We Govern*, New Haven, CT, USA: Yale University Press, p. 80.

70   Mayhew, D.R. (2011), *Partisan Balance: Why Political Parties Don't Kill the U.S. Constitutional System,* Princeton, NJ, USA: Princeton University Press, p. 168.

71   Mann, Thomas E. and Norman J. Ornstein (2012), *It's Even Worse Than It Looks*, New York: Basic Books, Perseus Group, p. xiii.

72   Beyme, op. cit., p. 62.

73   Verney, D.V. (1959), *The Analysis of Political Systems*, Chicago, IL, USA: The Free Press, p. 56.

74   Austin, op. cit., p. 144.

75   *Constituent Assembly Debates*, 22 January 1947.

76   Ibid., 29 April 1947.

77   Ibid., 8 November 1948.

78   Padover, op. cit., p. 68.

2

British System Was Deceptively Attractive

When the Indians began framing their Constitution in 1946, the parliamentary system had already been a work in progress in England for more than seven centuries. The evolution of parliament was excruciatingly slow, spread over a thousand years of England's bloody history. They developed it in fits and starts, being visionary at times, but mostly being expedient and opportunistic.

The parliamentary system developed due to a desire to take powers away from a monarch and give them to parliament. In the end, the country went from being ruled by the hegemony of king to an oligarchy of Cabinet.

The British parliamentary system was deceptively attractive. Almost all of its constitutional principles were specious. It portrayed itself as a system controlled by an elected legislature, but was in fact run by the executive. The parliamentary government worked in secret. It professed the collective responsibility of its ministers, but in fact it left no one accountable to the people. It claimed to separate powers, but concentrated powers to such an extent that a prime minister could easily become an autocrat. In the name of efficient government, it provided the majority the wherewithal to rule tyrannically. It was an inherently partisan system.

At the time the Indians were selecting their system of government, British constitutional scholars themselves had already written about their system's duplicity. In the late 1800s, Walter Bagehot called Britain 'a disguised republic.'[1]

Similarly, in his famous 1904 work *Governance of England*, Sir Sidney Low acknowledged that an inquirer into 'the real truth of things rather than an imaginary view of them' may conclude that 'there is no Constitution in England'.[2] In the 1950s, Professor Douglas Verney wrote of the parliamentary system's 'ingenuity', wherein 'the forms ... have been retained but the realities of political power have been transformed.'[3]

It is understandable why the British constitutional principles developed disingenuously, for this system was an outcome of political expediency. Dislodging king and Church from their seats of power was no simple task. The British people took advantage of every accident of history, every misstep of the monarch and every help from the outside to slowly extract powers from the king.

Had we taken a historic view of the British system, we would have known that it wasn't a system suitable for India's vastly different type of democracy. It was a difficult system to understand and replicate. It wasn't a system designed for self-rule, but for ruling others. Its democratization even in Britain was an arduous process.

SYSTEM BORN OUT OF EXPEDIENCY AND ACCIDENT

'The development of the English Constitution was of necessity slow,' wrote Bagehot, 'because a quick one would have destroyed the executive and killed the State, and because the most numerous classes, who changed very little, were not prepared for any catastrophic change in our institutions.'[4]

Bagehot's suggestion that the English developed their system deliberately, to avoid disastrous consequences, is, however, not accurate. The long haul was simply due to the fact that the task of removing monarchy and Church from their venerated positions was downright impossible. In the process England wasn't able to avoid the calamities Bagehot dreaded. The executive of early England, the monarch, did get destroyed. The nation did lose sovereignty to a foreign invader. And the elite rulers did find that the masses were not only prepared for, but actually demanded, drastic change in the political system. The executive was destroyed literally as well as figuratively; the monarch was dethroned several times and even beheaded in the bloody fights with parliament. Ultimately his executive powers were completely extracted. When in the end the English Constitution did extend vote to the masses, through a series of reforms in the 1800s, the democratized system which emerged was radically different.

The creation of parliament was nothing like the creation of the presidential system. Nobody set out to create parliament. There was no singular vision, nor was it based on experience. 'Parliamentary government first evolved in England without any comprehensive theory to inspire it,' writes Douglas Verney. By contrast, the US Constitution was 'the product of reflection and invention', he says. [5]

Since there was no design or vision, the parliamentary system developed in spurts, whenever an opportunity arose. How the king's inner council became the parliament of the United Kingdom is a long story involving revolts, wars, invasions, dethronings, beheadings, a regicide and even a king's love life. In the process, parliament, which used to be an event, became an institution. An institution that existed for the king's support, became his nemesis. Even the word 'parliament' – from the French word 'parler' meaning to talk and discuss things – completely transformed its meaning. From describing the consultative meetings of the monarch with a large group of his nobles, parliament came to mean an institution with supreme legislative and executive powers.

RULE BY PARLIAMENT ALONE FAILED

In the long history of establishing parliamentary supremacy, England's attempt to become a pure republic, however, failed miserably. In 1649, when after a bloody civil war King Charles I surrendered to the forces loyal to parliament, he was beheaded. The House of Commons abolished the monarchy and the House of Lords, and declared England a republic. It called it the Commonwealth of England. The Commons appointed a Council of State, led by Oliver Cromwell, to rule England in place of the monarch.

A ten-year experiment in rule by the House of Commons alone, without king or House of Lords, was a dismal failure. Cromwell came to prominence due to his military successes during the civil war. Within the first two years of the new regime, he was able to win big victories for England, albeit through vicious means. With the army solidly behind him, Cromwell began to show signs of despotism. He forcibly dissolved the House of Commons and replaced it with an assembly of individuals hand-picked by himself and his supporters in the army. Ultimately, he was appointed Lord Protector by his supporters under a new Constitution that provided the sovereignty of England to 'a single person and a Parliament'. Cromwell became king in all but name.

With a failed republic on their hands, the people of England chose to restore the monarchy. They were tired of upheaval and anarchy. After the death of Cromwell in 1658, the political order in England completely broke down. His son and successor Richard was no match for Cromwell and couldn't manage the army and the parliament. The people had had enough of military rule and desired once again a proper parliament and government. A new assembly was elected, and when assurances were given by Charles II (the exiled heir of the late king) that all decisions would be placed before parliament, it invited him to sit on the throne of England.

PARLIAMENT BECAME THE NEW SOVEREIGN

By the end of the sixteenth century, powers over lawmaking and money were firmly under parliament's control. And with the Act of Settlement in 1701, which passed the Crown to a distant relative of the current monarch, the parliament also took over the right of succession. This was a remarkable turnaround because now it was parliament that chose the monarch. The king was no longer the sovereign. He existed at the will of parliament and depended upon it for survival. The message was not lost on those who sat on the throne of Britain. They now offered their assent to the actions of parliament as a matter of routine. The last time the royal veto was used was in 1708.

The will of parliament now became the law of the land. The notion that laws were fixed or fundamental was abandoned, because parliament could make or change any law. It now held all authority – legislative, executive and judicial. In mid-1800s, Bagehot would declare that 'the Parliament of today is a ruling body'.[6]

Parliament was supreme, but it was still sorely undemocratic. A 1429 statute decreed that only men who owned freehold land had the right to vote. The landed elite joined with peers in the House of Lords to get their followers elected. The Lords thus dominated parliament. Another undemocratic feature of parliament was that women didn't have the right to vote at all.

The democratization of parliament began only at the dawn of the nineteenth century. The growth of urban areas and an increasingly aware working class demanded the change. Significant reforms had to be introduced. The unfair system of representation that paid no attention to the size of the electorate or population was abandoned. A series of Acts beginning in 1832 disenfranchised many boroughs; reduced many others to only one member; created new constituencies; broadened the property qualifications to include small landowners, tenant farmers and shopkeepers and reduced the property threshold. With the passing of the 1885 Redistribution Act, the notion of representation of communities was finally abandoned. Most constituencies were now single-member districts. Women, however, had to wait until 1918 for the right to vote, and another ten years before they were given equality with men in their voting qualifications. The principle of 'one man, one vote' wouldn't be applied completely until 1948.

The democratization of the House of Lords would take even longer. The Lords always had the right of veto over the House of Commons. But with the extension of the franchise by the reforms of the 1800s, a clash between the elected House of Commons and the unelected House of Lords became inevitable. In 1909, when a budget bill taxing large landowners was passed by the House of Commons but rejected by the Lords, the old system finally broke apart. The Parliament Act of 1911 split the conservatives who held a permanent majority in the Lords. In 1949, the second such bill further reduced the Lords' ability to delay legislation from two years to one. The process of appointing peers was modified next. Life Peerage Acts of 1958 and 1963 allowed the creation of peers for life, rather than on a hereditary basis, and opened the membership to women. Then, in 2005, the Lords were stripped of their judicial functions, by setting up a new independent Supreme Court.

Thus full control of the British system came in the hands of *elected* representatives only in the early 1900s. 'The story of English history is the record of the struggle of the House of Commons,' Sir Sidney Low wrote, 'first for freedom, then for power.'[7]

POLITICAL PARTIES' CONTROL MADE IT PERFECT FOR OLIGARCHY

The House of Commons now held unfettered powers. To it belonged all legislative authority, but since the drafting and passing of laws was in the government's control, which in turn was controlled by a political party, the parliament in essence began to reflect the will of a party.

Parties were well entrenched in the parliamentary politics of England from the time of Charles II. In 1679, a few members of parliament organized themselves under the banner of Country Party to oppose the king's attempts to influence parliament. Driven largely by religious undertones, this opposition developed a flair for organization and propaganda. The Whigs, as this group came to be known, won significant victories against the monarch. In reaction, the Tories emerged as a group in king's support. The Whigs and Tories continued to fight for dominance in parliament over the next several centuries. Over the years, many new parties emerged, and the names changed. Today, nearly all members of parliament represent a political party. In the last sixty years, all UK governments have been formed by either the Labour Party or the Conservative Party.

Thus, by controlling the new sovereign, the parliament, political parties gained uninhibited power under the British system. As Low said, 'Nowhere else is the power of that sovereign so little fettered. Democracy in America could not impair the validity of contracts, or prescribe a redistribution of all private property,' he wrote, 'but if the great majority of the English electorate were persuaded that such innovations were desirable, they could have them carried into effect by the ordinary process of legislation.'[8]

And that precisely was the rub. After a long history of extracting powers from the monarch, the British concentrated them in the hands of a faction to such an extent that it could do as it pleased. In short, the parliamentary system became an ideal system for an oligarchy.

'REPRESENTATIVE' GOVERNMENT, RUN BY OLIGARCHS

Parliament was inherently a legislature designed to deliberate on issues, not to run governments. Since it was not possible for an assembly to govern, a solution was found in having the elected members of the assembly, the House of Commons, appoint and control the executive. However, the executive was given the power to dissolve the lower House of parliament. This made government dominant over the House. Crucially, a coterie of the Cabinet or the prime minister alone could decide to dissolve parliament and call for a general election at any time. The parliamentary system thus functioned as an oligarchy.

As Bagehot acknowledged, 'of all odd forms of government, the oddest really is government by a public meeting.' He wrote, 'It is a saying in England, "a big meeting never does anything", and yet we are governed by the House of Commons – by "a big meeting."'[9] Sir Ivor Jennings made a similar remark in his 1941 work *The British Constitution*: 'Parliament cannot govern, it can do no more than criticize.'[10] Bagehot, however, offered an explanation: 'It may be said that the House of Commons does not rule, it only elects the rulers.'

The unfettered 'ruler' the House of Commons elected was the Cabinet, but that made the oligarchy worse because that made government completely partisan. The leader of the party with the most seats in the House was appointed prime minister and he chose members of parliament from his own party to form the Cabinet. 'The moment, indeed, that we distinctly conceive that the House of Commons is mainly and above all things an elective assembly,' Bagehot wrote, 'we at once perceive that party is of its essence.'[11]

A party government holding all executive and legislative powers, governing on a partisan agenda, and obtaining what it wanted by threatening to dissolve the assembly, only worked to make the oligarchy stronger. Even though the British justified it in the name of efficiency, it amounted to rule by fear. 'Efficiency in an assembly requires a solid mass of steady votes,' Bagehot explained, 'and these are collected by a deferential attachment to particular men, or by a belief in the principles those men represent, and they are maintained by fear of those men – by the fear that if you vote against them, you may yourself soon not have a vote at all.'[12]

Placing all powers in the hands of a partisan few also exacerbated the problem of elitism. This was the main reason why it took more than a century to democratize the British parliament. 'If we look at the body which really rules the Empire,' Low wrote, 'we see at once that it mainly represents one portion of the House, and that the undemocratic portion. In this respect our political system has preserved much of its oligarchic character. The effective power continues to be retained in the hands of a comparatively small body of persons ...'[13]

Worse still, the real oligarchy was even smaller than the Cabinet. 'And if we peer below the surface of things a little closer,' Low continued, 'we might even conclude that its chief functions have passed from the Cabinet as a whole, and that they have been transferred to an inner council or conclave, consisting of the Prime Minister and the three or four influential colleagues who share his confidence and are habitually consulted by him.'[14]

'PARLIAMENTARY SUPREMACY' JUST FOR SHOW

This oligarchic set-up turned a fundamental parliamentary feature, the supremacy of parliament, completely on its head. Control over parliament by a few was quite the opposite of the principle on which this system was based, that parliament was above all its constituent parts: the assembly, monarch and the government. Douglas Verney had warned: 'There are countries like the United Kingdom where the increasing tendency for the government to dominate parliamentary business may be departure from the parliamentary principle in the opposite direction.'[15]

A system whose raison d'être was to make government accountable to people's representatives was now controlled by government. Jennings had noted the contradiction as well. 'The theory is that the House controls the Government,' he wrote. 'It is equally true to say that the Government controls the House. ... The truth is, though, that a member of the Government's majority does not want to defeat the Government.'[16]

This was usurpation of power of the worst kind, for it was hidden. 'The House of Commons no longer controls the Executive,' Low admitted. 'On the contrary, the Executive controls the House of Commons. The theory is that the ministers must justify each and all of their acts before the representatives of the nation at every stage; if they fail to do so, those representatives will turn them out of office. But in our modern practice the Cabinet is scarcely ever turned out of office by Parliament whatever it does.'[17]

Again, what this exposed was the impracticability of the system. It relied on the members of a government's party to defeat their own government, and elected representatives to dissolve their own House. As Low said, 'Even when a party is broken by internal dissension, members are very reluctant to vote against the official leaders ... in practice the control of the House is largely inoperative.' Even when it came to the House's presumed powers of refusing money, Low was categorical: 'The refusal of supplies is a constitutional figment.'[18]

'SEPARATION OF POWERS' IN NAME ONLY

This usurpation of parliament's powers by a coterie exposed another brazen variation between the British system's façade and reality: its total lack of separation of powers. While it professed to separate the executive from the legislature, and both from the judiciary, in its functioning it did quite the opposite. In effect, this gave the executive total supremacy.

'There are two descriptions of the English Constitution which have exercised immense influence, but which are erroneous,' Bagehot noted. 'First, it is laid down as a principle of the English polity, that in it the legislative, the executive, and the judicial powers are quite divided. ... Secondly, it is insisted that the peculiar excellence of the British Constitution lies in a balanced union of three powers. ... The efficient secret of the English Constitution may be described as the close union, the nearly complete fusion, of the executive and legislative powers.'[19]

'RESPONSIBLE' GOVERNMENT BUT NO OVERSIGHT

Responsible government in the parliamentary context meant that laws were brought to parliament for debate and approval, and that the work of government was open to parliament's scrutiny. But when government held supremacy and it was guaranteed parliament's support, the whole notion of responsible government fell apart.

'According to the conventions of the Constitution, the Cabinet is the responsible executive,' Low wrote. 'If we look only at the actualities of the case, we might be inclined to say that the Cabinet, in its existing shape, is a committee not of parliament, but of one party in parliament ...'[20]

Even worse, the parliamentary system allowed government to operate from behind the mask of a Cabinet, under a shroud of secrecy. 'The most curious point about the Cabinet is that so very little is known about it,' said Bagehot. 'The committee which unites the law-making power to the law-executing power ... the most powerful body in the State ... is a committee wholly secret.'[21] Similarly, Low wrote: 'These characteristics are usually noticed in a rather grudging and hesitating fashion, but they have become established factors ... Secrecy and partisanship are elements of Cabinet government.'[22]

Parliamentary governments guarded the secrets of their Cabinet with vengeance. There were no registers, or clerks, or press statements, nor were there any reports of its discussions. It operated 'huddled away in a corner, and discussing the things of the party as well as the affairs of the country under the friendly cloak of darkness,' Low wrote. He quoted Lord Roseberry, who said: 'Of all anomalous arrangements for executive government, the strangest is the government of England by a Secret Committee.'[23]

'COLLECTIVE RESPONSIBILITY' WITH NO ACCOUNTABILITY

The idea behind Cabinet was that the responsibility was assigned to government as a collective. That is, ministers were jointly responsible to the assembly. A failure to pass any law or maladministration in any ministry was the failure of the entire government. Every legislative fight, therefore, was a fight for government's survival. But since the government operated under secrecy, a Cabinet could choose not to own a minister's action. And since it controlled parliament, a government could ensure that all its actions were sanctioned. Hence, to turn a government out for maladministration was nearly impossible.

Yet another principle of the parliamentary system was in reality impracticable. 'The Cabinet is said to be collectively responsible for the whole policy of the Government, whether it has been brought before the Cabinet or not,' Jennings tried to explain. 'In practice, however, the principle is never carried so far, because it rests with the Cabinet whether they shall accept or disown the ministerial decision.'[24]

And once again, the problem was that the notion of collective responsibility was impracticable. First, ministers in the parliamentary system were not appointed because of their knowledge or experience in the area, but because they were the political leaders of the parties in majority. They were politicians, and therefore, their view of responsibility was always political survival. If a measure were to lose, they just wouldn't bring it to vote. 'The merit of cabinet government,' Low noted, 'is that it defines and concentrates ministerial responsibility, and makes it possible to bring the popular judgement to bear upon the servants of the State ... But an English Cabinet is a group of political leaders, not a body of persons trained to administration ... they have risen to prominence by the arts of the platform ...'[25]

Second, collective responsibility was no check because defeating the whole government was something that most members of parliament didn't really want. It risked dissolution of their House and a new general election. As Sir Sidney asked: 'What is our check upon ministers ... The House of Commons cannot dismiss a minister, of whose acts it disapproves; it cannot even formally censure him, unless it is prepared to get rid of all his colleagues as well. Now, as a rule, that is just what the House is most reluctant to do.'[26]

'EFFICIENT GOVERNMENT' PUT ALL POWERS IN ONE OFFICIAL

The British system went against all these parliamentary principles, for one benefit: efficiency. The argument for concentration of powers was that a government must act with unity and energy. The monarchy offered both these attributes, but it was not reliable and was mostly oppressive. The mission of the parliamentary system was therefore to replicate the single force of the monarch but control it through people's representatives in parliament. 'The English Constitution, in a word, is framed on the principle of choosing a single sovereign authority, and making it good,' Bagehot famously declared. 'The American upon the principle of having many sovereign authorities, and hoping that their multitude may atone for their inferiority,' he chided.[27] Bagehot's sovereign authority, the House of Commons, could take any matter, executive or legislative, and 'despotically and finally resolve'.

He admitted that this 'lets forth a dangerous accumulation of inhibited power, which might sweep this Constitution before it, as like accumulations have often swept away like Constitutions'.[28] He would be proven right. Within two decades, Low would report that 'the Prime Minister does not often take all his colleagues into his confidence; or even consult them ... The growth of the Inner Cabinet is one of the most interesting developments of recent years.'[29]

As a result, a British prime minister would become all-powerful. Prime Minister Gladstone famously quipped that 'nowhere is there a man who has so much power with so little to show for it in the way of formal title or prerogative'.[30] 'An English Prime Minister,' Low wrote, 'with his majority secure in parliament, can do what the German Emperor, and the American President, and all the Chairmen of Committees in the United States Congress, cannot do; for he can alter the laws, he can impose taxation or repeal it, and he can direct all the forces of the state.'[31]

However, there was no one to judge a British prime minister's 'efficiency'. A parliamentary government was perhaps efficient, but since it was mostly non-inclusive and autocratic, it was ineffective. All external checks on a prime minister, of parliament or of king, had been nullified. Since the only control was that of his party, a prime minister resigned or dissolved parliament at a time opportune for his party, but no sooner. In a famous case, a government stayed in office from 1834 until 1841 despite being defeated in the House of Commons fifty-nine times.[32]

OPPOSITION VENERATED BUT TOOTHLESS

In another superficial feature, the British system gave the opposition a venerated position, but not much more. The so-called royal opposition was in name only, for it had no powers. It could ask questions and make speeches in parliament, but as for stopping a government from taking an action, or scrutinizing an executive department for wrongdoing, or subpoenaing a government official to provide evidence, it had no such authorities. Nor did it change any votes in parliament; the members almost always voted along party lines.

The opposition's right to call attention to government's abuses or bad policies was good theatre in parliament, but it rarely compelled a government to change course. In fact, questioning a government outside of parliament was more likely to affect a change, because inside, the issue was mired in politics. Commenting on the practice of raising questions in parliament, Low noted: 'If a person wants an administrative evil remedied, or a new project accepted, he may write about it to the papers, or he may get up a public meeting and have speeches delivered upon it; and by such methods he might well render more effectual help to his cause than if he requested the member for his division to ask a question in the House of Commons.'[33]

'Orators did not turn votes by their arguments,' Low wrote, 'nor would Cicero and Demosthenes have done so under like conditions. It is of the essence of our existing parliamentary system, as it has developed in recent years, that votes are not turned. A Member of Parliament is elected to vote for a particular Ministry, or to vote against it.'[34]

'POPULAR GOVERNMENT' BUT INHERENTLY PARTISAN

The claim that British governments were popular was the most specious of them all. The people of Britain didn't elect a government, they elected a party. Political parties were integral to the functioning of this system, but unlike its other institutions, parties were neither structured nor regulated under the Constitution. In order to function properly the system required two, and only two, parties. It didn't work so well when there were many parties. The party winning the most seats formed the government while the other sat in opposition. In this all-or-nothing system, the oligarchs of the party in power were given near-dictatorial authority. All in all, it was a perfect system for political parties, except that it was impractical and undemocratic.

In the name of efficiency, the parliamentary system was designed to be winner-take-all. The party in majority ran the Cabinet, and the Cabinet ran parliament. No separation of powers meant that the party forming the Cabinet held all powers. It was no exaggeration when Low called Cabinet a 'combination of a council of state, with a party directorate'.[35]

'The British system is perfected party government,' Woodrow Wilson, a future US president, wrote in early 1900s in his work *Congressional Government*. 'No effort is made in the Commons, such as is made in the [US] House of Representatives,' he said, 'to give the

minority a share in law-making.'[36] Low also noted: 'Government by
parties prevails to some extent under every free popular constitution;
but only in that of the United Kingdom, and those which are closely
modelled upon it, is it carried out in a thoroughly uncompromising
fashion.'[37]

An inherently partisan government made everything political. Every
legislative fight in parliament was a struggle for the political survival of
the party in power instead of a battle of ideas. The debates were political
speeches, not arguments for or against legislation's core issues or
quality. 'The nation is interested in what is being done mainly because
of its possible influence upon the fortunes of the parties and the party
leaders,' Low wrote. 'It follows that a quite disproportionate amount
of attention is paid to the electioneering side of ministerial projects.'[38]

Politics so dominated the British system that the House of
Commons wasn't really a legislative body; it became an electioneering
body. It was always in the process of making or unmaking governments.
'The main function of the House of Commons,' Bagehot admitted, 'is
one which we know quite well, though our common constitutional
speech does not recognize it. The House of Commons is an electoral
chamber; it is the assembly which chooses our president.'[39] Hence
parliament was in a perpetual mode of politicking. 'The main
difference is that the presidential electors [in the US], when they have
installed the President in office, have done with the matter,' Low wrote,
'whereas our ministerial electors continue to be busy until it is time to
choose another Prime Minister.'[40]

What made constant politicking even worse was that this system
allowed the party in power to pick its own timing in calling elections.
This placed political considerations over any others, in making any
legislative or executive decision. 'One of the peculiar features of the
true Cabinet system,' Low noted, 'is that you can always "find the
sovereign people," as it has been said, at the very moment when you
want it.'[41]

'DEMOCRATIC SYSTEM', BUT MAJORITY 'RULED'

In a system where party label was all that mattered, parties selected those who were loyal over those who were competent. 'The British political system differs from many other systems,' Jennings wrote, 'in that the local member is rarely the "favourite son" of the constituency. … They have been chosen by local political associations, but the associations are branches of national parties, and their main concern is to choose "good party men" who will support the national party in Parliament. … The qualities of the candidate therefore have little to do with his vote.'[42]

Once elected, a member of parliament was expected simply to follow the party line. 'They do not send him to Parliament to exercise his independence,' Low noted, 'they would be particularly annoyed and irritated if he did. … And the modern MP understands the conditions of his political existence so well that, in point of fact, he hardly ever does vote against his party.'[43]

Laws were passed without any contribution from members of the minority party. 'We have the curious fact,' Low noted, 'that nearly one half of the "Legislature"are not legislators at all. They can neither make laws nor prevent laws being made.'[44] Of course, the quality of laws suffered under this system because the focus remained on politics and because the passing of laws was almost always a fait accompli. 'Every member of the House, with the exception of a score or so who sit on the front benches,' Low noted, 'would admit, if he spoke the truth, that his influence over legislation was little greater than that of a private individual outside.'

Worst of all, a majority government was undemocratic because it was unrepresentative. Sir Sidney was unforgiving: 'We constantly profess that the Government of the day represents the House of Commons, and through the House of Commons the nation. In reality it does nothing of the sort; it represents, as a rule, rather more than one half of the electorate, and rather less than two thirds of the House.' He elaborated on it thus, 'The spectacle of millions of free men in a free state, habitually governed in opposition to their own will, and their own convictions, is so astonishing that we prefer to avert our gaze from it.'[45]

SYSTEM WORKS WITH ONLY TWO PARTIES

The British system's claim of functioning effectively under coalition governments was only ostensibly so. In reality, it worked well only when there were two political parties. Since at its core it was a majoritarian system, its success depended upon having a clear majority in parliament. A vague political environment, with multiple parties, threw the system off because it made the sharing of powers necessary. The parliamentary system, was an all-or-nothing system.

This worked in Britain because the society was structured along two major parties. 'The division into Whigs and Tories worked into a tradition,' Low said, 'and eventually into a national habit.'[46]

However, when there were more than two parties, a general election often resulted in no single party commanding a majority in the House of Commons. Every time this happened, the parliamentary system fell into a situation of no overall control, or a 'hung parliament'. Then either an unpopular government remained in power while the parties negotiated to build a coalition, or an attempt was made to run government with the support of the minority.

But the British system couldn't function properly even with as few as three parties. Commenting on a situation when there were three parties in the fray, Bagehot noted, 'The defining characteristic of that government is the choice of the executive ruler by the legislative assembly; but when there are three parties a satisfactory choice is impossible.'[47]

WHY THERE ARE TWO HOUSES

The House of Lords wasn't much of a legislative body, nor did it hold equal powers with the House of Commons. Before the Reform Act of 1832, the Lords were the bulwark of the monarchy in parliament, but after, they were defenceless against the Lower House. The Parliamentary Act of 1911 had further reduced their powers.

The parliamentary system worked when there was only one popularly elected assembly. The whole point of this system was that the assembly controlled the executive. No matter how necessary a revising assembly was deemed, the British system's design didn't allow two coequal chambers. One had to be in control, by the very definition of the parliamentary system. And that could only be the popularly elected House of Commons.

The House of Lords was not constructed to be a bulwark against the House of Commons or a safeguard against parliamentary tyranny. Bagehot admitted that such a revising assembly could be structured more effectively under a US-type federal system. 'A federal senate, a second House, which represents State unity, has this advantage,' he wrote, 'it embodies a feeling at the root of society – a feeling which is older than complicated politics, which is stronger a thousand times over than common political feelings – the local feeling. ... But in common Governments it is fatally difficult to make an unpopular entity powerful in a popular Government.'[48]

The theory that the two Houses held equal powers was never really the case with the British system. Here again, Bagehot accepted that the reality of the British system was entirely different from its theory. He wrote: 'When we cease to look at the House of Lords under its dignified aspect, and come to regard it under its strictly useful aspect, we find the literary theory of the English Constitution wholly wrong, as usual.'[49] Low was even more categorical: 'If the system of "checks and balances" is to save a country from the excesses of democratic violence, the House of Lords fulfils its purpose very imperfectly.'[50]

'CONSTITUTIONAL MONARCHY', NOT IN NAME ONLY

The British system was deceptive even in its pretension as a 'constitutional monarchy', for monarchy wasn't just a symbolic part of the system, it was essential. A king was needed in the parliamentary system, not while this system was functional, but when it was dysfunctional. Monarchy was the insurance against the system's failure. It atoned for the parliamentary system's three grave ills: latent dictatorship, structural instability and inherent partisanship. It also filled one of the parliamentary system's holes, the lack of a single individual as the symbol of the nation.

The first protection the British people needed was from parliamentary tyranny. They knew their system of government provided the wherewithal for one man with an overwhelming majority in parliament to turn into an autocrat. They had seen that happen, when in 1653 Oliver Cromwell had ended a ten-year rule by the House of Commons alone. England's attempt at becoming a full republic failed because parliament had lacked the capacity to check one man from becoming a dictator. It was only the revival of the monarchy which then provided an effective balance against parliament.

Instability in the British system was another serious problem for which the monarchy provided a solution. By convention, powers were reposed in the monarch every time Britain was without a government. Since a government could fall at any time, this was a crucial function that only an institution outside of parliament could fulfil.

The most crucial need that the British monarch filled, however, was that he provided a non-partisan institution in an otherwise blatantly partisan system. The king had influence because he was non-partisan.'The fundamental principle which governs his action,' Jennings noted, 'is that his prerogative is not to be used for purely partisan ends. He himself must neither be nor seem to be a partisan.'[51]

The reason the British monarch could fill these roles was because he represented the entire country. He was the singular symbol of the nation. The parliamentary system otherwise offered no single official, including the prime minister, who represented the whole of the people. This is precisely how Bagehot justified the monarchy: 'The best reason why Monarchy is a strong government is that it is intelligible government. ...the action of a single will, the fit of a single mind, are easy ideas; anybody can make them out, and no one can ever forget them.'[52]

But the British system couldn't reconcile the need for a single individual as a centre of power with parliamentary supremacy. The notion of 'constitutional monarchy' was both incomprehensible and impractical. Commenting on constitutional monarchy as a system, Low noted that '… it is extremely complex, mysterious, and artificial; so delicate, and so curiously adjusted, that it is scarcely possible to expose it to analysis without a sense of unreality.'[53]

Since it wasn't possible to fit monarchy within a democratic system, the extent and limit of its powers were left to convention. 'There is no authentic explicit information as to what the Queen can do, any more than of what she does,' Bagehot wrote.[54]

However, without clearly identifiable powers or functions, it became harder and harder to justify the monarchy. Silly arguments were presented in order to defend its continuation. Bagehot spoke of the monarchy's three rights vis-à-vis the government: the right to be consulted, the right to encourage and the right to warn. By 1904, Low was writing about a monarch's three functions: that all authority periodically returned to him; that he decided which of the leaders of the majority in parliament shall be entrusted with the premiership; and that he could demand or refuse dissolution of parliament. By 1941, however, Jennings had narrowed the powers of the monarch to just one: 'The Queen has one, and only one, function of primary importance. It is to appoint a Prime Minister.'[55] This too was puerile since the leader of the party with most seats in the House of Commons had to be chosen.

The fact of the matter was that the monarch was left with no control over the direction of national affairs. In nearly every case she acted as advised by the prime minister. The decisions were taken by the Cabinet. 'She must sign her own death warrant if the two Houses unanimously send it up to her,' Bagehot said about the queen.

But Bagehot knew of the real reason behind monarchy in the British system. It was a disguised safety net when the parliamentary system failed. 'Constitutional royalty … acts as a disguise,' Bagehot wrote, 'it enables our real rulers to change without heedless people knowing it.' Bagehot admitted that this was wrong. 'In the bare superficial theory of free institutions this is undoubtedly a defect,' he wrote. 'Every power in a popular Government ought to be known. A secret prerogative is an anomaly – perhaps the greatest of anomalies. That secrecy is, however, essential to the utility of English royalty as it now is.'[56]

ONLY THE RIGHT INGREDIENTS

Nearly every British constitutional scholar had cautioned that their system wasn't easy to imitate. Low wrote: 'Foreign observers, naturally desirous of improving their own institutions, have sometimes over-emphasized the merits of the English system. Perhaps they do not always see how much it depends upon circumstances which may be called local or accidental. The mixture contains numerous ingredients, "traces", as the analysts say, of many diverse elements, and if one is omitted, or introduced in undue proportion, the whole flavour of the resultant is altered.'[57]

Similarly, Bagehot had concluded that '[The English Constitution's] simple essence may, mutatis mutandis, be transplanted to many very various countries, but its august outside – what most men think it is – is narrowly confined to nations with an analogous history and similar political materials.'[58] And Douglas Verney, after an exhaustive analysis of the political systems of the world, cautioned: 'It is rather a subtle form of government and one hardly to be recommended to people who have just emerged from absolute rule.'[59]

The chief ingredient for its success was the existence of a cohesive polity with exactly two political parties. Other ingredients were no less important: a small nation, homogeneous population, unitary structure, monarchy, non-sectarian politics and no permanent majority. But a proper organization of political parties was so central to the functioning of the system that it just wouldn't be able to work without it. None of the ingredients – except perhaps one, a deferential society – was present in India at the time of the framing of her Constitution. Today even that is no longer present.

THE CONSEQUENCES OF A SECTARIAN GOVERNMENT

'Parliamentary government is, in its essence, a sectarian government, and is possible only when sects are cohesive,' said Bagehot. 'It is, in substance, subjecting the whole nation to the rule of a section of the nation,' he wrote.[60]

This was not a problem in England because the society was homogeneous, well informed and politically active. In India, the sectarian divide was violent and permanent; and the society politically suppressed after generations under the British rule. As we shall see, subjecting the nation to such an inherently sectarian system only added fuel to the fire.

That there were only two parties was not a sufficient condition for the success of the parliamentary system, they also needed to be non-sectarian. In England, the division of society between conservatives and liberals was not along strict lines. There were no issues of faith, or caste, or colour involved. The people of England were driven more by the leaders of parties and supported their favourite to bring him to power. 'Attachment to persons, rather than fidelity to principles, is the spirit of our party life,' Low wrote. 'The parties, therefore, instead of being two groups of believers endeavouring to propagate their own particular faith, are two armies of active combatants, each desiring above all things to follow its own chosen champion to victory.'[61]

India's parties were always sectarian. Even when they claimed to be secular, deep inside their vote-bank politics was always along religious or caste divisions. At the time of Independence, the conflict between the Congress party and the Muslim League was deeply communal.

THE PROBLEM WITH A PERMANENT MAJORITY

There was no way to work the parliamentary system successfully when a party was likely to be in permanent majority, as was the case in India under separate electorates.

In England, both parties had equal chance of coming to power and therefore each gave the other some room and respect while in power. 'Tolerance in this country is a principle of long standing,' wrote Jennings. 'It is, however, not tolerance alone that makes democratic government work. With us, the majority is not permanent. It is based upon differing views of personal and national interest, views which are susceptible of change and, in a sufficient number of persons, do change from time to time. ... This important fact must not be forgotten, for it enables the minority to submit peacefully and even cheerfully to the fulfilment of the policy of the majority.' Jennings expressed it succinctly thus: 'A Conservative Government might persuade me to become a Conservative overnight,' he wrote. 'It cannot change my ancestry, my language, my tribe or caste (if I had one), my religion, or even my economic status.'[62]

DEPENDENCE ON THE 'RATIONALITY' OF POLITICIANS

Bagehot described the conditions that were necessary for the system to work effectively; of course, none of them existed in India. 'The first prerequisite of elective government is the *mutual confidence* of the electors,' he wrote.'A second and very rare condition of an elective government is a *calm national mind* ... the third condition of all elective government is ... *rationality*. ... But the prerequisites of a Cabinet government are rarer still,' he noted:

> There are two kinds of nations which can elect a good Parliament. The first is a nation in which the mass of the people are intelligent, and in which they are comfortable. Where there is no honest poverty, where education is diffused, and political intelligence is common, it is easy for the mass of the people to elect a fair legislature. But suppose the mass of the people are not able to elect – and this is the case with the numerical majority of all but the rarest nations – how is a Cabinet government to be then possible? It is only possible in what I may venture to call *deferential* nations. It has been thought strange, but there *are* nations in which the numerous unwiser part wishes to be ruled by the less numerous wiser part. The numerical majority ... is ready, is eager to delegate its power of choosing its ruler to a certain select minority. It

abdicates in favour of its elite, and consents to obey whoever that elite may confide in.[63]

In short, a nation needed to be rich and peaceful, or an elite few had to run the government, for the parliamentary system to succeed.

By the same token, monarchy was vital for the parliamentary system because it was the most effective way to sustain people's deference in their government. A king was not necessary for the functioning of the system, but for this reason, and for having at least one non-partisan institution, he was immensely beneficial. Although Bagehot and others bent over backwards to show that monarchy was not essential, and that an 'un-royal' form of parliamentary system was possible, the filial feeling monarchy brought was crucial for its success.

An 'elective monarchy', something India attempted with the office of the president, was unviable. 'The mystic reverence, the religious allegiance, which are essential to a true monarchy are imaginative sentiments that no legislature can manufacture in any people,' Bagehot argued. 'You might as well adopt a father as make a monarchy. [64]

A UNITARY SYSTEM, UNFIT FOR A FEDERATION

A unitary government was also a necessary condition for the parliamentary system's success. The British system couldn't accommodate a federal structure of government because none of its institutions provided representation to local governments. Also, parliamentary sovereignty meant that all authority belonged to one national government. Every devolution of power to a local government came from an Act of Parliament, which could be withdrawn or altered by the same body. In such a system, local governments couldn't have constitutional sovereignty.

In England, all devolutions of authority – the creation in 1999 of a parliament in Scotland, and an assembly each in Wales and Northern Ireland – were acts of the UK parliament. They transferred some powers but retained authority over the devolved institutions. This was after a hundred years of prodding that parliament in England was incapable of managing local affairs. Low had noted in the early 1900s that 'some devolution on a large and systematic scale would be required in order to relieve the central parliament of burdens beyond its strength. Almost every great and progressive country ... has worked out the division between provincial and national institutions; and it seems inevitable that we shall be compelled to apply, in some shape, the federal methods which are in operation, in one form or another, in Germany, in the United States.'[65]

APOLITICAL BUREAUCRACY A MUST

Another crucially important factor in the British system's success was the existence of a bureaucracy that was meritocratic. Civil servants in England were not attached to politicians; they were appointed and promoted based upon merit. The British bureaucracy evolved after adapting to political changes over the centuries, but was also helped by the nation's deferential attitude towards its rulers. Civil servants were respected by the masses. The nation was small and it could find and monitor enough civil servants who were capable of sitting in key positions. None of these conditions existed in India.

Britain had overcome the 'spoils' system of appointing political supporters to administrative posts and promoting or transferring civil servants for their favours. 'The intrusion of politics is the first step towards the intrusion of corruption,' Jennings noted. 'Britain has avoided these problems, and it has done so by insisting on two principles which are aspects of the same principle. The first is that the Minister is responsible, morally as well as technically, for every action of his Department ... the second is that parliamentary criticism of a civil servant is fundamentally unconstitutional and objectionable.'[66]

BRITISH DECLARED PARLIAMENTARY SYSTEM UNSUITABLE FOR INDIA

For at least a decade before they granted India her independence, the British maintained that their system of government was not a good fit with this nation. Every time they spoke against India's ability to make a parliamentary government work, they were criticized by the Indian leaders for finding excuses to delay or deny their right to self-rule.

As early as 1933 the British had laid out exactly why the parliamentary system was unlikely to work under Indian conditions. A joint committee of the British Parliament, constituted to study Indian constitutional reforms, filed the following report:

> Parliamentary government as it is understood in the United Kingdom, works by the interaction of four essential factors; the principle of majority rule; the willingness of the minority for the time being to accept the decisions of the majority; the existence of great political parties divided by broad issues of policy, rather than by sectional interests; and finally the existence of a mobile body of public opinion, owing no permanent allegiance to any party and therefore able, by its instinctive reaction against extravagant movements on one side or the other, to keep the vessel on an even keel. In India none of these factors can be said to exist today. There are no parties, as we understand them, and there is no considered body of political opinion which can be described as mobile.[67]

Immediately before Independence, the British Cabinet Mission of 1946 recommended a plan which was not based on the contours of the parliamentary system. If anything, it was more likely to take India in the direction of the presidential system, for it envisioned a US-type federation.

NOTES

1   Bagehot, W. (2007), *The English Constitution*, SC, USA: Biblio Bazaar, p. 39, footnote.
2   Low, S. (1915), *Governance of England*, New York: G.P. Putnam's Sons, p. 2.
3   Verney, D.V. (1959), *The Analysis of Political Systems*, Chicago, IL, USA: The Free Press, p. 86.
4   Bagehot, op. cit., p. 228.
5   Verney, op. cit., p. 8.

6   Bagehot, op. cit., p. 229.
7   Low, op. cit., p. 55.
8   Ibid., p. 173.
9   Bagehot, op. cit., p. 139.
10   Jennings, Sir Ivor (1961), *The British Constitution*, London: Cambridge University Press, p. 84.
11   Bagehot, op. cit., p. 140.
12   Ibid., p. 141.
13   Low, op. cit., p. 186.
14   Ibid., p. 16.
15   Verney, op. cit., p. 33.
16   Jennings, op. cit., p. 78.
17   Low, op. cit., p. 81.
18   Ibid., p. 81.
19   Bagehot, op. cit., pp. 49–55.
20   Low, op. cit., p. 16.
21   Bagehot, op. cit., p. 57.
22   Low, op. cit., p. 34.
23   Ibid., pp. 35, 41.
24   Jennings, op. cit., p. 145.
25   Low, op. cit., p. 136.
26   Ibid., pp. 144–49.
27   Bagehot, op. cit., p. 197.
28   Ibid., p. 198.
29   Low, op. cit., p. 164.
30   Ibid., p. 161.
31   Ibid., p. 47.
32   Beer, S. H. (1982), *Britain Against Itself,* London: Faber and Faber Limited, p. 185.
33   Low, op. cit., p. 94.
34   Ibid., p. 64.
35   Ibid., p. 44.
36   Wilson, W. (2004), *Constitutional Government in the United States*, New Brunswick, NJ, USA: Transaction Publishers, p. 91.
37   Low, op. cit., p. 116.

38   Ibid., p. 103.

39   Bagehot, op. cit., p. 133.

40   Low, op. cit., p. 102.

41   Ibid., p. 113.

42   Jennings, op. cit., pp. 16–17.

43   Low, op. cit., p. 54.

44   Ibid., p. 60.

45   Ibid., p. 119.

46   Ibid., p. 125.

47   Bagehot, op. cit., p. 92.

48   Ibid., p. 121.

49   Ibid., p. 111.

50   Low, op. cit., p. 212.

51   Jennings, op. cit., p. 115.

52   Bagehot, op. cit., p. 70.

53   Low, op. cit., p. 274.

54   Bagehot, op. cit., p. 86.

55   Jennings, op. cit., p. 109.

56   Bagehot, op. cit., pp. 84-86.

57   Low, op. cit., pp. 45–46.

58   Bagehot, op. cit., p. 50.

59   Verney, op. cit., p. 86.

60   Bagehot, op. cit., p. 199.

61   Low, op. cit., p. 128.

62   Jennings, op. cit., pp. 30–31.

63   Bagehot, op. cit., pp. 214–22.

64   Ibid., p. 50.

65   Low, op. cit., Introduction.

66   Jennings, op. cit., p. 142.

67   *Report of the Joint Committee on Indian Constitutional Reform,* Vol. 1 (Part 1) Session 1933-34, p. 210, cited by A.G. Noorani in *Frontline,* 13 February 2010.

3

Predilection for a Parliamentary System

'India's greatest glory will consist not in regarding Englishmen as her implacable enemies,' wrote Mahatma Gandhi, '... but in turning them into friends and partners in a new commonwealth of nations.'[1] In his 1922 essay entitled 'Independence', Gandhi was asserting India's right for swaraj (self-rule). But even in this declaration of independence he held out an olive branch to the British. Nehru, and others inspired by Gandhi, began to take pride in their attempts to keep amity with the British. To them, uprooting the system of government that the British had installed was a discordant act. Besides, they were familiar with the parliamentary system, believing it to be effective for an efficient government. So when the need arose for a strong Central government, the Indian leaders were naturally inclined towards the parliamentary form.

Many political developments before and during the framing of India's Constitution made it glaringly obvious that the parliamentary system was ill-suited to India, but these were ignored. Gandhi's call for swaraj in 1922 was one such development. It changed the nature of India's struggle from a fight for representation to a demand for an entirely separate Constitution. While earlier the challenge was to tweak the system in ways that were acceptable to the British, in the struggle for swaraj the challenge was entirely different: to find a system that was acceptable to Indians themselves. Even after a call for independence, the Indian leaders didn't begin to develop such a system. Another opportunity to rethink the system of government was missed in 1937, when the British gave Indians their first chance to form provincial governments. Nehru opted to form Congress-only governments because the design of the parliamentary system didn't compel political parties to share power. This fiasco made the communal fight in India permanent.

A reconsideration of the parliamentary system was missed yet again at the very beginning of the process of framing India's Constitution. Since the Constituent Assembly was entirely under the control of one political party (the Congress), the minority party (the Muslim League) was apprehensive that the system chosen would suit only the majority. The parliamentary system was slated to be the choice precisely because it allowed the majority to hold all powers. Faced with the Congress leaders' predilection for the parliamentary system and with the bitter experience of 1937 fresh in their minds, the leaders of the Muslim League refused to even participate in the deliberations. Despite clamorous pleas to postpone the process of making the Constitution, even from the likes of Gandhi, the Congress party pushed on. It is astonishing that even as the nation burned, India's leaders never really considered a system which was fundamentally different from the parliamentary variety.

IT MADE SENSE AT FIRST

The basic tenet of the parliamentary system, an executive accountable to the legislature, actually made this system a sensible choice at the beginning of India's struggle. Then, the aim was to pry open the British government by gaining representation in legislatures, and thereby obtaining influence in executive decisions. The British rule was autocratic and the Indians needed a system of government that made it less so. The parliamentary system allowed Indians a semblance of representation in government.

The struggle for self-rule in India, however, began with a hapless first effort. The Home Rule scheme that sought to make the legislative councils in India on a partially elected basis, developed jointly by the Indian National Congress and a British member of parliament, Charles

Bradlaugh, in 1890, failed to pass the British parliament. The entire effort ended quickly with the death of Bradlaugh the following year. For nearly three decades, nothing constructive happened barring some superficial reforms in 1909. It was only after the First World War, when the British let some muted appreciation for the Indian contribution show, that the Indians had the heart to make another attempt.

In 1916, the 'non-official' Indian members of the Imperial Legislative Council managed to send a memorandum to the viceroy outlining a scheme of self-government for India. The Memorandum of the Nineteen, named after the nineteen of twenty-seven Indian members who signed it (among them a budding Muslim leader by the name of Jinnah) pleaded that while 'India does not claim any reward for her loyalty' during the war, 'she should no longer occupy a position of subordination but one of comradeship'.[2] The memorandum suggested that 'in all the Executive Councils, Provincial and Imperial, half the number of members should be Indians'. About the same time, both the Congress and Muslim League, on the initiative of Jinnah, jointly put forth a scheme demanding certain reforms. The Congress–League scheme asked for four-fifths elected and one-fifth nominated Indian members in legislative bodies.

AFTER THE SITUATION CHANGED

Even as the definition of self-rule began to move towards a vision of complete independence from British rule, there was no corresponding change in their vision of the system of self-government. The Indians sought to eliminate British tyranny, but not its chief instrument, their system of government. Every proposal for a new Constitution continued to envision a parliamentary system, despite the drastic changes in political circumstances. Gandhi's call for swaraj culminating in the National Demand in 1925, efforts to create a commonwealth of India, the Swaraj Constitution proposal, the Constitution embodied in the Government of India Act of 1935, and the calls for a Constituent Assembly, all either implied or proposed a parliamentary form of government.

This was remarkable, for in the two decades preceding the actual summoning of the Constituent Assembly, the political scene in India evolved from it being a colony of Britain, to a member of the British Commonwealth, to an independent federation, to a nation divided in two, before finally becoming a completely independent country. None of these phases, each hugely consequential to the nature of government, however, changed the British or the Indian thinking about the appropriate system of government to adopt.

Emboldened by the crowds Gandhi pulled by his call for swaraj, Indian leaders began to demand that Indians themselves be allowed to frame a Constitution, albeit within the framework of British parliament. A couple of years after Gandhi's call, the Indian members of the Central Legislative Assembly, led by Motilal Nehru, were able to pass a resolution recommending to the Governor General that a representative conference be summoned to develop a Constitution for India, and 'submit the same to the British Parliament to be embodied in a Statute'.[3] The adoption of the resolution became famous as the 'National Demand', for it was the first time a branch of the British government in India had supported the growing demand that Indians be allowed to create a Constitution of their own. In the Central Legislative Assembly, Motilal Nehru described the 'very minimum' required: 'We want the Executive to be responsible to the Legislature … Make us masters in our own home, but whatever else is outside the home and pertains more to your Imperial interests you are welcome to keep.'[4]

Similarly, attempts made directly in the British parliament to seek approval for a local framing of India's Constitution envisioned only a parliamentary form. A 1924 bill drafted on the initiative of Annie Besant, Tej Bahadur Sapru and Mahatma Gandhi, envisaged India as part of the British Empire. The Commonwealth of India Bill proposed that 'there shall be a Cabinet of not less than seven Ministers from among the Members of Parliament who shall be collectively responsible to the Legislative Assembly'.[5] The Bill found wide support among the members of the Labour Party and went as far as the first reading in the House of Commons at the end of 1925. However, the Labour Government lost in early elections and the fate of the Bill was sealed. A couple of years later, the British responded only by sending the seven-member, all-British, Simon Commission to examine whether Indians, mired in communalism, were fit for any participation in government. A furious Congress party set out to create a Swaraj Constitution for India.

The Swaraj Constitution, adopted by an All Parties Conference in 1928 under the leadership of Motilal Nehru, continued the tradition of imagining India as a British Dominion with a parliamentary form of government. The Nehru Report suggested a commonwealth of India along the lines of the Dominion of Canada, 'with a Parliament having powers to make laws for the peace, order and good government of India and an executive responsible to that Parliament'.[6] Motilal Nehru suggested a round table conference to discuss these proposals. India's freedom appeared near, with the minority Labour Party government in Britain agreeing to hold such a conference. But the British policy towards India changed again with the fall of the Labour government in 1931. The momentum built by the three round table conferences, however, resulted in a White Paper issued by the British outlining certain constitutional reforms.

The fall of the India-friendly government in Britain and the death of Motilal Nehru in 1931 dealt a serious blow to India's fight for a Constitution of her own, and to her struggle for independence in general. The 1933 White Paper didn't contemplate self-government, stipulating instead a bicameral federal legislature divided among appointed members from princely states, elected representatives from provinces and members nominated by the British; and a governor general who held 'special responsibilities' beyond the control of the legislative body. The seats for representatives in this federation of India were reserved on a religious basis. In one fell swoop, the British perpetuated the communal divisions in society, ended the special privileges of the princely states, bringing them under the same federal government, while ensuring at the same time that the British executive was not in any control whatsoever of the legislative body. The right-wing element of the Congress, the Swaraj Party, founded by Motilal Nehru in 1922 and now under a new president, called for the rejection of the White Paper proposals, and raised the first formal demand for a Constituent Assembly in India.

The British continued with their design, adopting the Constitution based upon a communal reservation system, in the Government of India Act of 1935. Next year, the demand for a Constituent Assembly became the 'cornerstone of Congress policy', as declared by Motilal Nehru's son, Jawaharlal, in his first address as president of the party. All the same, the Congress decided to participate in the first provincial elections to be held under the 1935 Act.

The Congress party's purpose in taking part in these elections was to wreck the Constitution embodied in the new Act from within. It worked hard to win control of the provincial legislatures and did manage an overwhelming victory in seven out of eleven provinces. As expected, it called for an immediate end of the Government of India Act,1935, and demanded that a Constituent Assembly be formed to frame a new Constitution for India. 'The Congress entered these elections with its objective of independence and its total rejection of the new Constitution, and the demand for a Constituent Assembly to frame India's Constitution,' the party stated in a resolution soon after its decisive victory.[7]

Nehru declared India's new resolve: 'We cannot entertain this idea of Dominion status in any shape or form; it is independence we want, not any particular status.' He reminded Congressmen that their aim was 'primarily to fight the Act and press and work for a Constituent Assembly', because the Government of India Act of 1935 'has been designed to perpetuate the subjection and exploitation of the Indian people and so strengthen the hold of British imperialism on India'.[8]

The 1935 Constitution was wicked not just because it perpetuated the communal divide in India, but also because it, by design, doomed the first Indian-only government to be ineffectual. Under the parliamentary form, the executive would be mired in political infighting if the legislative body that controlled it was perpetually and deeply divided. The Government of India Act of 1935 was designed to do exactly that. It structured a government in which the executive was put under the control of legislatures that were divided along religious lines.

The fight over the Government of India Act of 1935 made it clear that the parliamentary system was impractical as a system of government in a communally divided society. But the calls for a Constituent Assembly weren't accompanied by calls for the development of a different system.

JINNAH 'IRREVOCABLY OPPOSED'

In the elections held early in 1937, the Congress under the leadership of Nehru worked hard to win, for it aimed to end the very Constitution that was allowing the elections. But that the win would be so big was a surprise. The Muslim League didn't win even in Punjab or in Bengal, where Muslims were a majority. Of the 492 seats designated as 'Muslim' under the 1935 Act's Communal Award, the League won only 109. The Congress ran on the platform of supporting peasants against oppressive landlords, which drew huge support in the rural areas.

The Congress party had an implicit understanding with the Muslim League, under which the Congress avoided direct contests on several Muslim seats. The League expected that their winning candidates will be asked to join in the forming of governments. But in none of the provinces was the League given any share in power. The largest party in each province, following the example of the Congress, formed governments exclusively of their own. In denying any role to the League in the formation of cabinets, Nehru and his followers felt that 'the inclusion of the representatives of the Muslim League and other communal parties would have adversely affected the spirit of joint responsibility among the Ministers, and also weakened the national front ...' They also thought that 'a firm refusal to share power with the communal parties ... would also serve as a warning ... that with communal politics they would be eternally doomed to occupy opposition benches'.[9]

Soon after his big election win Nehru initiated a 'mass contact' programme to woo Muslims. Nehru wanted to rid India of political parties that were communal. 'We have too long thought in terms of pacts and compromises between communal leaders and neglected the people behind them,' Nehru declared in March 1937. 'It is for us now to go ahead and welcome the Muslim masses and intelligentsia in our great organization and rid this country of communalism in every shape and form.'[10]

The Congress party's policy of intimidation and exclusion from government was not limited to the Muslim League alone; princely states were also treated in the same fashion. Princes, even Hindu princes, resented the Congress's demands for popular reforms in their states. They became increasingly sympathetic to the Muslim League. The Maharaja of Nawanagar, the chancellor of the Chamber of Princes at the time, remarked: 'Why should I not support the League? Mr. Jinnah is willing to tolerate our existence, but Mr. Nehru wants the extinction of the Princes.'[11]

Faced with an uncompromising and overwhelming majority, the Muslim League rallied its core constituency, the communal Muslims, by raising the 'Islam in danger' cry. Jinnah made a public appeal to Gandhi to do something about the rapidly worsening Hindu–Muslim relations, but Gandhi seemed equally powerless.[12]

Muslim leaders began to paint Congress's refusal to form coalition governments as a breach of faith and launched a propaganda campaign. They raised two fears: that the non-inclusion of League representatives in the executive would necessarily lead to anti-Muslim policies; and that the Congress would forever exclude the Muslims from a share in power. Propaganda, mostly false, was even spread about 'atrocities' committed by the Congress governments against Muslims. The Muslims coalesced behind the Muslim League. In a number of by-elections in the Muslim constituencies, Congress candidates lost.

This further enhanced the League's standing among Muslims across the nation. Other minority parties and groups – even Hindu groups; the landlords, for instance – fearful of the Congress's domineering majority, came to rally behind the League. 'The strength of the Congress, it was felt, could be challenged with prospects of ultimate success, on the communal side.'[13]

Emboldened by an outpouring of support, and faced with the futility of gaining any share of powers in a parliamentary government, the League began to talk of a separate Muslim 'nation'. Jinnah, who once derided the League for being communal, now assumed leadership. He wrote to Nehru and Subhas Chandra Bose, the new Congress president, the League's three basic demands: that the League be 'the only authoritative and representative political organization of the Mussalmans'; that 'the Congress should accept the Communal Award'; and that 'coalition ministries should be formed in the Provinces'.[14]

All hopes for developing a common front against the British to fight for independence were now dashed. The Congress, of course, couldn't agree to relinquish its status as a national organization representing all people of India. The gulf between the Congress and the League was now unbridgeable.

India's first experiment with self-rule under the parliamentary system had failed miserably. The country's two principal political parties were locked in a stalemate. The fabric of the society was ripped apart by communal tension, the fight for independence was weakened, and there wasn't a semblance of consensus on the type of Constitution the Indians desired for their nation.

The parliamentary system's ineptness in sharing powers when both the majority and the minority seemed permanent made it appear that Indians were incapable of living under a system of self-rule. Even Gandhi began to view the situation with remorse, thinking that it was perhaps best that the British didn't leave India. 'India is a vast country,' he commented, 'you and your people can stay comfortably, provided you accommodate yourselves to our conditions here.'[15]

In reality, Pakistan was born in the wake of this 1937 fiasco with the parliamentary system. The fundamental tenet that a majority didn't have to share powers made the Muslim League's fight in India seem pointless. The League's status as a minority was never going to change, and hence it was forever doomed to sit in opposition. Faced with this stark reality, the League began to demand an autonomous Muslim nation. Pakistan, which until 1937 was merely Cambridge student Rehmat Ali's academic thesis, all of a sudden became a rallying point. 'The primary fact ... needs to be stressed that in 1937 there was singularly little support for the establishment of Pakistan. ... The growth of the Pakistan cult was phenomenal after the first general elections in 1937, and in three years the political scene in India underwent a radical transformation.'[16]

Before Jinnah committed to the formation of Pakistan, he set his condition for staying within a unified India in precise terms. In 1939, he had the Muslim League pass a resolution:

> It declared that Muslim India stood against the exploitation of the people of India and upheld the goal of a free India, but would be irrevocably opposed to 'any federal objective which must necessarily result in a majority community rule under the guise of democracy and a parliamentary system of government. Such a Constitution is totally unsuitable to the genius of the peoples of the country which is composed of various nationalities and does not constitute a national State.'[17]

Despite Jinnah's clear denunciation of the parliamentary system and his blunt refusal to work within it, the Congress leaders remained intent on their pursuit of that very system. In November 1939, the Congress ministries resigned over the issue of participation in the Second World War. In March 1940, the League's choice for Pakistan was sealed by the passing of resolutions demanding 'geographically contiguous' Muslim-majority areas that were 'autonomous and sovereign'.

Another outcome of the Congress party's decision to form majority-only governments in 1937 was that its calls for a Constituent

Assembly found no support among the minority parties. The calls for a Constituent Assembly became moot as soon as the rift between the Congress and the Muslim League erupted. While Nehru continued his efforts to renew those calls, Gandhi began to see that perhaps the best India was going to get for some time was this 1935 Constitution enacted by the British. He began to support the view that 'the Government of India Act of 1935 was an attempt, however limited it might be, to replace the rule of the sword by the rule of the majority'.[18]

But then, majority rule was precisely what landed India in trouble. An unfettered rule by the majority allowed under the parliamentary system had so deeply and permanently alienated a minority that by the time Gandhi turned around in late 1939 and supported the call for a Constituent Assembly, it was too little and too late. It was insufficient because Gandhi, like Nehru, failed to specifically address Jinnah's stand against the parliamentary system. In an article entitled 'The Only Way', Gandhi said that the only way out of the 'communal and other distempers' was to elect an assembly by universal suffrage to frame India's Constitution, but said nothing about the form of government such an assembly would contemplate. The only assurance he gave was that 'the Constituent Assembly will represent all communities in their exact proportion', which for a permanent minority was no assurance at all.

The tyranny of the majority that the parliamentary system permitted in 1937 was unmistakable. The winner-takes-all feature of this system allowed a majority party to establish a government entirely on its own, without any participation from the minority parties. As a result, within three years of India's first usage of the parliamentary system (1937–40), every aspect of the nation's political situation had worsened. The nation was at the brink of a vivisection, the freedom struggle was at a standstill, society was deeply divided and the political parties were deadlocked. The situation in India would have stayed the same for the foreseeable future, if not for the Second World War.

AMERICAN ADVICE IGNORED

Throughout the war years, there was little change in the thinking about what system of government India should adopt. The only noteworthy development was the failed Cripps Mission of 1942, led by Sir Stafford Cripps. A member of Churchill's War Cabinet, he was sent by the British, just months after the US entry into the war, to secure India's cooperation. The Japanese were rapidly approaching the shores of India and an invasion seemed imminent. The proposals that Cripps brought made promises for the future, but offered no concrete changes in India's status in the present. An Indian-only Executive Council was envisioned, but Cripps couldn't guarantee that the viceroy would not hold powers over it. As such, they were declined by the Indian leaders.

The Cripps Mission failed because it was only a show to satisfy the Americans. After the Japanese attack on America, the Americans were bearing the brunt of the war effort and were increasingly concerned about India falling to the Japanese. President Roosevelt of the US was putting pressure on Churchill to seek the Indians' cooperation in fighting the war.

The Cripps Mission fundamentally altered the nature of India's freedom struggle. The Indian leaders now realized that Britain had no intention of leaving India, and the only way to gain freedom was to push them out. 'The failure of the Cripps Mission,' Maulana Azad wrote in 1959, 'led to widespread disappointment and anger in the country. Many Indians felt that the Churchill Cabinet had sent Sir Stafford only because of American and Chinese pressure, but in fact Mr. Churchill had no intention of recognizing Indian freedom.'[19] Gandhi was particularly affected by the let-down. His faith in the sincerity of the British was now completely gone. While before he wanted not to embarrass the British during the war, after Cripps left, Gandhi didn't see any reason to wait. He began to plan a serious campaign to push the British out.

However, the Americans realized what was holding back India's freedom was the notion of majority rule and the disagreement between the majority and the minority parties. The American envoy Louis Johnson, who was sent to India to report on Cripps Mission, wrote to President Roosevelt: 'We must not assume that they will adopt the American or British systems. In view of the importance of guaranteeing protection to the minorities, a majority form of government may not be applicable and a coalition may prove to be the only practical way of guaranteeing internal harmony.'[20]

India remained a worry for the Americans until the very end of the Second World War, because while the Germans were defeated, the Japanese went on fighting. American pressure on the British to do something about India continued and resulted in another mission. This time it was spearheaded by the British viceroy Lord Wavell. The Wavell Plan was presented at a conference at Simla in mid-1945. The Simla Conference also failed in bringing an agreement between the Indian majority and minority parties. And the US envoy's thoughts about the form of government suitable for India fell by the wayside.

CLAMOURS FOR A DIFFERENT SYSTEM

It is astonishing that even in the clamour for a new form of governance, after Jinnah's public condemnation of the parliamentary system, every single proposal made was based on this very form. The British made efforts too, but as was to be expected, they were also based on parliamentary principles. By now, Jinnah had taken to opposing every scheme because none conceded the demand for a sovereign Pakistan.

Top Indian leaders considered at least fifteen proposals for a new system of government between 1940 when Jinnah's obstinate estrangement began and 1946 when the split became final. But none proposed a system that could resolve the principal issue of minorities sharing power. The only exception was an outline developed by the Muslim League in March 1940 that specified certain principles; sovereign states and mandatory safeguards for minorities, it felt, were necessary in a new Constitution. But the League was advancing its cause for a separate state of Pakistan, not these constitutional principles.

In August 1942, the Congress party's famous 'Quit India' resolution attempted to reassure the minorities, particularly Muslims, by declaring that India's Constitution 'should be a federal one, with the largest measure of autonomy for the federating units, and with the residuary powers vesting in these units'.[21] These were both – federal structure and residual powers with units – features of the US presidential system. But the Congress resolution was seen only as one party's political stunt. The British put almost all the Congress party leadership in jail and the proposal went nowhere.

Proposals to resolve the deadlock increasingly included elements of the US presidential system, but none followed the system in its entirety. Rajagopalachari, one of the first Congress leaders to realize that his party would have to concede the demand for Pakistan, developed a formula in April 1944 under which a state could separate from the Union. He suggested that 'in the event of separation, mutual agreement shall be entered into for safeguarding defence, and commerce and communication and for other essential purposes'.[22] The concept paralleled the American system's structure that allowed sovereign states to form a national Federal government with specific powers delegated to it. Rajagopalachari's proposal became the basis for the Gandhi–Jinnah talks in late 1944. The talks broke down in eighteen days because Jinnah didn't want to commit any part of his Pakistan's sovereignty to a national government.

Then a ray of hope emerged. It was from non-politicians. At the initiative of Tej Bahadur Sapru and his friends who represented an apolitical outfit, the Non-Parties' Conference, and with Gandhi's blessings, a committee was formed 'to understand the point of view of each party and to act as a sort of conciliation board'. The members of this committee were individuals who didn't belong to any recognized political party and who had not publicly committed themselves to any particular view. They included eminent Indians like S. Radhakrishnan, who would become the second president of independent India, and Sachchidanand Sinha, a former member of the Imperial Legislative Council, who would be the first chairman of India's Constituent Assembly.

The Sapru Committee attempted to develop a consensus on not just how to deal with the British, but also on the issue of Pakistan, and on a system of government suitable for India. Rejecting the idea of Pakistan, the committee stated in its recommendations released in 1945 that 'the partition of India would be an outrage justified neither by history nor by political expediency'.[23] It recommended that India be given immediate freedom as a British Dominion; that the popular ministries in provinces be re-established; that the largest party in the legislature be required to include other parties in forming governments; and that a Constituent Assembly be formed with an equal number of Muslim and non-Muslim members to frame India's Constitution. The committee then went further and suggested certain constitutional principles.

The Sapru Committee questioned the suitability of the parliamentary system – the first time a national body formally did so. As the committee asked its members whether the nation's executive should be 'parliamentary or non-parliamentary, removable or irremovable', it raised doubts about the parliamentary system: 'There is a school of thought in India which maintains that the parliamentary form of government, depending for its stability upon the support of the legislature, is not suited to the peculiar conditions of India, and that, for that reason, an irremovable executive at the Centre will be more appropriate.'

It turned out that the members of the Sapru Committee were not of one mind. While the majority of members favoured the British-type system, Chairman Sapru himself, along with the Sikhs on the committee, recommended a Swiss-type system with an 'irremovable executive'. What the Committee said in its report was most telling:

> We are bound to observe that since the time representative Government was introduced in India many decades ago, the Indian mind has been accustomed to the British type and indeed the whole of its education has familiarized it with that system, more

than with any other system. It is, therefore, easy to understand why there is such a decided and widespread tendency to favour that type. That type no doubt presupposes differences of political opinion based not on religious or communal considerations but on economic interests. Those who are opposed to the British model urge that the dominant feature of Indian life being the existence of communal and racial divisions, the British pattern of parliamentary government, based as it is on a large degree of homogeneity, is unsuitable and will not yield in this country those results which it has produced in England.[24]

The Sapru Committee's rejection of Pakistan, however, meant that it would not get the Muslim League's support. Similarly, its idea of parity for Hindus and Muslims in the Constitution-making body found little support among Hindus. But above all, the Sapru Committee's recommendations went nowhere because the British viceroy Wavell was busy developing his own plan.

More and more, the search for a solution to the incessant political stalemate was nudging India in the direction of the presidential system. The Wavell Plan was no exception. But it drew only from one of its features, the direct appointment of members of the executive. But at the Simla Conference Jinnah insisted that the Muslim League alone had the right to nominate all Muslim members of the Executive Council. No one, including Wavell, found that acceptable. Maulana Azad, the Congress party's chief negotiator, would note that 'the Simla Conference marks a breakwater in Indian political history. This was the first time when negotiations failed, not on the basic political issue between India and Britain, but on the communal issue dividing different Indian groups.'[25]

The necessity for an alternative to the parliamentary system was now acknowledged, albeit grudgingly, even by Nehru. He was now of the view that a Union of provinces was possible only when there was no coercion; and that safeguarding the rights of the minority would have to take a structural form – traits of the US system. A proposal incorporating these views was explored between B.N. Rau, a constitutional adviser and Nehru confidant, and the new prime minister of Britain, Attlee, near the end of 1945. Clement Attlee headed the first ever Labour government in Britain with a clear majority, which, to the world's surprise, had ousted Churchill. In the plan Rau discussed, the provinces could be structured along communal lines and their interests could be protected by an Upper House of the central legislature constituted on a provincial basis. This was akin to the structure of the Senate in the US system. In searching for options, Nehru looked to the Swiss system as well. To avoid the partition of the nation, he felt that the option of creating half-provinces with a degree of autonomy for each half, on the lines of half-cantons in Switzerland, should also be considered.[25] But with the calling of fresh elections in India at the end of 1945, these discussions ended.

The search for an alternative system of government acceptable to all was now taking on a sense of urgency. With each passing day, partition was looking more and more imminent. At the end of 1945, a close associate of Gandhi and a former president of the Congress party, Rajendra Prasad, took it upon himself to analyse all proposals to deal with India's communal divide. In his book, *India Divided*, he debunked the 'two nations theory'. In response to Jinnah's statement that 'Musalmans are a nation ... they must have their homelands', Prasad said 'it is impossible to have a homogeneous State of either the Hindus or the Muslims in any part of the country without a considerable minority of the other community in it'. Prasad proposed an alternative: 'Instead of seeking a solution of the Indian problem in the creation of national States of Hindus and Musalmans ... is it not better to allow India to continue as an unnational [sic] State that she is and has been?'[27]

It was telling that all alternatives to partition that Prasad summarized were based on a federal structure – perhaps what Prasad meant by 'unnational'. But none followed the model all the way. At the centre of all proposals was the typical parliamentary structure of a federal executive responsible to the legislature. Jinnah had already opposed all such schemes because 'the safeguards ... will be of no use', he said, 'so long as there is a communal Hindu majority at the Centre the safeguards will remain on paper'.[28]

The only proposal that spoke of a 'non-parliamentary' executive at the Centre was one made by B.R. Ambedkar, a constitutional scholar of repute and president of the Scheduled Castes Federation. His solution was based on the principle of granting relative majority to a community, but not absolute majority. As such, he proposed that no community should be granted more than 40 per cent representation in the nation's legislature. As for the executive, Ambedkar recommended that it 'should be non-Parliamentary in the sense that it shall not be removable before the term of the Legislature. ... Parliamentary in the sense that the members of the Executive shall be chosen from the members of the Legislature.' He declared that 'even the Constitution of the United States does not lend support to the absolutist rule of majority'.[29] Ambedkar also published his views in a pamphlet entitled *States and Minorities*, stating that 'the application of the British parliamentary system to India will ... make the majority community a governing class and the minority community a subject race'.[30]

Prasad, however, immediately rejected Ambedkar's proposal because he saw in it the same problem for the majority, that it will be unable to ever form a government of its own. Prasad argued that while Ambedkar considers majority rule in India untenable and unjust, 'he does not see any such difficulty in allowing a minority in combination with another minority to rule'. He pointed out that 'unless the Hindus and the Muslims combine they cannot form a government without the help of the Scheduled Castes but if any one of them combines with the Scheduled Castes it can establish its rule'.[31] Needless to say, the proposal didn't make much progress.

THE UNITED STATES OF INDIA

There was a sense of doom and urgency in the country after the Muslim League had gone to the 1946 polls on the platform of 'Pakistan'. It appeared that the League would capture almost all of the Muslim seats and the Congress all the others. The elections were essentially a plebiscite on the issue of Pakistan; the partition of the country seemed imminent.

In the last hours of despondency B.N. Rau took it upon himself to find a solution. In January 1946 as elections were still in progress, Rau presented his scheme for turning India into a federation, which he termed the United States of India. 'The essence of the scheme,' he wrote, 'is that while domination of one community by another is to be prevented, the unity of India is to be preserved for purposes equally beneficial to all.'[32]

Based on the premise that the Constitution for a united India must provide 'for the substance of Pakistan', Rau proposed that the nation be divided into three groups: central region, frontier regions and the states. The group comprising the frontier regions was drawn along the lines of Pakistan. Hindustan, Pakistan, and till such time that they acceded, the states, were to be the three territories. There was one federal legislature but Rau's plan allowed it to sit in parts in the three separate territories, so that 'the functions of the Federal Legislature in respect of each group of territories may be discharged ... by the members of that group alone'. The executive branch of the United States of India was organized as follows: 'The executive authority of the Federation is to be exercised by a Governor-General and there is to be a Privy Council of India to aid and advise him in the discharge of his functions. There shall be separate Executive Committees of the Privy Council for each of the three groups. The Governor-General, after consulting the executive committees of all three groups, is to make rules for the more convenient transaction of the business of the Federal Government.'[33]

Rau's United States of India took a leap toward making India a federation, but in every other respect it was business as usual. The British parliamentary principles drove the structure of government. 'This plan secures the federal principle better than the British convention and is at least initially better adapted to existing Indian conditions,' Rau wrote in commending the federation. 'It secures some measure of stability and continuity of policy,' he wrote, 'without destroying the element of responsibility to the legislature and it gives minorities a fair chance of obtaining representation in the executive.' And therein lay the rub, for under Rau's plan the executive was still under the control of legislative bodies. Also unresolved was the issue of sovereignty. Jinnah had explicitly refused to surrender any of it to a Union government of any sort in his talks with Gandhi.

In 1946 the Muslims of India voted overwhelmingly in support of Jinnah. Rau's proposal was never considered by India's political parties. His would be the last independent effort to devise a system of government that was markedly different from the British parliamentary system.

THE DEATH OF THE LAST BEST HOPE

India faced a bizarre and disgraceful situation at the beginning of 1946. For more than four years, a foreign power was willing to grant her independence but wasn't able to do so because the Indians couldn't agree on a system of government.

The British were getting frantic because not only did they have to rebuild a war-ravaged home, they also faced a hugely populated dominion that was ready to erupt in sectarian conflict. Within months of coming to power, Prime Minister Attlee sent three of his Cabinet colleagues to India to find a solution. The 1946 British Cabinet Mission put India firmly on the path to developing a Constitution.

The principles that the Mission advanced, or were generally expected to be adopted by the British-induced Constitution-making exercise, were based on the parliamentary form.

The Mission's first conclusion was that the idea of Pakistan made no practical sense. The three Cabinet members were quick to see that the establishment of Pakistan was not going to solve the communal problem in a nation where Hindus and Muslims lived together in every part. The British leaders pleaded with the Indian people to 'extend their vision beyond their own community or interest to the interests of the whole four hundred millions'. In a statement outlining their proposals in May 1946, the Cabinet Mission presented the stark reality: 'We and our Government and countrymen hoped that it would be possible for the Indian people themselves to agree upon the method of framing the new Constitution under which they will live. Despite the labours which we have shared with the Indian Parties, and the exercise of much patience and goodwill by all, this has not been possible. We therefore now lay before you proposals which, after listening to all sides and after much earnest thought, we trust will enable you to attain your independence in the shortest time and with the least danger of internal disturbance and conflict.'[34]

Instead of a federation of near-sovereign states, as was warranted not just by the demands for Pakistan but also by many princely states, the Cabinet Mission envisioned India as a union of provinces. These provinces were free to form groups, each governed by its own legislative and executive bodies. Together, these groups of provinces could determine the subjects that were provincial and those that were to be handled in common. There would also be a Union executive and legislature, constituted from representatives of British India and the princely states.

The British Cabinet Mission also structured India's Constitution-making body. The members for a Constituent Assembly, it suggested, should be selected by the provincial legislative assemblies recently chosen by the people of India in a nationwide election. The seats in this Constituent Assembly were allotted on a communal basis. First, each province was allocated a number of seats in proportion to its population, and then in proportion to each of the three communities, described as Sikhs, Muslims and General (everyone else). The communal representatives were to be elected by the members of that community in each province's legislature. The Mission went as far as recommending the initial groupings, although it granted that each province had the right 'to act according to its choice in regard to grouping'. It divided the provinces into three sections, grouping the six Muslim-majority provinces together and suggested that each section should develop a separate provincial Constitution for itself.

The cherry on the cake in the Cabinet Mission's plan was the recommendation that an interim government of India be formed in which all portfolios, including that of the war member, be held by the Indians themselves. This fulfilled the Congress party's long-standing demand that the substance of independence must be granted by the British in the immediate present.

Even though the system of government the Cabinet Mission proposed was fundamentally parliamentary, Jinnah initially accepted the plan because it offered the Muslim League two key benefits. Since almost all Muslim representatives had won the recent election as League's candidates, Jinnah saw that the League would be able to speak for Muslims exclusively. He also saw hope in the grouping together of the six Muslim areas in the Constituent Assembly, for it allowed them to have some form of autonomy or sovereignty. Anxious to consolidate his position, Jinnah quickly laid down two conditions for his acceptance of the Mission's plan: that the interim government must have Congress–League parity and that only the League will nominate all Muslim members. Quick on the uptake, the Congress party agreed to participate only in the Constituent Assembly part of the Mission's plan but not in the interim government.

The interim government became the first sticking point because, being parliamentary in form, it couldn't provide proper sharing of powers between a large majority and a much smaller minority. In rejecting this part of the plan, the Congress noted that it could 'never give up the national character of the Congress or accept an artificial parity or agree to a veto of a communal group'.[35] Jinnah argued that the Mission's plan for interim government and Constituent Assembly constituted 'one whole', and that the League wouldn't participate in one but not the other. Facing the deadlock again, the British disagreed with Jinnah. They withdrew the plan for provisional government but decided to proceed with the elections for the Constituent Assembly. Accusing the British of trying 'to appease the Congress', the Muslim League withdrew its acceptance of the plan. The viceroy invited Nehru to form the provisional government without the League.

In accepting this part of the plan, the Congress party took the position that the British couldn't force a province into the three groupings it had suggested. The British insisted that the Mission's intention was 'that the Provinces cannot exercise any option' with regard to grouping until a constitutional arrangement had been agreed to. The Congress refused to adhere to the British interpretation on the grounds that it was inconsistent with the principle of provincial autonomy. In a public statement in July 1946 Nehru divulged the Congress strategy of not allowing the groups to hold in the Constituent Assembly. Two of the six Muslim provinces grouped together by the British plan, Assam and the North-West Frontier Province, Nehru suggested, wouldn't vote with Bengal and Punjab.

Thus both the interim government and Constituent Assembly parts of the Cabinet Mission plan failed in safeguarding the rights of the minority. Jinnah now called for 'Direct Action', a code for unleashing sectarian violence. 'Due to the intransigence of the Congress on one hand, and the breach of faith with the Muslims by the British Government on the other,' he declared that the League was 'convinced that now the time has come for the Muslim Nation to resort to Direct Action to achieve Pakistan to assert their just rights, to vindicate their honour and to get rid of the present British slavery and the contemplated future Caste-Hindu domination'.[36]

India erupted in communal violence. Between July 1946, when Direct Action was initiated, and January 1947, when the League's withdrawal from the Constituent Assembly became permanent, everyone – the Congress, Nehru, the viceroy, B.N. Rau, even the British prime minister Attlee – tried to change Jinnah's mind, but failed. In September 1946, when the interim government came to power under the leadership of Nehru, prodded by the viceroy, Jinnah reconsidered his boycott, but only for a brief moment. Noting in a letter to the viceroy that 'it will be fatal to leave the entire field of administration of the Central Government in the hands of the Congress', Jinnah allowed a few Muslim League members to join the government. Within a month he would change his mind again and withdraw from the Mission's plan completely. He urged the British to postpone their plans for the Constituent Assembly. But now Nehru was determined to proceed.

With only three days remaining before the planned opening of India's Constituent Assembly in December 1946, the British prime minister made one last-ditch effort. At a conference in London he pleaded with Nehru to accept the view of the Cabinet Mission with regard to groupings, 'the view that the decisions of the sections should ... be taken by a simple majority vote of the representatives in the sections'.[37] Nehru didn't agree, and the London Conference failed as well. The Constituent Assembly began its work as planned at the end of 1946. A month later, the League passed a resolution that the Congress had 'converted the Constituent Assembly into a body of its own conception', and called for its dissolution.[38]

The Cabinet Mission of 1946 failed for want of two simple requirements: a way to provide autonomy to a people clamouring for it within the Union; and a way to share powers between a permanent majority and a minority. While a genuine federation could satisfy the former requirement, a structure of government in which a minority held real powers could satisfy the latter. The British plan offered neither.

NOTES

1   Cited in Rao, B. S. (2006), *The Framing of India's Constitution*, Delhi: Universal Law Publishing, Vol. 1, p. 33.
2   Ibid., pp. 21–22.
3   Ibid., p. 35.
4   Ibid., p. 41.
5   Ibid., p. 45.
6   Ibid., p. 59.
7   Ibid., p. 84.
8   Ibid., pp. 86–91.
9   Ibid., Vol. 5, p. 24.
10   Ibid.

11   Ibid., p. 26.
12   Ibid., p. 22.
13   Ibid., p. 26.
14   Ibid., p. 25.
15   Ibid., p. 26.
16   Ibid., p. 21.
17   Ibid., p. 28.
18   Ibid., p. 26.
19   Azad, A. K. (1988), *India Wins Freedom* (*Complete Version*), New Delhi: Orient Blackswan, p. 70.
20   Rao, op. cit., Vol. 5, p. 49.
21   Ibid., Vol. 1, p. 132.
22   Ibid., Vol. 5, p. 54.
23   Ibid., p. 58.
24   *Sapru Committee Report*, 1945.
25   Azad, op. cit., p. 117.
26   Rao, op. cit., Vol. 5, p. 64.
27   Prasad, R. (2010), *India Divided*, New Delhi: Penguin Books India Pvt. Ltd, pp. 35–39.
28   Ibid., p. 471.
29   Presidential address, May 1945, Ambedkar, B. R. (1979), *Writings and Speeches*, Volume 1, Bombay: Government of Maharashtra, pp. 357–79.
30   Ambedkar, B. R. (1947), *States and Minorities*, Bombay: Thacker and Co., pp. 36–38.
31   Prasad, op. cit., pp. 492–93.
32   Rao, op. cit., Vol. 1, p. 160.
33   Ibid., p. 161.
34   Ibid., p. 217.
35   Ibid., p. 279.
36   Ibid., p. 285.
37   Ibid., p. 347.
38   Ibid., p. 353.

4

Nehru Decides; Snubs Gandhi and Patel

The adoption of the parliamentary system by India's Constituent Assembly was a foregone conclusion, for it was the choice of an overwhelmingly dominant political party. The assembly merely went through the motions of debating it. The Indian National Congress, and its leader Jawaharlal Nehru, favoured the system for its ability to establish a centralized majority-party government. Nehru and his supporters equated such a system with strong government, which they had decided was the answer to India's troubles. From conception to birth, Nehru chaperoned the choice of the parliamentary system through the entire process of constructing a Constitution, fighting back or ignoring every objection. The committee that planted the seed of this system in India's Constitution and the one that adopted it as a principle, were both chaired by him.

Soon after the British Cabinet Mission's announcement about the formation of a Constituent Assembly, the Congress party appointed an Experts Committee, under the chairmanship of Nehru, to prepare the party for the upcoming Constitution-making exercise. The Committee had two sittings, in July and August of 1946, to gather and discuss the views of Congressmen regarding both the principles and the process of making India's Constitution. In its second session on 15 August 1946, at Vallabhbhai Patel's residence, K. Santhanam and K.R. Kripalani, both staunch Nehru supporters, presented a draft Constitution based on the parliamentary system of government. While the proceedings of the Experts Committee meeting do not record if any formal decisions were taken, it was widely believed that this meeting established the key elements of the plan the Congress party was to pursue in the Constituent Assembly.[1]

The Experts Committee meeting had two fateful outcomes. It placed India firmly on the road to adopting the parliamentary system, and it ensured that a Gandhian constitution wasn't even tried. It rejected Gandhi's advice that instead of copying the British system, India should adopt a unique home-grown system based on village panchayats. Dilip Kumar Chatterjee wrote in *Gandhi and Constitution Making in India*: 'Discarding the Gandhian plan as conservative and undemocratic, the Committee proposed a liberal democratic, parliamentary system of government with a federation. Nehru envisaged a centralized administration. In the course of a long exchange of letters between Gandhi and Nehru, in October 1945, Gandhi stressed the need for decentralized political institutions. ... But the Congress party and many of the Indian leaders were couching their demands for independence in terms of a parliamentary democracy, and many had participated in the modified forms of representative government which were introduced in British India.'[2]

ONE PARTY RULES THE CONSTITUENT ASSEMBLY

When India's Constituent Assembly began its work on 9 December 1946, the Congress party directly held 53 per cent of the 389 seats, while the Muslim League held less than 19 per cent. The only other large chunk, about 24 per cent, was held by the representatives of princely states. In the early days of the Assembly, when the Muslim League had refused to participate and the princely states were still in the process of negotiating their entry, the Congress party was in near-total control. As the political developments altered the total size and allocation of seats, the Congress party's dominance of India's Constitution-making body grew even stronger. When in January the Muslim League withdrew its representatives completely, the Congress's hold over the seats reached

67 per cent. This process of transformation continued throughout the life of the Constituent Assembly, ending only in November 1948. In the end, the Congress party, along with some Muslim and all of the Sikh seats, controlled at least 208 of the 324 seats.

The members of the Constituent Assembly were not directly elected, they were appointed by the provincial assemblies that came to power in recent elections. But since elections were held only in the provinces and not in the princely states, the states' representatives were nominated by the princes. To its credit, the Congress party took pains to include a fair representation of minority candidates among its ranks. At the insistence of Gandhi, the party even included a number of non-party candidates. As many as thirty members of the Assembly were drafted by the Congress from among India's men and women of eminence, including S. Radhakrishnan and B.R. Ambedkar, who would go on to be the chairman of the Drafting Committee.

In fact, Ambedkar was one of the first to point out that the Constituent Assembly was completely under the control of the Congress party. 'I do not know, what plans the Congress party, which holds this House in its possession, has in its mind,' said Ambedkar days after the start of the Assembly, as he argued that the deliberations should be postponed in view of the fact that the Muslim League was not participating. Commenting on the Congress's insistence on proceeding, Ambedkar said, 'it seems to me there are only three ways by which the future will be decided. Either there shall have to be surrender by the one party to the wishes of the other ... The other way would be what I call a negotiated peace and the third way would be open war.'[3]

The issue of one political party's dominance of India's Constituent Assembly was raised even in the British parliament, replete with a communal spin. Charges were made that the Assembly only represented one community, the caste Hindus. Rajendra Prasad, the Assembly's president and a staunch Congressman, refuted this as he opened the assembly:

In the course of the debates on India in the House of Commons and in the House of Lords in December last, certain statements were made detracting from the representative character of this Assembly during its last session. Notable among those who spoke in this strain were Mr Churchill and Viscount Simon. Mr Churchill observed that the Assembly, as it was meeting then, represented 'only one major community in India'. Viscount Simon was more specific and referred to the Assembly as 'a body of Hindus'. He went on further to ask 'whether this meeting of Caste Hindus at Delhi can be regarded by the Government as the Constituent Assembly they meant at all.

Prasad regretted that the Muslim League hadn't joined, but stated certain facts as evidence that the Assembly had fair representation: 'Out of a total of 926 Members who were to take part in the preliminary session, 210 Members attended. These 210 Members consisted of 155 Hindus out of a total of 160, thirty Scheduled Caste representatives out of a total of thirty-three, all the five Sikhs, five Indian Christians out of a total of seven, all five representatives of Backward Tribes, all three Anglo-Indians, all three Parsis and four Muslims out of eighty.'[4]

Ignoring the appeals of many, including Gandhi, to postpone the proceedings of the assembly until such time that the Muslim League joined, Nehru proceeded with the introduction of his Objectives Resolution within the first session in December 1946. It resolved 'to proclaim India as an Independent Sovereign Republic and to draw up for her future governance a Constitution', without going into the nature of that Constitution. Bending slightly to the headwinds, Nehru however postponed the Resolution's passing until the assembly's next session in January of the following year. With the boycott of the Muslim League now final, the Constituent Assembly proceeded with the appointment of a series of important committees, and then adjourned until April.

ELDER STATESMAN PRAISES AMERICAN SYSTEM

The opening day of the Constituent Assembly was full of promise despite the lopsided control of the House in the hands of the Congress party. A leading Congressman, J.B. Kripalani, led to the podium a non-Congressman to be the chairman of the Assembly. Sachchidanand Sinha was, in fact, an estranged Congressman who had left the party in the 1920s due to his inability to reconcile the positions he held within the British government with the freedom movement launched by Congress. Inviting Sinha to take the chair, Kripalani noted his eminent qualifications: 'Dr Sinha needs no introduction. You all know him. He is not only the oldest among us but also the oldest parliamentarian in India, having served, as you know, as a member of the Imperial Legislative Council from 1910 to 1920. He entered the Central Legislative Assembly in 1921 not only as one of its members, but as its Deputy President also. He was then entrusted with the portfolio of an Executive Councilor and Finance Member of the Government of Bihar and Orissa. So far as I remember Dr Sinha was the first Indian who was ever appointed as a Finance Member of a Province. He has a particular taste for education having been Vice-Chancellor of the Patna University for eight years. Over and above all this, Dr Sinha is the oldest Congressman among us. Up till 1920 he was a member of the Congress, being at one time its Secretary.'[5]

In his inaugural address, this long-time practitioner of the parliamentary system said, 'Under the British Constitution, there is no such thing as a constituent law, it being a cherished privilege of the British parliament, as the sole sovereign authority, to make and unmake all laws, including the constitutional law of the country.' Switzerland also 'had not had a Constituent Law, in the ordinary sense of that term, for it came into existence on a much smaller scale than it now exists ...' As for France, Sinha said: 'As a matter of fact, the French Constitution-makers, who met in 1789 at the first Constituent

Assembly of their country, were themselves largely influenced by the work done but a couple of years earlier in 1787, by the historic Constitutional Convention held at Philadelphia by the American Constitution-makers, for their country.'

It was the American Constitution that he urged the members to adopt:

'Having thrown off their allegiance to the British King in Parliament, [the Americans] met and drew up what had been regarded, and justly so, as the soundest, and most practical and workable republican Constitution in existence. ...

It may possibly be that in some such scheme, skilfully adapted to our own requirements, a satisfactory solution may be found for a Constitution for an Independent India, which may satisfy the reasonable expectations and legitimate aspirations of almost all the leading political parties in the country. ... Constitutions, as a governmental panacea, have come and gone; but it can be said of the American Constitution ... that the stream of time which has washed away the dissoluble fabric of many other paper constitutions, has left almost untouched its adamantine strength. ... What other form of government has better stood the test of time? ... my prayer is that the Constitution that you are going to plan may similarly be reared for immortality.'[6]

The high honour given to Sinha was, however, temporary. Two days later, the Assembly chose its permanent president, Rajendra Prasad, a Congress loyalist. Sinha was never to be heard from again during the proceedings of the Constituent Assembly. In his message of congratulations at the final adoption of India's Constitution, Sinha applauded Prasad and the Assembly for uniting the Indians behind so much in the new Constitution. He, however, noted that 'nothing in this world is or can be perfect', and that given the complexities that the assembly faced, 'it is not at all surprising that there are several problems unsolved'.[7]

APATHETIC MEMBERS GIVE ADVISOR FREE HAND

Soon after the January 1947 adjournment of the Constituent Assembly, the political situation in India underwent an earth-shattering change. The British government decided to grant India her freedom. A new viceroy, Louis Mountbatten, was being sent to make arrangements. When in March 1947 Mountbatten arrived in India, he found the atmosphere highly charged. The Muslim League's Direct Action was at its peak and the communal conflict had Nehru's inexperienced interim government in the doldrums. The Indians had no Constitution, and a government that was completely ineffectual.

The task of framing the Constitution now took on a sense of urgency. With the intention of speeding things up, Prasad appointed B.N. Rau as a constitutional advisor and asked him to send a questionnaire to members of the Constituent Assembly, seeking their views on the Constitution's most important questions. Rau's questionnaire asked members to send their responses before the Assembly was to resume work in April 1947, so that a draft Constitution with some consensus behind it could be prepared before the session began.

In the main, Rau wanted to know the structure of the Central government that the members desired. It was stated that the same structure would be applied to the provincial governments. Rau asked three key questions: 'How should the Head of the Indian Union be chosen?'; 'What should be the nature and type of the Union Executive? Should it be of the British type (parliamentary) or the American type (non-parliamentary) or the Swiss type (mixed) or any other type?'; and, 'If Parliamentary, should there be any special provision to secure a stable Executive?' In his accompanying notes, Rau explained that if the head of the Indian Union 'is to be a real Head, independent of the Legislature, he may have to be elected otherwise than by the Legislature as in the USA. ... This mode of election is presumably due to the theory of the American Constitution that the executive power must be completely separated from the legislative power.'

Regarding the nature of the Union executive, Rau wrote that 'from the point of view of practical administration this is perhaps the most important question in the framing of the new Constitution'. He worried about instability of parliamentary governments in a deeply divided India. Rau went so far as to quote an observation from the Simon–Attlee Report highlighting this danger:

> We think that under the conditions which have developed in the Indian Provinces, Ministers are too much at the mercy of hostile combinations against them for good work to be done. Ministers need to feel that they are assured of a reasonable period within which their policy may mature and its results may be judged; at present some of them are so much occupied in maintaining their position by securing the temporary support of this or that group of critics or malcontents that it must be very difficult to carry on the main work of ministerial government at all.[8]

In April, when the assembly resumed its work, Rau wasn't ready with his report for he had received no feedback. When on 30 April the Assembly appointed the two all-important committees, the Union Constitution Committee and the Provincial Constitution Committee, he sent his questionnaire to their members again. A month later he presented a draft Constitution to the Union Constitution Committee, but not one based on the members' responses. 'Replies to the questionnaire supplied to members of the committee,' he lamented, 'have been received from only one member (Sardar K.M. Panikkar). Another member (Professor K.T. Shah) has sent in a memorandum embodying general directives as well as a Draft Constitution. I have not, therefore, found it possible, as directed by the committee, to prepare a memorandum embodying what may be called the greatest common measure of the views of the several members. In these circumstances, the best course seemed to me to be to prepare an independent memorandum for the consideration of the committee.'[9]

The sole respondent to Rau's questionnaire in fact hadn't even bothered to answer the key question about how the head of the Indian

Union should be chosen. Rau's only feedback on that matter came from Shah's 'General Directives', ideas that were already well known to the Indian leaders. Shah wrote that his Directives were 'prepared originally at the instance of Pandit Jawaharlal Nehru in July last. It is based on a combination of American, British and French models.' In December 1946, he had sent a copy to Prasad as well. On the issue of electing the head of the Union, these Directives were quite precise: 'The Chief Executive or the Head of the Union of India or in any component part thereof, shall be elected by the votes of all the adult citizens of India…'[10]

Remarkably, Rau completely disregarded the only opinion he had received from a member of the Constituent Assembly. On the matter of the head of the Union, his draft described a chief executive that was an archetype of the parliamentary form. Rau attempted to explain his position: 'Since the President, under the proposed Constitution is intended merely to be a constitutional head, it seems unnecessary to provide for his election by direct vote of the people of the Union. Such an elaborate process might be appropriate for an all-powerful head like the President of the USA.'[11] In Rau's rendition, the head of the Indian Union, albeit called the 'President', would 'almost always act on the advice of Ministers…'[12]

The draft Rau prepared became the basis on which decisions were taken by the all-important Union Constitution Committee chaired by Nehru. A constitutional advisor's choice, developed without any formal input from the members of India's Constituent Assembly, thus became the country's system of government. In fact, B.N. Rau's May 1947 draft was essentially the first draft of India's Constitution.

THE NATION SPLITS IN TWO

Within three months of his arrival, Mountbatten reached the conclusion that if the British were to relieve themselves of India, partition was the only choice. His efforts to reconcile the political parties in India were as unfruitful as before. When on 3 June 1947 he announced that the British government had decided to hand over power to two separate nations, India and Pakistan, the political scenario in India was turned completely on its head. While before, the Indians had to devise a system that ensured regional autonomy and a Central government that shared powers, after that announcement, both requirements had essentially vanished.

With the troublemaking minority hived off into a separate nation, the majority found it even easier to establish a parliamentary government with powers concentrated in its own hands. Also, as attention shifted from placating a minority to diffusing separatist tendencies in other communities and princely states, this type of government – unitary and centralized – appeared more fitting to the fragmented nation. It was a remarkable paradox that the system of government that failed to unite the nation before partition was seen as the panacea for bringing unity and harmony to a still deeply divided, albeit smaller, country.

A strong Central government became the rallying cry for Indian leaders. Partition only vindicated their thinking. K.M. Munshi, a Congress party stalwart, said this in the Constituent Assembly: 'The plan of May 16 had one motive – to maintain the unity of the country at all costs. A strong Central government was sacrificed by the May 16 plan at the altar of preserving the unity, which many of us after close examination of the plan found to be an attenuated unity which would not have lasted longer than the making of it.'[13] Similarly, B. Shiva Rao wrote: 'The announcement of partition made a deep impact on the Assembly. It was as a last effort to maintain the unity of India that the Congress had accepted the Cabinet Mission's plan for a weak Centre.'[14]

The fact of the matter is that Indian leaders were preoccupied with the task of running a nation in turmoil. The framers of India's Constitution didn't have the time or the concentration to explore a form of government that was different from the one they knew. Since India's Constituent Assembly also functioned as the nation's legislature, the members' mindset was that of legislators. Nehru was not only the Congress party's chief strategist in the Constituent Assembly, he was also the prime minister of India's interim government. As India burnt in the worst communal violence in her history, the more pressing matters of containing the bloodshed and of governance took the Assembly's, and Nehru's, attention away from the task of making the Constitution.

Between April 1947, when the Union Constitution Committee undertook its initial deliberations, and July 1947, when it made its recommendations final, India went through mayhem. During this period the country's political ground shifted in truly fundamental ways. For instance, as the Union Constitution Committee was deciding whether India's Constitution should be unitary or federal, the British were announcing the country's partition. Politically the country was in a constant state of chaos and change. The plan which brought the Constituent Assembly into existence was withdrawn; the constitutional framework under which the first resolutions of the Assembly and the Union Constitution Committee were adopted was no longer applicable; the nation was partitioned; the provinces were being continually redrawn as the princely states acceded; and the country was granted independence. As Nehru submitted his committee's second report, because the first wasn't complete due to the drastic changes, he noted the difficulty: 'Momentous changes have since occurred. Some parts of the country are seceding to form a separate State, and the plan put forward in the Statement of the 16th May on the basis of which the Committee was working is, in many essentials, no longer operative.'[15]

The focus of the Constituent Assembly was blurred further when power was transferred to the Indian government on 15 August 1947. The members of the Constituent Assembly began to raise questions in the Assembly that were not concerned with the making of the Constitution. Within days, the president of the Assembly felt it necessary to appoint a special committee to look into the matter, asking: 'Is it possible to distinguish between the business of the Constituent Assembly as a constitution-making body and its other business?'[16]

The making of the Constitution and any consideration of a different system of government was far from Nehru's mind as well. When questions were raised in the Constituent Assembly regarding disturbances caused by some British military officers during the raising of the Indian flag, Nehru revealed a rare glimpse of his nearly impossible workload. To a member's question of whether he had received a telegram informing him of the matter, Nehru responded: 'I cannot say off-hand, because I have received 7,000 telegrams in the last four or five days … It is physically impossible for an individual or for a group of individuals to analyze them or even to read them quickly.'[17] This was before Nehru had to handle the eruption of the first Indo-Pakistan war in October; the arrival of millions of refugees; and the difficulties raised by the princely states, like Hyderabad, in acceding to the new nation.

India's Constituent Assembly was also pressed for time. It had to finish its task before power could be transferred. When the process of framing the Constitution began in earnest, in April 1947, the Assembly gave itself only until October. However, the country was in such a flux that the Union Constitution Committee was compelled to postpone decisions, while some decisions that it took in April were no longer appropriate in June. Although the pressure to complete a Constitution diminished after the British decided to transfer power to two separate nations, the momentum continued. The Assembly proceeded to adopt the recommendations of the Union Constitution and Provincial Constitution Committees as scheduled before, even if it was within a month of the game-changing announcement of partition.

The records show that even when there was more time, and even when the political situation had completely changed, the framers made no attempt to reconsider the system they were about to adopt.

A ONE-MAN DECISION

The complete story of how Jawaharlal Nehru single-handedly took his personal choice and thrust it upon the entire nation, and how he brazenly ignored the advice of India's most eminent men, has never been told.

The truth is, if not for Nehru, India would have adopted some form of the presidential system. A joint meeting of the Constituent

Assembly's two topmost committees essentially adopted the presidential system by embracing two of its principal features: autonomous provincial governments and direct election of the head of those governments. However, Nehru in his Union Constitution Committee continued to push for a typical parliamentary pattern for India's Central government. Alarmed by that choice, the president of the Assembly called another joint meeting. After a heated debate, the members again voted in favour of adopting the presidential system. Nehru was asked, officially and unambiguously, to reconsider his committee's decision. He never brought the matter up for reconsideration by his committee.

Here's what transpired in closed-door meetings.

Already the prime minister of India's interim government, Nehru was on his second stint as the head of a government functioning under the parliamentary system. He was intimately familiar with the benefits of centralized power that the system offered. Besides, he had spent his entire life under this system of government. So, when the Union Constitution Committee began deliberations with him as chairman and B.N. Rau as its constitutional advisor, and Rau's recommendations as its official draft, the adoption of the parliamentary form was a fait accompli.

Among the ranking members of Nehru's Committee was an outspoken critic of the US style federal system of government. K.M. Panikkar had become the most ardent and high-pitched supporter of a 'strong' Central government. The alternative, he felt, was dangerous for a fragmented nation like India. Therefore, as soon as the British Plan failed, Panikkar had a strong new opening to make his case. Within hours of the British announcement of their decision to partition the country, he issued a memo to his fellow members of the Union Constitution Committee, deriding the federal form and urging them to establish in India a unitary system of government instead. Coming only two days before the Union Constitution Committee was to open its deliberations, the memo was extremely well timed. Panikkar wrote on 4 June 1947: 'Federation, with limited powers for the Centre, was an unavoidable evil in India, so long as the Muslim majority Provinces had to be provided for in an All-India Centre. Now whether the partition comes, or whether a Hindustan Constitution is created with a loosely confederated Centre, the necessity for a federal Constitution has ceased ...'[18]

The question of whether India should be a unitary state or a federal union of states stumped everyone. Patel and his men at the Provincial Constitution Committee struggled with the issue in their meeting on 6 June 1947, but couldn't decide how to structure and organize the provincial governments without knowing the answer to this basic question first. This is when Patel decided to hold a joint meeting with the Union Constitution Committee to discuss the matter with Nehru and his colleagues in order to ensure that the two Constitutions proceeded along the same lines. In calling the joint meeting, Patel's Committee said that 'the primary question to be considered was whether India should be a unitary State with Provinces functioning as agents and delegates of the Central authority or whether India should be a Federation of autonomous units ceding certain specific powers to the Centre'.[19]

Nehru's Committee also grappled with the issue of centralism versus federalism in its separate meeting on the same day, but ended up mystifying it further. The members of the Union Constitution Committee reached a baffling decision 'that the Constitution should be a Federal structure with a strong Centre'. Going a step further, the committee members also decided how such a government was to be organized: 'It was accepted as a general principle that the executive authority of the Federation should be co-extensive with its legislative authority.'[20]

When members gathered the following day for the joint meeting called by Patel, they were presented with the perplexing decision – 'Federal structure with a strong Centre' – taken by the Union Constitution Committee the day before. After deliberations, the members of the two topmost committees of the Constituent Assembly jointly decided to accept the decision in principle, but they were hard-pressed to describe exactly how this peculiar system would work. With the able and experienced Prasad in the chair, the members of the joint meeting persisted. They agreed to a set of principles on which the provincial governments should be based in order to have both a strong Central government and provincial autonomy. The members of the joint meeting decided the basic principles for India's system of government:

> a) There should be a Governor at the head of every Province; b) the Governor should be appointed by the Province, and not by the Central Government; c) The Provincial executive should be of the Parliamentary Cabinet type, with such suitable modifications appointed by indirect election on the basis of adult franchise through a special electoral college.[21]

This was most significant because India's highest Constitution-making committees had adopted the presidential system's two main features: autonomous state governments, and a directly elected head of government. Granting a degree of independence to provincial governments was especially significant coming as it did after a decision to partition the country was already taken. Apparently the members of the joint committee concluded that providing autonomy to provincial governments was important even after the Muslim League's demands for sovereignty were no longer a factor. The adoption of the second feature of the presidential system – appointing the chief executive through an election by people rather than by legislators – was also historic.

But as soon as the two committees went their separate ways, the agreement to adopt the American method of selecting the chief executive began to unravel. The day after the joint committee meeting, on 8 June, the Provincial Constitution Committee proceeded along the decision that the governor of each provincial government shall be elected by the people. It decided that the election be held by 'adult franchise through a special electoral college'. But the Union Constitution Committee in its meeting on the same day chose an entirely different method of electing the president. It decided 'that the President shall be elected by an electoral college consisting of ... the members of the lower chamber of the Federal Legislature, and ... by the Legislature of [each] unit, by the lower chamber'.

In other words, Nehru's committee decided that while the states' executives could be elected by the people, the nation's chief executive would be elected by the legislators. Following the typical parliamentary pattern even further, the committee decided that the nation's chief executive was to be controlled by the national legislature. They established that 'the President's power to dissolve the lower chamber of the Federal Legislature should be exercised only on the advice of the Ministers'.[22]

Faced with these contrary decisions taken by Patel's and Nehru's committees, K.M. Munshi, a member of both these committees, decided to intervene. He wrote to the president of the Assembly, Rajendra Prasad, urging him to call another joint session to resolve the matter. He had this scheme to propose:

> I also think that the only occasion when the citizens of India irrespective of the differences of British Provinces and Indian States can mobilize themselves into a nation is the occasion of Presidential election. I realize the force of the argument that elections should not be multiplied and a way can be found by which the President and the Heads of the Provinces can be elected simultaneously. The question of the election of the President and the Heads of the Provinces is, therefore, so interlinked that the matter may well be considered in a joint meeting of the Union Committee and the Provinces Committee. I, therefore, request you to arrange for a joint meeting of both the Committees where the following scheme may be considered: 1) Every five years, electors shall be elected by the adult citizens of India throughout its territories in the proportion of one elector to one hundred thousand citizens. 2) These electors shall at the same elections elect the President of India and the Heads of the respective Provinces. 3) In the event of there being a vacancy either in the office of the President of India

or of the Head of that Province within a period of five years, the same electors shall elect the successor.[23]

But this was also when Nehru was working to make his choice final. On 9 June, the day Munshi wrote his letter to Prasad, the two committees made their divergent choices even harder to change. In their meeting in the morning, the Provincial Committee appointed a subcommittee to further develop the idea of an electoral college to elect a governor directly by the people. In the afternoon, the Union Constitution Committee, with Nehru in the chair and Prasad in attendance, brought up the relevant question from Rau's questionnaire and with hardly any explanation made the decision in favour of the parliamentary type. The committee went out of its way to say that the decision was final: 'It having been agreed already that the Union Executive should be of the parliamentary type no further decision on this item is necessary.'[24]

Nehru's committee attempted to close the debate on the issue despite Prasad's mentioning of Munshi's letter and suggesting that a joint meeting with the Provincial Constitution Committee was warranted. It is most interesting that the minutes of the Union Constitution Committee meeting on 9 June didn't record Prasad's raising of the issue.

NEHRU IGNORES RESOLUTION TO 'RECONSIDER'

Patel, however, wouldn't let go of the matter. He wanted the Union Constitution Committee to revise its decision. On the evening of 9 June, secretary of his committee circulated a note requesting a joint meeting with the Union Constitution Committee the following day. Setting the agenda, the note said:

> The following point mentioned by the President at today's meeting of the Union Constitution Committee: The President of the Union, according to the decision of the Union Constitution Committee, will be a purely constitutional Head of the State.

On the other hand, the Governors of Provinces, according to the decision of the Provincial Constitution Committee, will have certain powers to be exercised by them in their discretion. Should this distinction be maintained? ... Mr. Munshi has sought permission to revise the decision reached by the Union Constitution Committee on the mode of election of the President.[25]

At the insistence of Patel, India's most eminent men debated once again about what form of government India should have, and once again, Nehru lost. In their joint meeting, the members of both the Union and Provincial Constitution Committees decided that the chief executive of India should be chosen directly by the people.

This was the second time a joint session had reached the same conclusion. More crucially, he was asked to go back and change his committee's decision. Held over a two-day period, 10 and 11 June, this historic meeting was chaired by Prasad and included thirty-six luminaries; the likes of Jawaharlal Nehru, Sardar Patel, B.R. Ambedkar, Gobind Ballabh Pant, Jagjivan Ram, K.M. Munshi, Syama Prasad Mookerjee, Alladi Krishnaswami Ayyar, K.M. Panikkar, J.B. Kripalani and, of course, Rau. Nehru and his supporters protested that a joint committee meeting had no power to bind a constituent committee. In view of Nehru's standing, the joint committee couched its resolution as a mere suggestion:

It was decided by a majority vote to recommend to the Union Constitution Committee that they should reconsider their decision for the indirect election of the President through an electoral college. It was made clear that the decisions of the joint committee, in so far as they were in conflict with the decisions taken in either of the two committees, could only be considered as the recommendations of the joint committee to the committee concerned. It was then open to the committee concerned either to accept or to reject the recommendation when making its report to the Constituent Assembly.[26]

Munshi recalled the fateful day more than a decade later, even remembering the main points on which Nehru lost the argument. His summary of why Patel and others wanted an elected president was one of the best descriptions of the presidential system's main benefits:

> In the Joint Committee, a hot debate followed on the position and status of the President, and if I remember aright, by two or three votes the proposition that the President should be elected on the basis of adult franchise, was carried.
>
> The points urged by the protagonists of the proposal were: (1) If the President were elected by the Parliament, he would be a creature of the majority in power, and a pale replica of the Prime Minister, and therefore no better than a figurehead as in France or Ireland. (2) The character of the quasi-federal Union would be completely destroyed if the President were a mere representative of the party in power at the Centre. (3) The President should have powers of safeguarding the Constitution as also those necessary to maintain the machinery of the Government effectively in a crisis which might be created by an absence of a single majority party in power at the Centre, or by that party acting unconstitutionally, or by the country being exposed to external dangers. (4) The whole country going to election to select the President would tend to usher in a two-party system which is essential for the ultimate success of democracy.
>
> When the protagonists of this view gained their point, those who were opposed raised a protest that the Joint Committee had no power to bind the Union Committee by its decision.[27]

Nehru had lost the argument despite the fact that he came to the joint meeting armed with a so-called compromise. To give provincial governments some say in the selection of the chief executive of the nation, Nehru and his supporters decided that the president of India would be elected not just by Central legislators but by all legislators of the nation, including those of the provincial governments. Evidently, this formula, developed a day before the joint meeting, didn't impress the members of the two committees. It still left the president of India as a creature of legislative bodies, and at the mercy of the majority party.

Clearly vindicated in his view that the chief executive of India's governments, at the Centre as well as in the states, should be elected directly by the people, Patel was quick to act. In his Provincial Constitution Committee, within hours of the joint meeting, he finalized how the governors of India's provinces were to be selected:

> That there should be direct election on the basis of adult suffrage; that the duration of the office of the Governor should be coterminous with the life of the Legislature; and that there should be simultaneous election with the election of the members of the Lower House.[28]

Remarkably, despite the sharp rebuke, Nehru completely ignored the joint committee's decision. About the resolution passed by India's most distinguished men that he should change his committee's decision from a parliamentary type executive to the presidential type, Nehru did absolutely nothing. The next meeting of the Union Constitution Committee, held only a few hours after the joint committee meeting, started without him in attendance. Filling in for Nehru, Ambedkar chaired the meeting and brought up the matter of the election of the president, but mentioned nothing of the joint committee's decision. Instead of reconsidering their decision, the twelve members of the Union Constitution Committee openly defied the joint committee's resolution and adopted the so-called compromise developed by Munshi's subcommittee the day before. Nehru did join his committee's meeting later that afternoon and took the chair, but said and did nothing about reconsidering a matter of the highest importance in the making of India's Constitution.

The Union Constitution Committee would meet for one more session before finalizing its report to the Constituent Assembly, but it would never reconsider its decision about the type of executive. That choice would remain parliamentary until the final adoption of

India's Constitution. On 4 July 1947, when the Union Constitutional Committee sent its final report to the Assembly, its recommendation for India's chief executive read as follows:

> Head of the Federation: (1) The Head of the Federation shall be the President (Rashtrapati) to be elected as provided below: (2) The election shall be by an electoral college consisting of (a) the members of both Houses of Parliament of the Federation, and (b) the members of the Legislatures of all the units or, where a Legislature is bicameral, the members of the Lower House thereof
> ....
> Council of Ministers: There shall be a Council of Ministers with the Prime Minister at the head to aid and advise the President in the exercise of his functions.[29]

The matter was sealed. India was to have a government based on the parliamentary system.

NOTES

1   Rao, B.S. (2006), *The Framing of India's Constitution,* Vol. 1, Delhi: Universal Law Publishing, p. 331.
2   Chatterjee, D.K. (1984), *Gandhi and Constitution Making in India,* New Delhi: Associated Publishing House, p. 25.
3   *Constituent Assembly Debates,* 17 December 1946.
4   Ibid., 20 December 1946.
5   Ibid., 9 December 1946.
6   Ibid.
7   Ibid., 26 November 1949.
8   Rao, op. cit., p. 434.
9   Rao, op. cit., Vol. 2, p. 471.
10   Ibid., p. 458.
11   Ibid., p. 474.
12   Ibid., p. 503.
13   *Constituent Assembly Debates,* 14 July 1947.
14   Rao, op. cit., Vol. 5, p. 112.

15   *Constituent Assembly Debates,* 5 July 1947.

16   Ibid., 20 August 1947.

17   Ibid.

18   Rao, op. cit., Vol. 2, p. 534.

19   Minutes, Provincial Constitution Committee, 6 June 1947, Rao, op. cit., Vol. 2, p. 646.

20   Minutes, Union Constitution Committee, 6 June 1947, ibid., p. 554.

21   Minutes, Joint Meeting, 7 June 1947, ibid., p. 609.

22   Minutes, Union Constitution Committee, 8 June 1947, ibid., Volume 2, p. 555.

23   Munshi, K. M. (1997), *The President Under the Indian Constitution,* Mumbai: Bhartiya Vidya Bhavan, pp. 18–21.

24   Minutes of the Union Constitution Committee, 9 June 1947, Rao, op. cit., Vol. 2, p. 556.

25   Note circulated by secretary, Constituent Assembly, to members of the Union and Provincial Constitution Committees, 9 June 1947, Rao, op. cit., Vol. 2, p. 611.

26   Minutes of Joint Committee Meeting of the Union and Provincial Committees, 11 June 1945, Rao, op. cit., Vol. 2, p.612.

27   Munshi, op. cit., pp. 22–24.

28   Minutes of the Provincial Constitution Committee, 11 June 1947, Rao, op. cit., Volume 2, p. 652.

29   Report of the Union Constitution Committee to the Constituent Assembly, Rao, op cit., Volume 2, pp. 578–80.

5

A System Favoured by Party Oligarchs

India's Constituent Assembly breezed through the adoption of the most important fundamental principles of the Constitution, almost exactly as prescribed by the Union Constitution Committee, within a week. It was then simply a matter of drafting. The process slowed down significantly when the Constitution entered the drafting phase, because the country was undergoing what Nehru would call 'humiliating times',[1] a period of despicable violence. The Assembly wouldn't meet again for more than a year.

For the most part, once the assembly had adopted the recommendations made by Nehru's committee, any lingering opposition to the parliamentary form was seen as sheer obstructionism. Conditions in India were worsening with each passing day and no one wanted to stir up settled issues. Besides, a feeling was taking hold that a strong Central government based on a system that was familiar to all, and with powers concentrated in the hands of the prime minister, was the need of the hour.

More crucially, the time for debate had passed, for India now desperately needed a fully functional and effective government. Within days of adopting the fundamental principles of the Constitution at the end of July 1947, Nehru's inexperienced government began to face enormous new challenges. First, he and his colleagues had totally underestimated the viciousness of the Muslim–Hindu violence that was spreading in the countryside. Then in October, the first war over

Kashmir began, which also caught the Indian leaders unprepared. Patel, as home minister, had his hands full too with his campaign to persuade the princely states to join the Union.

In January 1948, India suffered another blow when a right-wing Hindu assassinated Mahatma Gandhi. One of the biggest impacts of his death was on the internal workings of the government. Gandhi had been instrumental in keeping the rift between Patel and Nehru from turning into an all-out feud.

On top of it all, there were issues relating to the unrepresentative character of India's Constituent Assembly. It functioned as a political house under the control of a political party. A handful of Congress leaders controlled the outcome of every vote taken.

These conditions were not in the least conducive for a reappraisal of the system of government India ought to adopt.

THE PARTY DIKTAT

From the very beginning of India's Constituent Assembly, voices were raised about how it was not representative of the entire nation. To begin with, there was the issue that members of the Constituent Assembly were not elected for the specific purpose of making the Constitution. Barring a few who were handpicked by the Congress for their eminence or constitutional scholarship, the rest were general representatives of their constituencies. Also, since the elections were only held in the British India provinces, not in the princely states, the legislatures represented only 15 per cent of India's population. Representatives of the princely states slowly began to trickle into the Assembly, but they were also cherry-picked by the princes. Further, Muslims were under-represented in the Assembly because the Muslim League chose not to participate at all.

The issue of the Constituent Assembly's unrepresentative character came to a boil as it neared the final adoption of the Constitution. In November 1948, two amendments were moved in the Assembly seeking to postpone the consideration of the draft until a new, more representative and competent house was formed. The amendments came from two entirely unrelated members, one Muslim the other Hindu. Maulana Hasrat Mohani wanted 'a fresh and competent Constituent Assembly on the basis of joint electorate and the formation of political rather than communal parties in India'. Damodar Swarup Seth, a Congressman, suggested postponement because 'the final Constitution of free India should be based on the will of the entire people of India'. 'I am afraid that this amendment of mine may displease some of my friends,' he said, '[but] when 85 percent of the people of the country are not represented in this House ... it will be in my opinion a very great mistake to say that this House is competent to frame a Constitution for the whole country.'[2] As Mohani's and Seth's amendments were defeated, they were both attacked with questions about why they joined the Assembly in the first place.

To make matters worse, members of India's Constituent Assembly could not vote freely. Appeals to members' conscience were common inside the Assembly because they were under pressure to vote along party lines. In a practice unheard of in a Constitution-making body, India's Constituent Assembly functioned under a system of whips, diktats issued by political bosses. As the Congress held an overwhelming majority in the Assembly, a small number of party bosses dominated the entire constitution-making exercise.

Many members spoke out in the Assembly against the practice of issuing whips. In December 1948, moving his amendment to limit the powers of the Central government vis-à-vis provincial governments, Mohamed Ismail Sahib noted that 'if only Members are given the right to vote as they please, and if they are given the freedom of vote on this particular question at least, I know ... many Members will vote for these amendments'. A Congress leader sitting in the chair immediately stopped Sahib: 'May I suggest that these remarks are not called for here?' Similarly, in May 1949 when the Assembly reversed an earlier decision regarding the method of selecting governors, Muhammad Sa'adulla objected: 'This august House has a total of 303 Members at present, if I remember aright ... the Congress party controls 275 votes and if members of the party are to follow the ukase, there is no chance for any other opinion to prevail.'[3]

'I would remind honourable Members that the duty we have to perform here is a very sacred one and that we are answerable to God,' said Pocker Sahib Bahadur in another exchange regarding whips. 'If the defence is that we did not act according to our conscience on account of the whip that is issued,' he said, 'it is no defence at all.' A Congressman objected: 'Is it necessary to make all these references?' The chair tried to intervene, but Bahadur continued: 'Well, Sir, I hope the Honourable Vice-President will not compel me to dilate more on this topic. Anyhow, I take in that the Honourable Vice-President knows that Party Whips are issued and Members are being guided by these Whips, to put it in a nutshell.' T.T. Krishnamachari replied: 'I have no desire to answer ... Whips may be issued. We know what is being done. It is a matter of convenience. If some of us do not congregate together and get through the work that is to come before the House by mutual agreement, I am afraid this House will have to sit for three or four years.'[4]

The same justification that party whips were necessary to avoid chaos was as at hand when Ambedkar spoke in the Assembly on the final day before India's Constitution was adopted. 'The task of the Drafting Committee would have been a very difficult one,' he said, 'if this Constituent Assembly has been merely a motley crowd ... It is because of the discipline of the Congress party that the Drafting Committee was able to pilot the Constitution in the Assembly with the sure knowledge as to the fate of each article and each amendment.'[5]

The issuance of whips, however, had a serious impact on the quality of debates. Since the Assembly functioned as a normal legislative body, the decisions once taken could only be reviewed if they were brought up by the president of the Assembly or by the leaders of one of the top committees. These leaders controlled and choreographed which decisions were taken when. They brought issues to the floor of the house in a sequence that suited them, knowing that they could get them passed regardless. For instance, the Provincial Constitution was brought to vote before the Union Constitution; and the Preamble of the Constitution was discussed near the very end of the process. At times, decisions were taken selectively on some clauses while others of the same article were postponed because they posed difficulties. When members objected, or submitted amendments in the Assembly, they were manipulated through the party machinery. As a result, thousands of amendments were notified but not actually moved on the floor of the House. Of the 7,635 amendments to the draft Constitution that were tabled, only 2,473 were in fact moved. Mostly, when members spoke in the Assembly they were making a political or sycophantic speech, or they were simply establishing a record for posterity that they had spoken in the historic Assembly.

PATEL ON A KEY PRESIDENTIAL PRINCIPLE

In a bizarre move, Patel came to the Constituent Assembly first to get his Provincial Constitution approved before the principles of the Union Constitution were adopted. He had won the argument that India's chief executive should be elected directly by the people, but had failed to compel Nehru to change his Union Committee's decision. He then faced the nearly impossible task of developing a Constitution for the provinces that allowed for a directly elected chief executive. It was his final effort to include at least one presidential principle in India's system of government. It wouldn't last long, but at first Patel succeeded.

He recommended that, 'for each Province there shall be a Governor to be elected directly by the people on the basis of adult suffrage'; and that, 'there shall be a Council of Ministers to aid and advise the Governor in the exercise of his functions except in so far as he is by or under this Constitution required to exercise his functions or any of them in his discretion'.[6]

There were two principles Patel was after, and both were well known doctrines of the presidential system. One, state governments should be independent of the Central government; and two, executive authority must be independent of the legislature. However, both his aims were incongruous with a system configured on the parliamentary pattern, and with a Central government which itself didn't have independent executive. If governors reported to a president who was under the control of the Central government, it brought the entire system under the control of that one government. Similarly, a governor acting on the advice of a council of ministers was hardly an independent executive. Still, Patel pushed on.

Of his two aims, Patel apparently thought it was more important to have independent state governments than to have independent executives. Patel's vision for India was a federation of autonomous states, each with a parliamentary-type government.

Patel acknowledged the difficulties involved in direct elections, but considered them necessary because of 'the dignity of the office which a popular Governor will hold and naturally a Governor who has been elected by adult franchise of the whole province will exert considerable influence on the popular ministry as well as on the province as a whole'.[7]

Members were unaware of what had transpired on this issue of direct election between Patel's and Nehru's committees. Referring to their joint meeting, a member asked: 'May I know whether this clause was also considered and is it a fact that that Committee was of the opinion that the election of the Governor should not be held directly by adult franchise but he should be elected by the Provincial Legislature…?' Patel was given the perfect opportunity to disclose to the entire Assembly how this was a matter of deep discord, and how he had won. But he chose not to address the issue at all. Prasad, who was chairing the session and was familiar with the entire debate also simply moved on; 'that is a question which the Mover may answer if he wishes', he said. Patel never did. The clause as proposed was put to a vote, and adopted.

But the hybrid of presidential and parliamentary systems that Patel proposed created the difficulty of reconciling two directly elected officials, a governor and a chief minister, both engaged in the same branch of government. This was a recipe for constant friction. The issue sparked one of the Assembly's most heated debates. The members argued back and forth between granting and limiting governor's powers. They faced most difficulty in describing exactly when and how a governor could take control from the council of ministers. 'We cannot by any means reconcile the Presidential and the Cabinet systems,' exclaimed a wearied Hriday Nath Kunzru.

Kunzru was remarkably prescient in that statement, for Patel's formulation would ultimately be turned on its head. Nehru's decision to have a figurehead chief executive at the Centre had already put paid to Patel's attempt of establishing a genuinely federal system. Given a unitary system at the top, it was unfeasible to have truly independent state governments. Then, there was the matter of having two executive officials. This raised the obvious question: why have both, if one was to act as advised by the other? These questions would haunt the Assembly and compel it to revise the entire scheme Patel had developed so assiduously.

ASSEMBLY NEVER VOTED ON FORM OF GOVERNMENT

When Nehru came to the Assembly to get his Union Constitution approved, he came with all guns blazing. After his defeat in the joint committee meeting, he was taking no chances. There were those who could argue forcefully against the parliamentary system, but either chose not to or weren't allowed. Those who began to oppose, withdrew. The process was so completely managed at this stage that not a single vote was taken in the Assembly on a principle different from those proposed by Nehru. As a result, the question whether India should adopt the parliamentary or the presidential system of government was never put to a vote in India's Constituent Assembly.

The fundamental problem with Nehru's proposal was that the parliamentary system required a non-partisan head of state who drew power from a source different from that of the head of government. When both top officials in a government were elected, and both engaged in executive functions, it was nearly impossible to make the system work without making one subservient to the other. As such, Nehru proposed a figurehead president, but that created a head of state submissive to a head of government.

Nehru struggled with this issue as soon as he began discussing his Union Constitution in the Assembly. He rationalized it thus:

> We have given anxious thought to this matter and we came to the very definite conclusion that it would not be desirable, first because we want to emphasize the ministerial character of the Government that power really resided in the Ministry and in the Legislature and not in the President as such. At the same time we did not want to make the President just a mere figurehead like the French President. We did not give him any real power but we have made his position one of great authority and dignity. You will notice from this draft Constitution that he is also to be Commander-in-Chief of the Defence Forces just as the American President is. ...
>
> Some people suggested, why have even this rather complicated system of election that we have suggested? Why not the Central Legislature by itself elect the President? That will be much simpler, of course, but there is the danger that it will be putting the thing very much on the other side, of having it on too narrow a basis. The Central Legislature may, and probably will be dominated, say, by one party or group which will form the ministry. If that group elects the President, inevitably they will tend to choose a person of their own party. He will then be even more a dummy than otherwise. The President and the ministry will represent exactly the same thing. It is possible that even otherwise the President may represent the same group or party or ideas. But we have taken a middle course and asked all the members of all the legislatures all over India, in all the units to become voters. It is just likely that they will be choosing a party man. Always that is possible of course.[8]

In one breath Nehru described a president of India who was going to be both a commander-in-chief and a dummy, but there was no uproar in the Assembly. It was partly due to the fact that Nehru had picked his timing well. He had interrupted Patel's discussion of the Provincial Constitution to begin a clause-by-clause review of his committee's report in the afternoon of 21 July, leaving no time for deliberations to begin the same day. The following day was scheduled for the Constituent Assembly to adopt independent India's national flag. Nehru himself was scheduled to unveil the new flag. In a highly emotional patriotic speech, he would bring the whole Assembly to its feet. After a day's gap, Nehru's proposals were taken up for debate, but once again in the afternoon.

There was another reason why members were not up in arms about a president who would be chief executive in name only. The members of India's Constituent Assembly were never told that in a joint session Nehru was officially asked to reconsider his committee's decision.

But there was another darker reason why members wouldn't denounce Nehru's proposals inside the Assembly, because outside measures were being taken to stifle the opposition. The first indication of that came when chief proponents of the presidential form went absent during the two days of proceedings when the all-important Clause 1 of the Union Constitution was being adopted. None of the so-called rebels of the Congress party – H.V. Kamath, P.S. Deshmukh, R.K. Sidhwa, K.T. Shah, H.N. Kunzru – participated in the debate over the most important principle of India's Constitution while it was being adopted. Kamath, Deshmukh and Sidhwa were present in the Assembly but chose not to participate in any significant way. Sidhwa was even careful to clarify, 'Mr President, I had no desire to enter into this debate but for one point ...,' as he went on to talk about a minor issue. It is not clear whether Shah, who would later miss not a single opportunity to push for presidential principles, was present, for he didn't speak at all.

When it came to amendments with regard to Clause 1 of Nehru's report, all those who were against the establishment of a puppet president felt compelled to drop their amendments. Remarkably, every single amendment seeking to establish a directly elected president in India was withdrawn. Members had given notice of these amendments when the clause was introduced, but refused to press them on the floor of the Assembly when discussions opened after a day's gap. In fact, all amendments to Clause 1, except those of very little consequence, began to fall by the wayside as soon as the president of the Assembly opened the session. 'I have got a very large number of amendments of which notice has been given,' noted Prasad as he declared Clause 1 open for debate, but within minutes many just dropped. Of the first eleven notified amendments (Nos 61 through 71) not one was moved or pressed on the floor; then two were moved (No. 72 sought a president by rotation from the north and the south of India, and No. 73 sought a drafting change from 'as provided below' to 'in the manner set out below'); and then again the next ten were not moved. This pattern continued, so that out of a total of thirty-seven amendments for which members had sent notice, only seven were moved in the Assembly and put to vote. Of the seven, only two were acceptable to Nehru and accordingly only those two were adopted by the Assembly. Both were essentially drafting changes, leaving Nehru's Clause 1 intact in its principle that the president be elected by the nation's legislators.

The fact that the members were being pressured to drop their amendments may never have come to light if not for Shibban Lal Saksena, a Congressman from United Provinces. Not only did Saksena announce in the Assembly that the reason he was not pressing his amendment was because he was 'not free in the matter', but he also had the courage to present his arguments about why a directly elected president was what the country needed. He also reminded the Assembly that it had just passed the Provincial Constitution based on principles different from the ones being proposed by Nehru's committee. 'This is a very serious matter and I deeply feel that the scheme that we have accepted in the Provincial Constitution in regard to the election of Governors should be adopted in the Union Constitution as well,' he said. Saksena pointed out why: '… for fulfilling our pledge for re-establishing unity in our country, which is broken up today and may be further broken up in view of the present efforts of some States, the election of the Rashtrapati by adult suffrage will be very helpful.'[9]

Another member, Gopi Krishna Vijayavargiya, of Gwalior state, argued that since the legislatures in the princely states are 'very faked up and crude', they will negatively affect the election of the president if that election were held by legislative bodies. 'Therefore, I moved an amendment,' he said, 'that the Union President should be elected directly on the basis of adult franchise, so that the people even the poor ones may have the opportunity of exercising their votes for the election of the President. Now I do not want to press my amendment in view of the opinions expressed here ...'

Members seemed resigned to the fact that a presidential-type chief executive was not going to be adopted by this Assembly even if the nation demanded it. Politely, a member expressed the sense of the Assembly: 'There has been a fairly decent amount of opinion in favour of the President of the Union being elected on adult franchise, but since the whole Constitution is based on the Ministerial type of Government rather than the Presidential type, it is as well that we should elect our President by an electoral college.'[10]

However, Syed Kazi Karimuddin was indignant and continued to protest: 'I want to bring home to the House why this election should be made on the basis of adult suffrage ... in India, looking to the conflicting political parties, diverse ideologies and many diverse factors, for the maintenance of peace and tranquility and for the effective representation of all parties in the Cabinet, it is necessary that there should be a non-parliamentary executive. The only reason that has been advanced why adult suffrage should not be introduced is that a huge machinery will have to be set up for dealing with the elections and the energies of the nation will be consumed in holding these elections. But that is absolutely no reason.' A nationwide election will 'educate the masses ... momentous economic problems ... will be brought to the forefront', said Syed Karimuddin, and lamented that as proposed, the president 'will be puppet of the majority party'.

The next speaker, Mahomed Sherif, too urged his fellow members to rethink.

However, at this point arguments in the Assembly were no longer about the parliamentary versus presidential system; now there was a Hindu–Muslim undercurrent. In late July, when the Assembly was taking decisions on the most important fundamental principles of India's Constitution, the partition-related violence in the nation was at its absolute worst. Inside the Assembly, members' nerves were frayed and the proceedings frequently witnessed resentment and anger. There was an unspoken assumption that having accomplished an independent Pakistan, the Muslims now desired a weak India and therefore a weak government in India. Since a parliamentary government was viewed as the strongest form of government, any argument against it was seen as an argument for a weak government in India. So, if a Muslim member spoke against the parliamentary form of government, he was simply wasting his breath. The pursuit of a parliamentary form of government in India was now seen as an effort to establish a strong government for a beleaguered nation.

Nehru himself bothered to speak on the matter only once, at the beginning while introducing his committee's report. As acting prime minister, Nehru felt that he knew best, as he was the one who utilized the strength of a parliamentary government each and every day. He was anxious for the Assembly to stop debating, so that his government could focus on the urgent tasks at hand. 'I am not prepared to believe that adult franchise is absolutely essential,' he said at the end. 'Obviously, the number of those who will elect the members of the Assembly will be in millions and they are expected to be proper persons. Therefore, when the members of the Assembly themselves are being elected by the votes of millions where is the necessity for electing the President by adult franchise? Therefore if you desire to frame and promulgate your Constitution without necessary delay, then we should avoid complications; otherwise we will not be able to frame our Constitution in the least possible time, and act on it.'[11]

Without any further delay, Clause 1 of the Union Constitution Committee's report was adopted.

'WE CANNOT GO BACK UPON IT'

Once the concept of a figurehead president was approved by the Constituent Assembly, its opponents faced an additional hurdle: the argument that having adopted this system's main principle, the Assembly cannot reverse itself. All future efforts to bring non-parliamentary concepts for consideration would now end with this admonition. Still, the proponents of the presidential form had one hope: to establish a president who had discretion. This ended with the old argument that any dilution of the prime minister's powers described a weak government.

When on 28 July 1947, only sixteen days before Partition, Clause 10 of the Union Constitution Committee Report came up for consideration, the members were not interested in long speeches. In moving the clause, Nehru said nothing: 'This is a very simple clause ... There shall be a council of ministers with the Prime Minister at the head, to aid and advise the President in the exercise of his functions.'

To those who wanted a president with discretionary powers, the 'aid and advise' clause represented the last opportunity. But once again the biggest supporters of the presidential system did not participate in the day's proceedings. As a result, the debate quickly deteriorated into a Hindu–Muslim spat. Of the four amendments that were moved regarding this clause – two from Muslim and two from Hindu members – the Muslim amendments sought to have some control over the appointments of the prime minister and his council of ministers, while the Hindu members sought just the opposite.

Both amendments moved by Hindu members were in fact drafting changes designed to make the clause even more precise in establishing the prime minister as the only centre of power. One of the movers, Thakur Das Bhargava, didn't mince words as he moved his amendment: 'It should be clearly stated in the Union Constitution that the voice of the Prime Minister would be the final voice and the President will merely echo it.' Sir N. Gopalaswami Ayyangar, himself a member of Nehru's Union Constitution Committee, had an amendment similar to Bhargava's and was the one that the Assembly adopted: 'The Prime Minister shall be appointed by the President and the other Ministers shall be appointed by the President on the advice of the Prime Minister. The Council shall be collectively responsible to the House of the People.'[12]

Both amendments moved by Muslim members suggested that the entire Cabinet, including the prime minister, be elected by the national legislature. They wanted to have a say in the selection of the executive instead of giving the prime minister a free hand.

But one amendment went further: it suggested a non-parliamentary executive. Kazi Syed Karimuddin wanted to add the following to the end of Clause 10: 'that the executive of the Union shall be non-parliamentary, in the sense that it shall not be removable ...'[13]

As Congressman H.V. Kamath raised the familiar bogey of weak government in opposing Karimuddin's amendment, he ended up giving one of the best arguments in favour of the presidential system. 'The most elementary as well as the most fundamental principle ... of a democratic, efficient and dynamic government,' said Kamath, 'is that while every shade of political opinion and every school of thought should be adequately represented in every legislature, because in a legislature two heads are better than one, twenty heads are better than two and two hundred heads are better than twenty, in the case of the executive, especially when we are planning a dynamic executive, the reverse is the case.' In short, it was best to have a single executive. Exactly what the presidential system offered.

The raising of such fundamental issues against the parliamentary system impelled Nehru to stand and make a declaration: the adoption of the system was now irrevocable. Referring to Karimuddin's amendment, Nehru pointed out: 'So far we have been proceeding with the building up of the Constitution in the ministerial sense and I do submit that we cannot go back upon it and it will upset the whole scheme and structure of the Constitution.'

An unequivocal statement from Nehru still didn't stop a member from saying in despair: 'Constitutions are made, although there is an element of finality about them, only for a time; and I hope to live and see the British model dethroned, just as British power is being dethroned, and the better model adopted.'[14]

But the parliamentary system was now so firmly entrenched as India's choice that an inquiry into its substance seemed futile. As a result, no one asked whether a president was bound by the advice he receives from a prime minister. Even worse, no one asked why a president with absolutely no discretionary powers was even necessary.

AMBEDKAR'S 'ADMIRATION' FOR PARLIAMENTARY SYSTEM

As soon as the Constituent Assembly adopted the Union Constitution Committee's principles, B.N. Rau was asked to prepare a draft Constitution. He didn't take long since they were essentially his recommendations that the Assembly had adopted. In October 1947 Rau's draft was turned over to the Drafting Committee, chaired by Ambedkar, for 'scrutiny'. However, there was one problem: Ambedkar had publicly opposed the parliamentary form of government.

As recently as March 1947, only seven months before he began his work as chairman, Ambedkar had written that 'there is no doubt that the British type of executive is entirely unsuited to India'. In a memorandum to the Assembly's subcommittee on Fundamental Rights, Ambedkar outlined a proposal for a 'United States of India'. He recommended a form of government that had many similarities with the US-style presidential system. In language reminiscent of the American Declaration of Independence, he said that 'the British type of Executive will be full of menace to the life, liberty and pursuit of happiness' for India's minorities.[15]

This was not the first time Ambedkar had denounced the British parliamentary system. In 1945, in a speech on India's fundamental problems, he had declared that 'majority rule is untenable in theory and unjustifiable in practice'. He suggested that India must have a non-parliamentary executive. He said that there must be certain governing principles instead of just a 'series of methods', before India's communal problem can be permanently solved. Along these lines Ambedkar outlined the principles on which India's government should be based: an 'Executive power assumes far greater importance than the Legislative power'; 'the Executive should cease to be a Committee of the majority party'; and 'the Executive should be non-Parliamentary in the sense that it shall not be removable'.[16]

Ambedkar decided that the parliamentary system was entirely unsuitable for India, not unlike Jinnah, when in 1937 Nehru refused to include any other party in the first Indian-only provincial governments. While Jinnah, after that incident, went in the direction of Pakistan, Ambedkar even declared that British rule was better than having a majority-only government of the parliamentary type. He even took his suggestion to the British. In a secret report of a meeting, the British viceroy recorded Ambedkar's strong opposition that 'the parliamentary system would not do in India'. 'I asked him whether he would say that in public,' the viceroy wrote, 'to which he replied that he would be perfectly ready to do so, with the utmost emphasis. He was 100 per cent opposed to self-government at the Centre and would resist it in any possible way.'[17]

But now Ambedkar not only joined the Constituent Assembly he opposed, but became the chief proponent of the very system of government he denounced. The fact was that Ambedkar had very little support outside the Assembly. In both 1937 and 1946 elections, he had lost big. He became a member of the Constituent Assembly only because the Congress party chose to support him.[18]

Ambedkar, who could very well have been the parliamentary system's most capable opponent, now became a committed promoter. As for his push for a non-parliamentary executive, when the matter came up for consideration in the subcommittee on Fundamental Rights, Ambedkar chose not to be present.

When in February 1948 Ambedkar's committee submitted its draft to the Assembly, the parliamentary clauses were essentially the same as written by Rau. In fact, the one area where the parliamentary principles weren't fully applied, he proposed a change. The provision for directly electing the governors was approved by the Assembly but it didn't fit well with the purely parliamentary scheme. Going beyond his committee's authority 'to scrutinize the draft', Ambedkar proposed an alternative method of appointing governors. He suggested that 'the Legislature should elect a panel of four persons (who need not be residents of the State) and the President of the Union should appoint one of the four as Governor'.[19] It was astonishing, for his suggestion was based on an entirely different principle than the one approved by the Assembly.

On 4 November 1948, as Ambedkar presented the draft in the Assembly, he seemed subdued. He noted how the minorities of India 'have loyally accepted the rule of the majority', and went on to describe a Constitution that openly centralized powers in the hands of the majority. In building his case for such centralization of power in the hands of the majority, Ambedkar played down the whole notion of a majority and a minority. He declared that if the majority stopped discriminating, the minorities would simply 'vanish'.[20]

The parliamentary system was inherently unitary and as such Ambedkar's most difficult task was to refute the arguments for granting more autonomy to state governments. He suggested that the 'rigidity' and 'legalism' of federalism would raise difficulties for governments because frequently they would require judiciary's intervention. He argued that the draft Constitution had struck the right balance between the state and Central governments otherwise the modern world required even more centralization.

India was going to be a 'flexible federation', said Ambedkar. India's Parliament will have powers 'to legislate on exclusively provincial subjects in normal times'; and 'a very large part of the Constitution ... can be amended by Parliament ... [which] does not require ratification by the States'. The Indian federation was going to be 'special' in other ways too: it will avoid 'diversity in laws, in administration and in judicial protection'. Ambedkar admitted that these features, common to most federations, 'may be welcomed as being an attempt to accommodate the powers of Government to local needs and local circumstances, but this diversity when it goes beyond a certain point is capable of producing chaos'. And then he raised that bogey again: 'Such a state of affairs not only weakens the State but becomes intolerant to the citizen who moves from State to State.'[21]

In order to show that a unitary structure was better, Ambedkar also claimed that the mother of all federal systems, the US, had weaknesses or features unsuitable for India. He attempted to do so by highlighting the US concepts of dual citizenship and separate Constitutions. Both concepts raised concerns in India that they could become tools for inflaming separatist tendencies. There was a school of thought in the country that a nation so fragmented could only be kept together with an iron hand.

The crux of Ambedkar's advocacy of the parliamentary system, however, was in showing why it was necessary to have only one centre of power. He did so by making his famous 'responsibility versus stability' argument. He declared that a government behaved responsibly only if it was always fearful of losing power. According to him, it was not possible to have a system that guaranteed both, a government staying in power while at the same time staying responsible. Therefore, one has to choose. The choice they had made is to have a government that was more responsible at the expense of it being less stable. The reason all executive and legislative functions were fused into one centre of power was to ensure that the entire government fell if it behaved irresponsibly. He argued that multiple centres of power diluted government's accountability and therefore it was best to deny the president any powers.

The parliamentary system was therefore chosen for its one and only benefit: the 'daily assessment' of responsibility. Ambedkar presented the essence of this argument: 'The daily assessment of responsibility which is not available under the American system is, it is felt, far more effective than the periodic assessment and far more necessary in a country like India.'

However, Ambedkar's claim that a daily assessment of responsibility was 'not available under the American system' overlooks one of that system's principal features, the significant powers of legislative oversight. Constant governmental scrutiny was one of its hallmarks because it separated powers between the executive and legislative branches. Similarly, the American system's greatly superior 'periodic assessments' provided for more representatives per citizen, in more frequent elections, and in more branches of government, than the parliamentary system.

It was ironic that Ambedkar reposed all powers in the very branch of government, the legislature, in which he had the least amount of faith. 'Democracy in India is only a top dressing on an Indian soil, which is essentially undemocratic,' Ambedkar noted as he justified the inclusion of a large number of administrative details in the Constitution instead of leaving them to the legislature's discretion. 'In these circumstances,' he said, 'it is wiser not to trust the Legislature to prescribe forms of administration.' And yet he was leaving the entire administration in the hands of the legislature.

The proof of democracy was in the electing. But Ambedkar was advocating a system that itself weakened people's electoral powers. The daily assessment of responsibility was consequential only through periodic assessments of elections. However, the Indian system gave people fewer representatives in government and no ability to elect the executive directly. Gaining inconsequential powers of probing governments, at the expense of weakening the powers of electing them, was to weaken democracy.

In making their choice for the parliamentary form, Ambedkar and his backers were really making the following assertions: 1) that a daily threat over a government's survival was necessary; 2) that is was possible to reach final conclusions about a government's effectiveness on a daily basis; 3) that it was practically possible to throw a government out at any time; 4) that the advantage of this daily threat should be gained at the expense of people's electoral power; 5) that there were some conditions peculiar to India that made it possible or effective to dismiss a government at any time; and 6) that a power to force a government out was better than the power that forced a government to reform.

These affirmations raised a whole slew of fundamental questions. What made a government responsible, insecurity or oversight? Was it fair to judge a government each day based on the passing or failing of legislation? How, in a nation of a permanent majority, would a majority-controlled government really fall? How did limiting the people's representation and participation in government make a government more responsible? How could a centralized system govern a large nation with a history of strong local governments? What power in a nation of an overwhelmingly domineering political party could dismiss a party government at any time? What mechanism would improve the quality of laws when the minority had no say in government?

None of these questions were addressed in India's Constituent Assembly as 'daily assessment of responsibility' was chosen as the primary aim of India's system of government.

Then there was the inexplicable proposal of a president who, as Ambedkar described, 'occupies the same position as the King under the English Constitution'.[22] This elected-king of India couldn't possibly meet the British king's two fundamentally necessary and inherent features: hereditary 'divine' powers and a non-partisan nature. The 'king of India' on the other hand was not only elected by the legislature, he had absolutely no discretionary powers. The introduction of this puppet chief executive altered the British parliamentary system into an entirely different form of government.

Ambedkar finished his speech claiming that the Constitution embodied in the draft was perfect. 'If things go wrong under the new Constitution,' he announced, 'the reason will not be that we had a bad Constitution. What we will have to say is that man was vile.'[23]

'WILL CREATE HELL IN THIS COUNTRY'

Nearly a hundred members rose to speak after Ambedkar's commendation of the draft, but most were simply making speeches. Their favourite topics were the importance of India's villages and the language used to draft the Constitution. Members wanted to show their nationalistic fervour and lectured Ambedkar for his derogatory remarks about the mentality of India's villages, or for choosing a foreign language.

Not one member spoke unconditionally in favour of the draft Constitution and none rose to praise the parliamentary system of government in particular. There were many members, however, who went out of their way to speak in favour of the presidential system as a whole or to highlight some of its features as especially suitable for India.

Most interestingly, it was a Congressman, Ramnarayan Singh, who unleashed the most scathing attack on the choice of the parliamentary system. 'I say emphatically that this Constitution is not what is wanted by the country,' he announced. He said that the parliamentary system envisioned under the Constitution 'will develop surely into the party system of Government which has been a failure in the west', and 'will create hell in this country'.[24]

Shibban Lal Saksena elsewhere too thought the presidential system more suitable because 'stability of Government was the first need of the Nation today'. Mahboob Ali Baig Sahib Bahadur concurred; governments under the parliamentary system were 'so unstable … it is there that the seeds of corruption are sown', he said. Ministries are 'so much engaged in cajoling, in satisfying its Parliament that there is hardly time to look after its administration'. Besides, 'a parliamentary executive … cannot reflect the several sections of the country', Bahadur noted. K. Santhanam simply declared: 'In many cases I think the presidential type is superior and much better suited to India.'

Experienced members were especially enraged. 'By this centralization of power,' worried Lokanath Misra, 'I do not know what will happen in the future ... but from my present experience I must say that the Government that we are now having has been so centralized and our people in power have become so greedy of power that in the name of law and order, peace and unity, they are liable to go astray easily if the country is not vigilant.' P.S. Deshmukh didn't mince words either: '... if the present Constitution can be described in a nutshell it is one intended to fit in with the present administration. ... It is to fit in with the administration left by the British in this country.'[25]

'I have had experience as a Minister with eight nominated Governors,' said an alarmed Rev. J.J.M. Nichols-Roy from Assam, 'I am strongly of the opinion that an elected Governor will be a better substitute.' Commenting on the Drafting Committee's proposal for nominating governors, Dakshayani Velayudhan from Madras quipped: 'the remedy they have suggested is worse than the disease. ... We find that this direct recruitment to Governorship is taken from the Government of India Act and it shows that we have not left out even a comma from it.'

Hussain Imam took exception to the fact that in his presentation to the Assembly, Ambedkar was less than forthcoming about the strengths of the US presidential system. He noted that he was 'surprised that a learned pundit of Constitutional law like Dr Ambedkar should have skipped over the fact that the responsibility of the non-parliamentary executive is not less than that of the parliamentary executive. If it is examined it will be found that the committees of the House of Representatives and the Senate in U.S.A. exercise far greater control than the control exercised by the House of Commons.'

Some members were astonished at how Ambedkar had relinquished his long-held views against the parliamentary system. 'I was really surprised to hear Dr Ambedkar while he was introducing the Draft Constitution,' said a bewildered Kazi Syed Karimuddin, 'praising the system of parliamentary executive, while in his book *States and Minorities* he has advocated that the system of non-parliamentary executive is best suited to protect the minorities ...' Another member reminded Ambedkar what he himself thought of legislative bodies. 'I will use his own words,' said Z.H. Lari, '"…It is wiser not to trust the legislatures to prescribe forms of administration." With respect, I say he is mainly right.'[26]

These were all mere speeches now; the draft Constitution was easily adopted. The draft's acceptance by the Assembly meant that not just the fundamental principles of the Constitution but also its articles were now fixed. Any wholesale change was no longer possible.

Except, of course, a change that would make the system even more centralized, or to some, more parliamentary.

NOTES

1   *Constituent Assembly Debates,* 17 May 1949.

2   Ibid., 4–5 November 1948.

3   Ibid., 31 May 1949.

4   Ibid., 30 December 1948.

5   Ibid., 25 November 1949.

6   Ibid., 27 June 27, Principles of a Model Provincial Constitution.

7   Ibid., 15 July 1947.

8   Ibid., 21 July 1947.

9   Ibid., 23 July 1947.

10   K. Chengalaraya Reddy, Ibid.

11   *Constituent Assembly Debates*, 24 July 1947.

12   Ibid., 28 July 1947.

13   Ibid.

14   Ibid.

15   Rao, B.S. (2006), *The Framing of India's Constitution,* Vol. 2, Delhi: Universal Law Publishing, pp. 84–104.

16   Presidential Address, All India Scheduled Castes Federation, 6 May 1945, B.R. Ambedkar, (1979) *Writings and Speeches*, Vol. 1, pp. 357–79.

17   Viceroy's to the Secretary of State, Linlithgow Papers, MSS. EUR.F/125/8, 7 October 1939, cited in Shourie, A. (2009), *Worshipping False Gods: Ambedkar, and the Facts Which Have Been Erased*, New Delhi: Rupa & Co, p. 24.

18   Ibid., p. 55.
19   Rao, op. cit., Vol.3, p. 513.
20   *Constituent Assembly Debates*, 4 November 1948.
21   Ibid.
22   Ibid.
23   Ibid.
24   Ibid., 5 November 1948.
25   Ibid, 5–8 November 1948.
26   Ibid., 8 November 1948.

6

A Major Reversal in the Constituent Assembly

Despite the insurmountable odds against its adoption, the suitability of the presidential system continued to haunt the Constituent Assembly until the very end. There were members like K.T. Shah who attempted to instil features of presidential form of government in every relevant article. And then there was the matter of direct election of governors that Patel had managed to push through the assembly. But ultimately, all such efforts failed. Until there was nothing but a 'centralized federation with a façade of parliamentary democracy', as one member put it in the end.

A 'LONELY BATTLE' FOR PRESIDENTIAL FEATURES

K.T. Shah, a member from Bombay, was the odd man out in Nehru's coterie. He was the only member of Nehru's Union Constitution Committee who openly favoured the presidential system and continued to fight for its adoption all the way to the end.

The fact that Shah didn't find much support in the Assembly didn't stop him from trying to introduce presidential principles into the draft Constitution through amendments and new clauses. Each attempt faced sure defeat at the hands of an extremely disciplined Congress party, but Shah carried on. He moved his amendments in the Assembly and pushed for their passage with eloquent speeches favouring the presidential form of government.

His comments in the Assembly were some of the most informed and fervent appeals for the adoption of the presidential system. 'I know that my voice almost appears as a voice in the wilderness,' he said. 'But I think it my duty to place this on record that, after a close study of the working of Constitutions elsewhere, after a close study stretching over perhaps thirty-five years of the development of political institutions in this country and their influence on our public life, on our public morality, on even our private relations, I venture to suggest that this is not a very healthy example we are copying; and that the sooner we get rid of the combination of executive, judiciary and legislature in some supreme Cabinet, in some supreme authority, the better for us it would be.'[1]

Shibban Lal Saksena frequently broke ranks and rose in support. He startled the Assembly by declaring: 'If left to ourselves we would have copied the American system.' Even 'Dr. Ambedkar ... if it were left to his choice, he would have preferred the American system,' he said.[2] Similarly, when a member argued that the separation of powers might create disharmony, Kazi Syed Karimuddin retorted: 'Under parliamentary system, it is not a harmonious structure, but a structure in which political opponents are crushed. A harmonious structure is one in which ... the opposition is accommodated.'[3]

Ambedkar always responded to Shah's attempts with the same old arguments. The direct election of the president wasn't necessary because he is 'only a figurehead'. On the separation of powers, Ambedkar raised doubts about its functioning in the US. He suggested, inaccurately, that there was a movement to change that in that country. He was downright misleading in giving members the impression that the US system didn't allow the legislature the benefit of executive's counsel, for in reality the two had to work together given the US president's power of veto.

An irritated member finally rose to put Shah in his place. 'Sir, Prof. K. T. Shah has been fighting such a lonely battle that I hardly like to criticize him,' said K. Santhanam, '[but] ... he has taken upon himself too much of a task and that too quite unnecessarily. ... I humbly make the suggestion to Prof. K. T. Shah to concentrate on points where it will be practicable to improve the Constitution without trying to put forward an alternative constitution.'[4]

THEN, A MAJOR PRINCIPLE IS REVERSED

The differing visions of Patel and Nehru about India's system of government came to a final confrontation as soon as the Assembly began adopting the Draft's provincial government clauses. In these clauses, a feature of the presidential system – direct election of the chief executive – was still very much in place. Two years earlier, when Nehru was asked to reconsider the Union Constitution's principle of having the president elected by the legislature, he hadn't done so. But now the tables had turned. Now, it would be the Provincial Constitution that would undergo reconsideration and that too by the entire Assembly.

In a major reversal, and the only one of its kind, the Assembly would drop a fundamental principle that it had already adopted. Instead of electing governors directly by adult franchise, the Assembly would alter the provisions so that the governors are appointed by the president. Not only that, the governor's discretionary powers would be taken away, making him also a mere figurehead in his provincial government just like the president was at the Centre.

Patel, who had fought so hard for the inclusion of this key presidential tenet, was nowhere to be seen in the Assembly during the two days when it decided to reverse his biggest contribution to India's Constitution.

The tables had turned partly because Patel was weakened. The first year and a half of India's independence had taken a heavy toll on him. As deputy prime minister under Nehru and the minister of home affairs, Patel was the man directly responsible for bringing together a nation in deep turmoil. Violence raged across the land throughout this period. But it was the assassination early that year of Mahatma Gandhi that affected him most. Gandhi was the main reason he continued to serve in government alongside Nehru. His estrangement from

Nehru was getting worse. Within a couple of months of Gandhi's assassination, Patel had suffered a heart attack. He recovered, but never regained the same will to fight. By the beginning of 1949, a much younger Nehru had hit his stride as the all-powerful prime minister of the nation.

The stage for a major reversal in the Assembly was in fact set by Constitutional Advisor Rau himself. In his report accompanying the first draft, Rau had alerted members of a mismatch between the principles of the Union and Provincial Constitutions that the Assembly had adopted. He had pointed out that while the president was to be elected indirectly, governors of states were being elected directly by the people.

In a bold, unprecedented move, Ambedkar's Drafting Committee wrote in the draft an alternative clause for the selection of governors – an alternative based on a principle that was the opposite of the one the Assembly had approved. It altered the mode of selection of governors from 'direct election' to 'appointment'. As the Assembly prepared to adopt the clauses of the Provincial Constitution, the Drafting Committee however notified that, based on the suggestions it had received since the draft was open to the public, it was willing to accept an amendment that 'the Governor should be directly appointed by the President ...'

Over a two-day period, some of the Congress party's heaviest hitters and allies – K. M. Munshi, H. V. Kamath, Alladi Krishnaswami Ayyar, P.S. Deshmukh, T.T. Krishnamachari, B.R. Ambedkar and even Jawaharlal Nehru himself – came out in full force in favour of dropping the concept of directly elected governors. But not Patel. Only two months before, Patel had defied death again. In March 1949 he was involved in an airplane emergency. The plane carrying him and the maharaja of Patiala had engine trouble and landed in the deserts of Rajasthan. No one was injured; Patel and his entourage had walked to safety. So it was odd that an apparently active and healthy Patel was absent from the Assembly on the very day it was to decide on his signature contribution to the Constitution.

A few members tried to stop the Assembly from reversing its decision on the grounds that it was not authorized to do so. But those efforts were too feeble to succeed.

Basically, members were presented with two arguments in favour of appointing governors instead of electing them: one, that locally elected governors would stoke separatist tendencies in the provinces; and two, that having two elected officials in a state – a governor and a chief minister – was a recipe for permanent conflict. 'The crux of the matter here is this,' said H.V. Kamath, '… if the Governor were to be elected by the direct vote of all voters in a province he is very likely to be a party-man with strong views of his own, and considering that he will be elected by the whole province – by the entire adult population of the province – he will think that he is a far superior man and a far more powerful man than the Chief Minister … There will be two conflicting authorities within the State.'[5]

Members thus faced a fundamental issue. To function properly, the parliamentary system required a figurehead, but then a figurehead, by definition, couldn't have direct mandate from the people. 'Wherever there is responsible government,' said P.S. Deshmukh, 'it necessarily means that the representatives of the people should have the authority to alter the executive any day or at any time … Therefore it necessarily follows that even if you have election for Governors, the Governor will have to be a figurehead.'

In the system India was devising, the concept of an elected governor was absurd for another reason. India's federal structure made it necessary that the Centre had a way to control state governments, and that was possible only when governors were appointed. India was a Union of states rather than a federation of sovereign states. If both the governor and the chief minister of a state were locally elected, the Centre was left with no mechanism to control provincial governments.

All this exposed a grave risk at the heart of India's parliamentary system: it could turn into a dictatorship. Hriday Nath Kunzru, the president of an independent outfit called the Servants of India Society, was one of the very few willing to bring this up in the Assembly. 'If you entrust the Central Executive with power to exercise control over the Provinces in all important matters,' he noted, 'and make them fall in line with the policy of the Centre, there is the serious danger of the country falling under a dictatorship.'[6]

The proponents really had no answer to this risk of dictatorship in India's system. Kunzru himself thought that by eliminating governors' powers over the day-to-day administration this risk would be minimized. He opposed the two articles in the draft Constitution which granted such powers, arguing that 'the Governor should not be able to exercise the power of setting aside his Cabinet and taking the administration into his own hands which he was to have when he was to be elected'. But since even as figureheads the governors had the power of dissolving their state's government, and the Centre had the power of imposing President's Rule, the system remained exposed to a prime minister turning the whole thing into a dictatorship.

PATEL'S CONSPICUOUS ABSENCE

Many members, especially those with experience in state administration, were not convinced that the Assembly should go back on a principle of such importance. They argued that a fundamental principle adopted after many days of debate, and at the insistence of a leader of Patel's stature, should not be taken so lightly. Prominent among these members were Rohini Kumar Chaudhuri, a former minister from Assam; Biswanath Das, former premier of Orissa; Muhammad Sa'adulla, former premier of Assam and B.G. Kher, former premier of Bombay.

Those who opposed going back on Patel's principle were especially irked that he was not in the Assembly. Biswanath Das was nominated to the Assembly by the Congress, but he couldn't hold back his disdain. He rattled the Assembly on all the touchy issues: that maybe there shouldn't be a governor at all; that the Congress party was having its way; and that perhaps Patel wasn't aware that such wholesale changes were being made to the Constitution.[7]

Suddenly, no one was interested in the key point that, even though the parliamentary system needed a figurehead, that figurehead could fulfil his purpose only when he had the dignity granted by the direct support of the people. The members were now only interested in the insinuations made by Das. They wanted to know about Patel and his thoughts on the matter.

First, the Congress party's most effective troubleshooter, K.M. Munshi, tried to clear the air. He explained how the Union and Provincial Constitution Committees had gone their separate ways, but now that 'we have adopted the British model, the election of the governor by adult franchise in the province remained an anomaly, a completely out-of-date and absurd thing.'

Noticing that the members were still sceptical, Nehru himself rose to address the issue. This was highly significant, for Nehru rarely spoke in the Assembly on individual clauses or issues. First, he reminded the members of how difficult the past two years had been, and that this change 'should not appear to be a strange thing to do, for we have had a great deal of experience, bitter experience during this period'. He then declared that 'even those like Sardar Patel, who themselves put forward in this House the other view, felt that a change would be desirable'. Nehru cited three reasons for the change. One, 'an elected Governor... would to some extent encourage ... separatist provincial tendency'; two, 'he might be some kind of a rival...[to] the government of the province'; and three, 'there will be these enormous elections'.[8]

Once Nehru spoke, it was all over for the provision of direct election of governors. Those who still wanted to debate, like Syed Muhammad Sa'adulla, were literally heckled. And the motion was adopted.

A FAÇADE OF PARLIAMENTARY DEMOCRACY

In the six days following Ambedkar's motion to adopt the final draft, the mood inside the Assembly was sombre. Speaker after speaker came forward to praise the many significant firsts embodied in the

Constitution, its many accomplishments that were a matter of pride for India's Constituent Assembly, yet there persisted the feeling that something was amiss.

There was no denying that the Constitution broke significant new ground and established some worthy principles. Adult suffrage, in a nation of 400 million mostly illiterate and destitute inhabitants, was a substantial accomplishment. Ending the chief cause of communal cancer in India's polity – separate electorates based on religions – was also a major achievement. So was the ending, or nearly so, of reservations based on communal grounds. Then there was the abolition of untouchability, which made discrimination illegal for the first time in history. The new Constitution was also instrumental in reducing India's fragmentation by putting an end to princely India and thus creating the largest democratic republic (in terms of population) on the planet. To do all this in a society deeply and violently divided along language, religion, caste and economic lines was no small matter. There was also a general feeling both inside and outside the Assembly that the framers of the Constitution had laboured hard. It had taken them three years, during one of the most gruelling periods in India's history, while they also functioned as the nation's legislators. During this time they deliberated as the Constituent Assembly for a total of 165 days.

So when hundreds of members rose in the Assembly in praise of the achievements of the Constitution, many were genuinely admiring. What was really extraordinary, however, was how many members rose to criticize the new Constitution. Nearly a third of the speakers who took the floor did so to say something disparaging.

Most of them had serious misgivings, but some were downright livid at what the Assembly was about to pass. One member [Kamalapati Tiwari] called the Constitution 'futile and lifeless', another [Lakshminarayan Sahu] called it 'queer and unwholesome'. One noted that 'democracy of this country has yet to be realized, and certainly not in this Constitution' [K.T. Shah]. Several members described certain provisions as 'a farce', [Damodar Swarup] or 'a clear deception', [Sardar Hukam Singh] or 'a façade' [H.V. Kamat]. The criticism was so persistent that a member exclaimed, 'far from having any sense of satisfaction, I am feeling extremely depressed' [Seth Damodar Swarup].[9]

Even Congressmen came forward to speak with an openness they had not shown before. Nandkishore Das, a Congressman, described the general feeling: 'It has got to be admitted however that the Constitution, in spite of being one of the best paper Constitutions in the world, has failed to evoke sufficient enthusiasm in the country and a suspicion lurks in the minds of even the most ardent admirers of the Constitution that something is wrong somewhere and things are not proceeding in the way they should.'

The best overall perspective of the Constitution's shortcomings, as well as its achievements, was presented by Kamalapati Tiwari, a Congress leader from the United Provinces. 'After all, what have we done so as to deserve this self-praise and mutual congratulations,' Tiwari asked his colleagues. 'We shall have reason for self-gratification only when the nation praises us.' He then bared the truth behind the Constitution's three 'most noteworthy' achievements: granting of universal franchise; abolition of untouchability; and of religion based-separate electorates. He said, 'If you had not included these broad features in the Constitution, what else would you have included in it?'. ... The principle of adult franchise is a well-known principle,' and its usefulness has already been demonstrated elsewhere. ... We accepted a well-recognized principle and have done but our elementary duty.' On untouchability, Tiwari said: 'Today we say that we have abolished untouchability through this Constitution. I ask had we not done what Bapu [Gandhi] had asked us to do and what had met general approval, how would we have kept face with our people?' Similarly, on the abolition of separate electorates, he asked: 'Our history of the last one hundred and fifty years bears testimony to the fact that no other problem has been so much responsible for ruining the country as that of separate electorates. ... Would we have provided for separate electorates even now?'

'Many petty mistakes' can be pointed out but 'I shall only point out the fundamental defects,' said Tiwari as he began his criticism. 'The first fundamental defect of the Constitution appears to be that it is terribly Centre-ridden. … A tree is being planted with its roots above and its branches spreading downwards.' Second, Tiwari continued, 'it appears that the Constitution has been framed only to meet the exigencies of the times.' The third shortcoming according to Tiwari was this: 'Is it not true that there are many clauses in this Constitution which infringe and encroach upon the Fundamental Rights of the citizens?'

CONCENTRATION OF POWER CRITICIZED

Extreme centralization of power was the Constitution's most criticized characteristic. Speaker after speaker worried that such centralization would kill initiative among the people, would become the cause of corruption in society, and would run the risk of dictatorship.

'Not that I do not want a strong Central Government,' exclaimed N.G. Ranga, 'all of us want it. But just contemplate for a moment what is likely to happen if another Hitler were to arise and take charge of the Central Government.' Hukam Singh said that the concentration of powers in the Constitution will 'facilitate the development of administration into a fascist State'. He prayed, 'May we be saved from such contingencies!' H.V. Kamath was equally scathing in his criticism: 'I may describe it as a centralized federation with a facade of parliamentary democracy'.

Fascism was not the only worry members had. 'If such a control continues, the initiative will be gone,' declared Algu Rai Shastri. Equally damning was a statement made by Lokanath Misra: 'This Constitution really tends to make the people irresponsible.' T.J.M. Wilson gave perhaps the best description of how over-centralization actually weakened the nation. 'Many people mistakenly think that strength lies in centralization and a strong Centre. I repeat that democracy of conscious effective citizens is much stronger and more efficient.'

Even a member of the Drafting Committee came forward to reveal how vexed he was with the whole process. 'The Drafting Committee was not a free agency,' exclaimed Syed Muhammad Sa'adulla, 'they were handicapped by various methods and circumstances from the very start. We were only asked to dress the baby. … It does not lie in my mouth to criticize individual provisions of the Draft Constitution as I am as much responsible as any other member of the Drafting Committee … but yet I am sorely tempted to draw your attention to only two or three things in this Constitution which are entirely repugnant to a free democratic constitution.' He then went on to talk about over-centralization, the limitations on Fundamental Rights, and the lack of financial independence in the provinces.

As member after member revealed their inner thoughts against over-centralization, K.T. Shah reminded the Assembly how he tried so hard to bring about separation of powers in the Constitution. He closed by saying, 'the working democracy of this country has yet to be realized, and certainly not in this Constitution'.

MANY DERIDED THE PARLIAMENTARY SYSTEM

Severe and open criticism wasn't limited to over-centralization alone; the parliamentary system itself also came under heavy fire. Members attempted to expose its reality, that in practice it was nothing but a party system of government which was not suitable for a country with many parties and that it was especially dangerous when there was one dominant political party.

'If there are two parties and two parties only,' said N.V. Gadgil, 'I have not the slightest doubt that this experiment will succeed to a substantial extent. But if there are more than two parties the life of the Cabinet will become very precarious.' Ramnarayan Singh, however, was ready to declare that 'the parliamentary system of government or the party-system of government has been provided for in this Constitution … it does not suit India'. 'Unfortunately there are already too many parties in our country,' he said. 'There have been parties on the basis of the caste-system for a long time. Now if you introduce a new party-system what will be the outcome? ... The result will be that some scoundrels and capitalists will combine and manage to monopolize all the votes.' Similarly, Kazi Syed Karimuddin thought that if the president is not directly elected, 'he will be a creature of the majority party'.

The harshest criticism was aimed at the parliamentary system's most defining feature, its reliance on legislature. One member was enraged and reminded the Assembly what Ambedkar had said, that it was 'wiser not to trust the legislature'. Another thought it absolutely necessary that the fundamental rights 'must be taken out of the jurisdiction of the Legislature'. Some thought that India's parliamentary system was doomed because while it depended on legislators' wisdom, it didn't place any qualification requirements for them.

'In our Constitution a compromise has been effected which is impossible,' Hukam Singh declared. 'We have imposed prohibitions on the Legislature, thus conceding that there is danger from that side, and then proceeded to permit the legislature itself to restrict the liberty. The feared robber is made the judge and the possible trespasser the sole arbiter. This is a clear deception.'

Some members even dared to say the unspeakable and declared that the parliamentary system was being adopted only to satisfy the existing government. In fact, most of those who commented that the Constitution was nothing but a copy of the Government of India Act, 1935, were essentially saying the same thing. The Constitution kept a foreign ruler's centralized system in place in which the government at the Centre held all the powers.

The Constitution was 'not even the case of pouring old wine into new bottles, but of old wine and old bottles', said Ajit Prasad Jain, declaring that 'both the laws and the administrative machinery under the new dispensation will not be much different'.

As to why India was adopting a system that suited the existing government but not the people, Shibban Lal Saksena, by now a Congress party rebel, had the answer. 'Under the procedure adopted,' he said, 'the Drafting Committee could not get the advantage of the free opinion of the whole House and decisions of the Congress party alone became binding upon it.' He went further: 'I personally feel that the constitution has very much suffered on this account. Out of about 10,000 amendments which appeared on the order paper ... I think this House had opportunity for discussing hardly a few hundreds. The rest were all guillotined inside the Congress party. ... Congress party meetings became meetings of the real Constituent Assembly, and this real Assembly became the mock Assembly ...'

When Rajendra Prasad made his closing remarks, he still held out the hope that India's system would not be over-centralized. Mindful of the general feeling in the Assembly, Prasad expressed the view that since for the first time India was to have an 'elected' president, he would also have some say in government. He pointed out that there were no specific provisions in the Constitution 'making it binding on the President to accept the advice of his Ministers'.

It was truly remarkable that, in the end, India's Constitution was based essentially on a hope. On the all-important issue of balance of powers between the two topmost officials of government, the prime minister and the president, the Constitution was ambiguous. It left the matter on this hope that conventions would develop to clear it up. As was to be expected, those hopes were soon dashed.

NOTES

1   *Constituent Assembly Debates*, 10 December 1948.
2   Ibid.
3   Ibid.
4   Ibid., 30 December 1948.
5   Ibid., 30 May 1949.
6   Ibid.
7   Ibid., 31 May 1949.
8   Ibid.
9   All quotes in this section are from *Constituent Assembly Debates*, 17–24 November 1949.

7

A Case of Systemic Failure

The country's political system today is completely broken – 'rotten', according to many, including Rahul Gandhi, the new custodian of the Nehru–Gandhi legacy.

Arbitrary or unrestrained exercise of power – tyranny – can only be checked by distributing powers among many. It is possible in a parliamentary democracy, Bertrand Russell, the famous British philosopher and Nobel laureate, admitted, 'for the majority to exercise brutal and wholly unnecessary tyranny over a minority'.[1]

Mahatma Gandhi was perhaps the only Indian leader who fully understood how truly tyrannical the British parliamentary system could become. 'Indeed, my recent visit to England has confirmed my opinion,' he wrote to the British secretary of state in 1932, 'that your democracy is a superficial circumscribed thing. In the weightiest matters decisions are taken by individuals or groups, without reference to Parliament … My whole being rebels against the idea that in a system called democratic one man should have the unfettered power … To me this is a negation of democracy.'[2] He predicted that if India copied this system, 'she will be ruined'.

Once in power, the majority in this system ran amok. As the framers of India's Constitution began their work, it was clear that in all three watershed moments in recent history – the first time the British people voted for an India-friendly government (1924); the first time Indians themselves formed local governments (1937); and the first time India needed a truly federal government (1947) – the parliamentary system failed to deliver. Similar experiences would continue after Independence too. The first time India needed the top two officials in its government, the prime minister and the president, to work together, it made one subservient to the other. The first time India needed to select a prime minister after Nehru, permanent fissures developed in the entire system. Then, when a prime minister won with overwhelming support, the system let her become a dictator. When democracy was in true danger, only providence brought it back. If a coalition government was needed, this system failed to deliver both stability and accountability. Governments rode roughshod over the Constitution, which the system was helpless to defend. Corruption and quality of life continued to deteriorate and the system offered no means of remedy.

Leaders of the majority could act on momentary passions or sinister designs with impunity. The insidious communal division, the demoralizing partition, the corrupting licence raj, the unlawful Emergency – all of these were the results of unfettered majorities acting with callous disregard for the minority opinion. To those who argued that blaming all these ills on the parliamentary system is an oversimplification, I say study the history of India objectively. The facts show that the parliamentary system failed at every turn.

TWO ELECTED HEADS

Within days of adoption, the new Constitution began to show signs that India's peculiar parliamentary system with two elected officials at the top, the president and the prime minister, was a recipe for disaster. The silent tug of war between Jawaharlal Nehru and Rajendra Prasad, India's first prime minister and president respectively, began immediately and would continue for a whole decade. It would diminish the office of the presidency to such an extent that, in the end, India's president would become nothing but a figurehead.

Even as the Indian Constitution was being drafted, a famous British constitutional scholar, Sir Ivor Jennings, had cast doubt on the workability of this feature. 'The Indian Constitution,' he wrote in a 1948 paper for the Commonwealth Prime Ministers' Conference, 'provides for an elected President who is apparently intended to be a constitutional monarch without the trappings of a monarch. This is perhaps a somewhat hazardous experiment. Constitutional monarchy has been evolved in Great Britain by a long and at times stormy process of evolution. It is easy to translate this system through the appointment of a Governor-General, but it may be less easy where an elected President, presumably a politician of some ambition, assumes royal functions.'[3]

The matter was 'hazardous' especially because nowhere in the Constitution was it made clear whether the president was bound to act as advised by the prime minister. Two different interpretations began to take hold across the country. Those who saw the Indian president as a copy of the British monarch argued that the president was a mere figurehead with no discretion whatsoever. Others found this view unfathomable, for there was absolutely no similarity between an elected president and a hereditary king. Eminent jurists and those in the know, however, were aware that the Indian president was meant to have a real say in government.

Many, including Prasad himself, had tried during the framing of India's Constitution to make the provisions more explicit, but to no avail. When Prasad became the acting president of India's provisional government, he began to take personal interest in the powers assigned to his office. In April, he wrote to the constitutional advisor to the Constituent Assembly, asking him to make the president's position clear. He wanted to know whether 'the President is not bound by the advice of his Ministers at all in any case or that he is bound to act in all cases?'[4] When no response was forthcoming, Prasad wrote to Rau. This time he asked a specific question: whether the president could, in his discretion, withhold assent from a bill passed by a state's legislature and referred to him by the governor.[5]

This time there was some movement. A couple of months later, the Drafting Committee gave notice that it wanted to add a new clause: 'In the choice of his Ministers and the exercise of his functions under this Constitution, the President shall be generally guided by the Instructions set out in Schedule IIIA, but the validity of anything done by the President shall not be called in question on the ground that it was done otherwise than in accordance with such instructions.'[6] It also circulated an elaborate draft of the Instrument of Instructions that was to be Schedule IIIA. The Instrument gave the president the power 'to appoint a person who has been found by him to be most likely to command a stable majority in Parliament as the Prime Minister', a provision that was earlier rejected by the Union Constitution Committee.

The Instrument of Instructions clause had satisfied most in the assembly, for it not only gave the president significant leeway, it made his powers explicit and it also left parliament with the final say. At this stage, the draft had appeared to find the right balance. This clause combined with two other provisions in the draft – the president's power to block legislation and his two-term limit – gave both sides enough to go on. In December, the clause incorporating the Instrument was adopted by the Assembly without much ado.

Then suddenly, in a remarkable series of events, the draft Constitution began to change again in the direction of establishing the prime minister's supremacy over the president. First, in May 1949, the provision giving the president the authority to block legislation was dropped from the draft. It had been adopted only a few months before, in December, with only one dissenting voice. The assembly now decided to allow re-passage of legislation over a presidential veto. 'Nowhere in the Assembly Debates is there an explanation of this extraordinary affair,' Austin wrote.[7] Then, in October, the president's restriction of two terms in office was suddenly and quietly omitted. In the version of the draft printed on 28 October 1949, the relevant article was modified to read simply that the president was 'eligible for re-election to that office'. This was also 'an unpublicized change in the Constitution, which was apparently not debated by the Assembly'.[8] It was a subtle change, for it removed the general impression that the

Constitution sanctioned a president to continue in office for only two terms.

But the biggest reversal, which forever enfeebled the office of the presidency, was when the Assembly decided to drop the Instrument of Instructions from the Constitution altogether. Only ten months after it was adopted, at the insistence of Drafting Committee chairman Ambedkar himself, the very same committee decided that the Instrument was no longer needed. 'Why? The Assembly never in so many words gave the reasons.'[9]

This last-minute change gravely altered the balance of power in favour of the prime minister, but they were so surreptitious and hurried that the Assembly as a whole didn't quite grasp their real meaning. The purposely vague prescription that the Assembly had finally passed ('There shall be a Council of Ministers with the Prime Minister at the head to aid and advise the President in the exercise of his functions.') left the president at the mercy of the more popularly elected prime minister.

For Nehru, however, this wasn't sufficient; even before the Constitution was inaugurated, he began actively opposing Prasad's candidature for president. 'Nehru had seen enough of Prasad to know that the latter was against many things which he stood for, including his brand of socialism, his secularism in actual practice and his views on important matters of policy concerning home as well as foreign affairs,' wrote a distinguished journalist, H.N. Pandit, in his 1974 book *The PM's President*. 'Above all,' Pandit wrote, 'Nehru himself was against the President's belief that the President of India had much more power under our Constitution than the British monarch ... Nehru was intent on not having as President a person who would never stop trying to upset the status quo in the balance of power under the Constitution.'[10] Instead of Prasad, Nehru proposed the name of C. Rajagopalachari (Rajaji), a Congress leader from the south whom he had brought to Delhi to become Governor General after Mountbatten left in June 1948. It was a conceited move on Nehru's part because neither the Congress party nor Rajaji himself was interested. Rajaji had, in fact, suggested that Nehru himself should become president and let Patel be the prime minister. 'Consequently, Nehru resorted to what he usually did under such circumstances. He wrote to Prasad suggesting that he should decline the office of the head of state. Prasad refused to oblige and cleverly added that he left it to Nehru and Patel "to edge me out". Only then did it dawn on Nehru that Patel, with his enormous influence in the party, was backing Prasad.'[11]

As it became evident that in the system India had adopted, party bosses controlled the appointment of the president, a miffed Nehru immediately expanded his campaign to gain supremacy in his party as well. Being the most popular leader of his party and the prime minister who brought some stability to a nation in upheaval, Nehru chose an interesting course of action: he threatened to resign. Only three weeks after he took the oath of office, Nehru wrote to Patel: 'I am quite convinced that I could serve the cause of our country much better today in a private capacity than in the public office I hold.'[12] Patel responded the following day, saying that he could appreciate Nehru's sense of oppression, 'but we should do nothing which would make confusion worse compounded'.[13] But Nehru was not about to let go. Within six months, Nehru was openly clashing with the incoming Congress president, Purushottamdas Tandon, when he appointed certain members to the newly formed Working Committee who were opposed to Nehru. He was particularly infuriated because of Patel's support for Tandon.

Patel died in December 1950, but the dispute simmered into the summer of 1951. In August that year Tandon wrote to Nehru that 'the Prime Minister and his Cabinet are responsible to the Congress'. Once again Nehru resorted to his self-serving tactic; he announced his decision to resign from the Working Committee and the party's Central Election Committee. He also began to rally the chief ministers of state governments behind him. 'The major problem has seemed to me,' Nehru wrote to them, 'how to bring about some kind of communion between those in government or outside, who give the lead, and the masses of our people. That lead has to be realistic.'[14] By

September 1951, Tandon capitulated and Nehru was elected president of the Congress party.

The concentration of power was now complete, and within days Nehru had the Congress Plenary Session pass resolutions affirming his economic and social policies, and confirm 'the pre-eminent role of the Prime Minister' and reinforced the boundaries of the office of Congress president ... as limited strictly to organizational affairs with no special responsibilities for policymaking.'[15]

A CONSTITUTIONAL CRISIS

India's peculiar parliamentary system landed the nation in a crisis within months of its adoption. The confrontation between the top two offices, the PM and the president, began just days after the inauguration of the new Constitution.

On 14 February 1950, Nehru's Cabinet sent a note to Attorney General M.C. Setalvad asking him about the president's powers in the case of legislation passed by a state government, the Zamindari (Landownership) Abolition Act. A month later, President Rajendra Prasad raised his own questions in a paper entitled 'Questions relating to the powers of the President under the Constitution of India'. In the main, he wanted to know 'Does the Constitution contemplate any situation in which the President has to act independently of the advice of his Ministers?[16] When no response was forthcoming from Setalvad or the office of the prime minister, Prasad persisted, because with each passing day important new laws were being made, like the abolition of zamindari, and far-reaching new precedents were being set. After waiting five months, Prasad wrote again, this time to Deputy Prime Minister Patel. With Patel he was more assertive, noting 'that the President could advise ministers not on matters of detail but generally on matters of policy'. Prasad wished, therefore, to have a senior staff person to inform him 'if there is any matter in which I should have a discussion with ministers'.[17] It appears that even Patel didn't respond to Prasad.

When no one was willing to specify what powers the Constitution really granted to the president, Prasad became impatient. In September, after having waited more than six months for a response to his 'Questions' and nearly two weeks after writing to Patel, Prasad finally took the matter directly to Nehru. In a letter to the prime minister, on 8 September, Prasad questioned certain elements of the Bihar Zamindari Bill and went as far as expressing his reluctance to grant his assent. Unbeknown to the public, a feverish and angry exchange of letters ensued among India's top officials, which brought their government to a near collapse.

The crisis was averted only because the president chose to back down. Somehow Patel learnt of Prasad's letter to Nehru and, realizing its gravity, decided to intervene before Nehru had a chance to react. He wrote a strongly worded note to Nehru, stating that in view of Prasad's 'rather strong convictions on this problem', the request for presidential assent to the Bihar Bill should be delayed until the matter was reviewed by the law and home ministries, and that 'the cabinet should avoid giving the impression that it had given Prasad's well-considered note summary treatment'.[18] The same day, Prasad wrote to Nehru again, raising the pitch even higher: 'When I am asked to sign a document, I must satisfy myself and not sign blindly,' he said.

With both Prasad and Patel standing together in opposition, Nehru moved fast. The day he received Prasad's letter, he threatened to resign. This was his third such threat within the first year. To Patel he wrote that 'the cabinet – with all present save Patel, who was unwell in Bombay – had considered Prasad's note and decided that he should give his assent from both the constitutional and practical points of view'. Nehru warned that if the president didn't assent to the Bihar Bill, he and his ministry would resign. At once Prasad returned the Bill with his assent, commenting that he was doing so because of the 'urgency Nehru attached to the matter'. Prasad's letters and related documents were not circulated, nor were they included in the official records – as Nehru told Patel, 'to preserve secrecy'.[19]

By yielding to Nehru, Prasad avoided the collapse of government within its first year. But soon they were at loggerheads again, this time over the Hindu Code Bill, an omnibus measure to reform laws regarding marriage, divorce, inheritance of property, etc., but only for the Hindus. Nehru had chosen the Bill as his signature effort to establish his credentials as a 'secularist'. Prasad, on the other hand, took the view that the Bill was 'highly discriminatory', for it reformed Hindu traditions but not Muslim and other traditions. He took the stand that such 'revolutionary changes' should be postponed till at least the first general election was held under the new Constitution and a more competent and representative Parliament was in place.

Once again, there was an angry exchange of letters. Once again, Nehru threatened to resign. And once again, the feud resulted in an important legislation being delayed rather than improved. In a top secret letter, Prasad wrote to Nehru that he would send to parliament a message if he thought the Bill was inappropriate, and clearly stated: 'My right to examine it on its merits when it is passed by Parliament before giving assent to it is there.'[20] Nehru shot back a response the same day, that this raises 'serious matters of great constitutional importance', and that 'the President has no power or authority ... to go against the will of Parliament ... Otherwise the question would arise as to whether Parliament is the supreme legislative authority in this country or not.'[21] Nehru shared the letters with members of his Cabinet but asked them to keep the matter 'absolutely secret'.

As was to be expected, the secret war came out in the open. In 1957, Nehru openly opposed Prasad for a second term. He was chosen only because Maulana Azad put his foot down.[22] In November 1960, Prasad chose to go public with his view of the constitutional powers of the president. In a speech, in the presence of Nehru, he stated that while 'it is generally believed that like the Sovereign of Great Britain the President of India is also a constitutional head and has to act according to the advice of his Council of Ministers ... The question I should like to be studied and investigated is the extent to which and the matters in respect of which, if any, the powers and functions of the President differ from those of the Sovereign of Great Britain.'[23]

Three years later, in 1963, K.M. Munshi took it upon himself to carry forward Prasad's contention that, the president was not merely a figurehead, by writing the book *The President Under the Indian Constitution*. Munshi, a key member of the Constituent Assembly, debunked the notion that the Assembly had created a powerless president.

By now, however, the precedent was firmly established that the president always acted as advised by the prime minister. Contentions over presidential powers continually declined after May 1962 when Prasad departed from the scene. The voices of Munshi and others were lost in oblivion. Prasad's unanswered 'Questions' soon became moot, for the concentration of powers in India's parliamentary system – in the hands of a single individual, the prime minister – would extinguish democracy itself.

A SINGLE CENTRE OF POWER

India's system was so prone to becoming a monocracy that within a decade of Nehru's death, democracy in India came to a complete halt. The failure of the system was glaring, for it failed in its first full run. The first time a political party came to power with an overwhelming majority, its leader Indira Gandhi was able to convert India's democracy into a dictatorship with ease.

The amassing of all governmental powers in one person was so complete that Indira Gandhi was able to rule India as a despot during an eighteen-month period in the mid-1970s, a period that became infamous as 'Indira Gandhi's Emergency'. In a series of horrifying manoeuvres, Gandhi and her coterie were able to amend, or debase, the Constitution so drastically that it bore no resemblance to the original.

Any semblance of separation of powers in the Constitution was expunged. All confusion about the president's powers was removed. He was now required by the Constitution to act only as advised. That democracy survived in India after this episode was not a testament to India's Constitution, but due to a miscalculation by Gandhi when she decided to hold elections again. The restoration of democracy, however, didn't mean the restoration of the Constitution. The political leaders who came to power after Indira Gandhi repealed many of the changes made during the Emergency, but decided to keep those that concentrated powers in the hands of the majority party. India's parliamentary system thus became even more party-centric.

The Indian system's tendency towards totalitarianism turned into a frenzy soon after Nehru's death in May 1964. The reason for that was simple: the system provided the wherewithal for a prime minister to acquire dictatorial powers, if he or she was pushed to the wall. As Sir Ivor Jennings had written in 1951, 'the flexibility of the cabinet system allows the Prime Minister to take upon himself a power not inferior to that of a dictator'.[24] Many in India's Constituent Assembly had also warned about the danger of this system turning into a dictatorship. So it was no surprise that as soon as a prime minister came to power but was not secure in office, which was the case with Indira Gandhi in 1966, the seizing of all powers began.

Grabbing control of the presidency took centre stage first. Given the circumstances of her ascent and the likelihood that the president might still have some discretionary powers – Prasad's 'Questions' were still unanswered – Indira Gandhi considered it crucial to have a pliant president. She wasn't the Congress party's consensus candidate. A few powerful Congress leaders from the states, who became collectively known as the 'Syndicate', were able to determine who should become prime minister after Nehru's death. But when Lal Bahadur Shastri, Nehru's successor, suddenly died in office, they were unable to come to an agreement on any one candidate. Indira Gandhi was then chosen to be the prime minister by a secret ballot, but her election left the party deeply fragmented.

To make matters worse, Indira Gandhi was unable to win the people over in the general elections of 1967. The Congress party's majority in the Lok Sabha was reduced to a very slim margin of only twenty-five, and it lost control of eight state assemblies. Indira Gandhi quickly resorted to populist measures under the guise of socialism. She issued a Ten-Point Programme which included measures such as the nationalization of banks and insurance companies, and limitations on urban incomes and property. This further alienated the right wing of the Congress party, led by a member of the old-guard who was also the deputy prime minister and minister of finance, Morarji Desai. The stage was now set for yet another struggle for power within the Congress party.

When Zakir Hussain suddenly died in office in 1969, the leaders of the Congress party – Indira Gandhi on one side and the Syndicate on the other – decided to draw their battle lines over who became India's next president. The old guard in the Congress party nominated a member of the Syndicate, Sanjiva Reddy, for president, instead of the acting president V.V. Giri who had assumed office after Hussain's death. Indira Gandhi favoured Giri; she considered him to be 'friendly'.[25] She decided 'to give the confrontation the look of ideology and principle' and 'chose Morarji Desai as her victim'.[26] Desai was relieved as finance minister and within days he resigned from government altogether. He told the Lok Sabha that he didn't want to be 'a silent spectator to methods that may endanger the basic principle of democracy on which our parliamentary system is established'.[27] A month later Giri was elected president by a narrow margin. Soon after, the Congress party split into two.

The consequences of this battle over the presidency were huge. While before this fight, India's system was at least able to masquerade as one based on two centres of power, after it was over, that pretence was completely gone. A handful of leaders had fought over who was to be president, when he ought to have been 'elected' by the people's representatives. This contest to control the only other centre of power that had any chance of standing against the office of the prime minister would change the fundamental nature of India's system. From one in which the president and the prime minister were engaged in a tussle, the system was now completely controlled by the latter. The battle would also begin an era of fragmentation in political parties, because it was the party bosses who held powers. This was the main reason behind the splitting of the Congress party. The fight also began an era of subjecting the nation to minority or unstable governments; of political horse-trading for power; of promising devastating populist handouts to acquire or retain power; and, most consequentially, of allowing the majority to pass laws without any constraints whatsoever.

With a 'friendly' president in office, the Indian system's propensity for autocracy began to show in many other ways. For instance, its feature that a government could engineer its own timing for coming back to power was now exposed as a major shortcoming. Indira Gandhi used this over and over again, dissolving parliament early or extending its life, as she found most suitable for her party. President Giri obliged her every single time.

Worst of all, this system allowed a prime minister who held sway over the presidency to pass any legislation or take any administrative action. Each time her agenda ran into difficulty, the president was there to remove it. For instance, in 1969, acting president Giri promulgated an ordinance nationalizing banks and in 1970 he approved a 'midnight order' derecognizing the princes despite the defeat of a bill to that effect in parliament.

As a result of her radically egalitarian programmes and slogans, Indira Gandhi's popularity grew. In the 1971 elections, her party won big; gaining a two-thirds majority in the Lok Sabha by winning 350 of the 520 seats. Later that year, her popularity received a fortuitous boost due to India's overwhelming victory over Pakistan in the Bangladesh War. The following year her Congress party won from 52 to 83 per cent of the seats in all but three small states in the assembly elections.

The Indian variety of parliamentary system now had all the ingredients for a total monocracy. There was a hugely popular prime minister, who was the undisputed leader of her party, who controlled more than two-thirds of the seats in the Lok Sabha, who controlled a majority of state assemblies and who had a pliant president in the office.

As a result, the migration of power to the prime minister's office in general, and Indira Gandhi in particular, now began in earnest. Gandhi began by bringing government's intelligence and investigative agencies under her direct control. The concept of collective responsibility of the Cabinet too collapsed. Once the powers were centralized in the hands of the prime minister, the other ministers were no longer responsible, or even relevant. By early 1971, the Cabinet secretariat was rendered insignificant; ministers now reported directly to the PM's secretariat (PMS). Sanjay Gandhi (Indira Gandhi's younger son) and his handful of friends 'had virtually hijacked the government' and the real power had shifted from the PMS to the PMH (PM's house).[28]

India's system had allowed a prime minister to amass personal powers to such an extent that she was able to turn India into a police state. She was now able to exercise authority with full immunity. She extended the state of national emergency which was put in place due to the war with Pakistan, even though the war had already been won. She would keep it in force for six more years. She re-enacted a detested preventive detention law (MISA, Maintenance of Internal Security Act) which was earlier rejected by parliament. A.B. Vajpayee, a leader of the opposition party, Jana Sangh, declared that it was 'the beginning of a police raj' and 'the first step towards dictatorship'.[29]

Like any other dictator, Gandhi set out to fix the one thing that stood between her and permanent total control: the Constitution. India's Constitution had instigated the fight for supremacy between the prime minister and the president because it wasn't explicit about presidential powers. So, of course, the fix was to restrict the president's powers explicitly. Within the first week of taking office after the March 1971 elections, Gandhi instructed her newly appointed law minister to proceed with the drafting of a series of constitutional amendments. In the guise of socialism, the thrust of all these amendments was to further entrench the concept of parliamentary supremacy. Especially over the two remaining forces she hadn't yet completely vanquished: the presidency and the Constitution. When, in July 1971, the sweeping twenty-fourth amendment – providing that 'notwithstanding anything in this Constitution, Parliament may ... amend ... any provision' and that the president 'shall give his assent' – was presented in the Lok Sabha, it took only two days to pass.

If there was any doubt left that India's parliamentary system was absurd, the passage of the twenty-fourth amendment completely removed it. When parliament had unlimited power to change the Constitution, which even the president couldn't restrict, it was senseless to have a written constitution, or, for that matter, to have any other branch of government. A political party with two-thirds majority in parliament could amend the amendment provision itself, or remove a branch of government altogether, or outlaw every other political party, or repeal the entire Constitution, and so on. The system in India had now become so ludicrous that Gandhi and her coterie knew that it wasn't going to last. Sooner or later, they knew, the constitutionality of their amendments would be challenged in court. So now, having tamed the Constitution, the last remaining power that stood in their way was the judiciary.

Here again, the Indian system itself gave Gandhi the way to overpower the judiciary. The prime minister had the power of appointing justices to the Supreme Court, and the president merely followed her advice. She and her men began appointing pliant judges to pack the Supreme Court.[30] As a result, in a key challenge to her amendments, in the famous Kesavananda Bharati case, the majority of judges mollified the government by upholding all three amendments. But in the same decision the court also dared to rule that an amendment could not alter the basic structure of the Constitution. Pointing to the absurdity of the government's position, Chief Justice Sikri noted that 'if the claim is accepted that there is no limit to the power to amend the Constitution, Article 368 [the amending provision] can itself be amended ... a political party with two-thirds majority could debar any other party ... establish totalitarianism ... enslave the people'.[31]

The very next day, on 25 April 1973, Indira Gandhi replaced the Chief Justice of India, a day before he was to retire. She appointed in his place a judge, Justice A.N. Ray, who was fourth in line in terms of seniority. In what became famous as 'supersession of judges', the prime minister had shocked the nation by breaking a well-established convention of appointing the seniormost judge as chief justice. A.R. Gokhale, Mohan Kumaramangalam and S.S. Ray, Indira Gandhi's in-group on legal matters, had 'recommended Ray according to most accounts because he was expected to be pliable as well as liberal'.[32]

By the end of 1973, her brand of socialism was beginning to show its true colours. The country faced a recession, rising unemployment, rampant inflation and scarcity of food and almost every other item. Prices rose 22 per cent in 1973 alone. There was a drop in power generation, and in agricultural as well as industrial production. All this led to unrest. Many colleges and universities closed for extended periods. The law and order situation deteriorated. Corruption seeped into high offices because of extreme centralization.

As her popularity began to wane, Indira Gandhi's need for eliminating critics and removing threats to her authority became even stronger. She replaced President Giri who was beginning to speak out against the government. When his term ended, she ensured that a man even more obedient than Giri sat in the president's office. The appointment of Fakhruddin Ali Ahmed as India's fifth president was a watershed moment because it changed forever the opinion of the high office in the minds of the people. While before, the office was viewed as one designed for eminent men, after Ahmed it came to be seen as suitable only for extreme loyalists. In his book published the same year, H.N. Pandit wrote that 'it seems reasonably certain that India will never again have a really first-rate public figure as the head of the state'. 'In the matter of choosing the nominee the Prime Minister's opinion alone will prevail,' he wrote, '...it will be the man with tail-between-the-legs look who will be finally chosen.'[33]

Grim forebodings of a constitutional system gone awry were now being openly discussed in the Indian media. Soon after Ahmed was sworn in, Palkhivala, a renowned constitutional expert, wrote in a column entitled 'The Mess We Are In'[34]: 'The danger facing India is that it combines economic stagnation with fragile institutions and a Constitution which is looked upon by politicians as so pliant that it can be bent to any whim or caprice of the ruling clan.' Similarly, Pandit concluded his book by declaring: 'Today our Constitution is in serious trouble' because 'by providing two elected heads of state, the makers of the Constitution have laid the infrastructure for a never ending series of crises … The presidency seems destined to prove the Achilles heel of the Indian Constitution'.[35]

Anyhow, Indira Gandhi's hold over power was now complete. But she had only begun.

THE ALL-POWERFUL PM

Prime Minister Indira Gandhi began to rule by diktat, by means of presidential decree if necessary. She introduced several harsh measures to deal with the rising disturbances and economic decline. The scope of MISA was expanded; a new law Conservation of Foreign Exchange and Prevention of Smuggling Activities Act (COFEPOSA) was enacted, allowing detention for hoarding and smuggling without a court order; and then a few months later, the right to appeal for persons detained under COFEPOSA was suspended. She would even have the president use his emergency powers – the state of emergency declared in 1971 for the Bangladesh war was still in force, four years after hostilities had ended – to suspend the right to move the courts for protection of certain Fundamental Rights. So much so, she had the president issue an ordinance forcing savings on individuals.

The Indian parliamentary system also allowed Indira Gandhi to blatantly disregard the federal structure of the Constitution. An already suspended Gujarat legislature was dissolved and the state was put under President's Rule. Fresh elections to the Gujarat Legislative Assembly were postponed more than once. Morarji Desai had to go on an indefinite fast in April 1975 to force elections. Jayaprakash Narayan, who had joined Desai in opposition to Indira Gandhi, began calling the Central government a 'one-woman government, reduced to a dictatorship under the façade of democracy'.[36]

With such limitless powers at her disposal, it was only natural that Indira Gandhi and her closest advisers began to consider what could be done with regard to her election case. She was accused of indulging in corrupt practices during her 1971 parliamentary election campaign. In January 1975, S.S. Ray 'mooted' the idea of declaring an 'internal emergency' as a way to deal with the matter if the verdict went against Indira Gandhi.[37] When in June 1975, Justice J.L. Sinha of the Allahabad High Court ruled that Indira Gandhi was guilty of two corrupt practices – using an official of her secretariat to further her election prospects and obtaining the assistance of state government officials – all hell broke loose. 'Mrs Gandhi Unseated' ran the newswires. Her inner circle began to consider whether she should resign. Since Justice Sinha had granted her twenty days in which to appeal to the Supreme Court, Indira Gandhi decided not to resign. 'By staying in office she could at least have some opportunity to direct the course of events.'[38]

There was no provision in India's system to force a prime minister out of office as long as his or her party held a majority in parliament. The opposition parties among them had no more than sixty seats in a 518-seat House. But by precedent Indira Gandhi should have resigned. Many state ministers as well as members of parliament and state assemblies had lost their seats when they were found guilty of using government officials for election purposes. 'Mrs Gandhi herself had asked Channa Reddy, her Cabinet minister from Andhra Pradesh, to resign when he was held guilty of corrupt practices.'[39]

Powers were so completely in the grip of Indira Gandhi that within three days of the Allahabad verdict, her son and two or three others were able to control the entire government from the prime minister's residence. They launched a plan to 'set things right', as Sanjay confided[40] to a friend. The thinking done earlier about declaring an internal emergency also came in handy. S.S. Ray confirmed to the prime minister that the way to 'do something' was to declare an 'internal' emergency which the president was empowered to do under Article 352 of the Constitution. This would give the Central government emergency powers to silence the press, to detain opponents, to give any direction to state governments, and above all, to suspend Article 19 (Fundamental Rights) of the Constitution. Indira Gandhi's secretary, P.N. Haksar, had already set up a mini-government in the prime minister's secretariat. 'Not even a deputy secretary was appointed without its concurrence.'[41]

Additionally, about 700,000 security personnel of various police forces were under the direct control of the Central government. The country's intelligence unit, RAW, had already been put under the prime minister's direct charge. It was ready with dossiers on all of Indira Gandhi's opponents. Lists were prepared with names of those who were to be detained. Chief ministers in the states were told to make preparations for arrests of those individuals. An already strengthened MISA was the law under which arrests were to be made to avoid having to produce charges before a court. Arrest warrants were prepared; some were even signed blank. The date set for action was 25 June, the day after the Supreme Court would uphold the Allahabad High Court's decision. What was truly remarkable was that she and her men were able to do all this in absolute secrecy; the opposition leaders were completely oblivious until the very last day.

The system had gone so badly astray that no one thought it necessary to consult, or even inform, the one man who was to proclaim the Emergency. Indira Gandhi was so confident that there would be no trouble from President Ahmed that only four hours before the midnight deadline, she drove to Rashtrapati Bhavan to get the president's signatures. The Constitution required that the president act as advised by the council of ministers, but Indira Gandhi hadn't even consulted her Cabinet. Within minutes, the president had signed a proclamation that 'a grave emergency exists whereby the security of India is threatened by internal disturbances', and granted the government a slew of emergency powers.[42] 'He did not think of demurring. He was indebted to Indira Gandhi for elevating him to the highest position in the country.'[43]

The parliamentary system's much touted 'collective responsibility' of government was of no use either since the Cabinet wasn't even informed. 'I have decided to declare an emergency. The President has agreed,' Indira Gandhi simply announced to her secretaries, and 'I shall inform the cabinet in the morning.' The third branch of government, the courts, were of no consequence either. All of Indira Gandhi's opponents were placed in custody under a legitimate law (MISA) passed by Parliament, and all their Fundamental Rights were suspended under a constitutionally valid proclamation signed by the president. India's court system was unitary; the entire system was under one apex court, the Supreme Court of India. And sitting at the top of the Supreme Court was Indira Gandhi's own man, Chief Justice Ray.

'With the sweep of her hand, Mrs. Gandhi had snuffed out democracy. Repression would be piled upon repression.'[44] 'The action was sudden, quick and ruthless and it had all the ingredients of a coup. … In Delhi, opposition leaders were woken up between 2.30 and 3 a.m., shown orders of arrest and driven to a police station, ironically not far from Parliament House. They were detained under MISA, the same Act under which smugglers were detained. Those arrested were from all parties … the only opposition party left untouched was the pro-Moscow Communist Party of India, an ally of the Congress. … Most of the Delhi newspapers did not appear because the power supply to their presses was cut off before midnight … it was nearly as drastic as imposing martial law – it was "police law".'[45] The news was the same all across the nation. Jayaprakash Narayan and Morarji Desai were among the first to be arrested; the official figure was 676 arrested in the first two days. In all, more than 100,000 would be detained. That was not all. There were instances of torture. Then there were the pet projects of Indira Gandhi's son Sanjay: beautification and population control. To make India's cities look better, shanty towns were demolished; private properties were grabbed to widen streets; and edicts were issued prescribing what colour buildings could be painted. The poor and the middle class were subjected to the terror of a forcible sterilization programme. 'Sterilization targets were assigned to chief ministers, who, in their efforts to gain favour, were reported to have exceeded them'.[46] It was most ironic that the parliamentary system would allow Prime Minister Gandhi to use the parliament itself to end democracy in India. To give her actions an air of democratic legitimacy, she had parliament approve the proclamation of Emergency. Since almost all senior members of the opposition were behind bars, the resolution passed easily. As it passed, Era Sezhian of the DMK noted: 'Sometimes I think some of us even feel why have a parliament? Why should 500 members come here to take a decision which one person can take? That was what Hitler thought.'[47]

By the end of 1975, it was hard to imagine that it could get any worse, but it did.

AN AUTOCRAT PERVERTS THE SYSTEM

The process of amending the Constitution to protect Indira Gandhi now began with utter disregard for any norm or convention of parliamentary democracy. The thirty-eighth amendment removed the proclamation of Emergency from judicial review. Only four days before the hearings were to begin in her election case, the Constitution (Thirty-ninth Amendment) Bill was introduced in parliament. It sought to remove the court's authority to adjudicate election petitions, thus altering the law under which Indira Gandhi was found guilty – retroactively. Her hold over parliament was so strong and terror so pervasive that the Amendment bill passed both the Lok Sabha and Rajya Sabha without a single vote against it. 'Even thirty years afterwards, the audacity... chills one's spine,' wrote Arun Shourie in 2007.[48]

Indira Gandhi's appeal in the Supreme Court succeeded; in a five to four majority decision in November, the judges validated her 1971 election. It was astonishing that the court accepted the concept that laws could be changed by parliament retroactively. The only saving grace for the judiciary was that a part of the thirty-ninth amendment, that divested the courts of power to adjudicate on the election of a prime minister, was nullified. The judges held that it violated the basic structure of the Constitution.

Denied their perpetual 'parliamentary' supremacy, Indira Gandhi's men declared war on the judiciary. The time for them to make permanent changes to the Constitution was running out. This was the end of 1975; parliamentary elections were due in March of the following year.

An anonymous paper entitled 'A Fresh Look at Our Constitution' began to make ripples. It proposed that 'all judges in the country should be appointed by the President in consultation with the council of ministers'; and that a Superior Council of the Judiciary be set up with 'the authority to interpret laws and the Constitution'. 'In other words, the Supreme Court would no longer be supreme, and the executive and legislative branches, in conjunction under India's parliamentary system, would sit in judgement over themselves'.[49] In December, the court was to hear many appeals in the habeas corpus cases coming from several high courts which had allowed them on the grounds that the government could not suspend the right of detainees to know the cause of their detention. When the verdict was announced in April, it shocked the nation. In a four to one majority decision, the judges held that no citizen had a right to challenge the legality of his detention under MISA and the president's ordinance.

As it became apparent that the court was intimidated, it became obvious once again that it was due entirely to the prime minister holding exclusive control over appointments and transfers of judges. As soon as the hearings in the habeas corpus case began, Indira Gandhi had started taking punitive actions against those judges in high courts who had ruled against the government in preventive detention cases. Justice Chandrachud would later admit that 'the Court was hard-pressed to maintain its independence'.[50] The lone dissenter, Justice Khanna, would be superseded for the position of chief justice of India a year later. With the judiciary on the run and ready to do her bidding,

Gandhi was now a dictator in all but name. After the habeas corpus decision was announced, Jayaprakash Narayan, the leading voice of the opposition, noted that the decision 'has put out the last flickering candle of individual freedom ... Mrs. Gandhi's dictatorship both in its personalized and institutionalized forms is now almost complete.'[51]

To make her autocracy permanent the Constitution needed to be changed, and now it was only a matter of time before the judiciary succumbed to pressure and allowed parliament to amend the Constitution as it pleased. To gain more time, in January 1976, prime minister Gandhi extended the state of emergency and postponed elections. 'Parliamentary democracy has been twisted and perverted,' screamed a member of parliament, P.G. Mavalankar, as the parliament extended its own term.[52]

'THE LIGHT GOES OUT OF THE CONSTITUTION'

With only a handful of close associates, Gandhi now managed to clandestinely draft a massive amendment to the Constitution and get it enacted within a matter of six months. The speed was remarkable, especially because in between the amendment's introduction and passage, the parliament had to extend its own term, its second such arbitrary extension. The amendment was huge even in size. It was twenty pages long. Its fifty-nine clauses added nine new articles to the Constitution and amended fifty. But what was really remarkable was how vast it was in significance.

With the forty-second amendment, Indira Gandhi changed not just the letter but the spirit of India's Constitution. Any semblance of separation of powers, even the ostensible, was taken out. The parliament, the president, the judiciary, all now had one constitutional master: the prime minister. 'The drafters concentrated on increasing the central government's and the Prime Minister's authority, willing to sacrifice democracy for this greater cause'.[53] The amendment gave Directive Principles precedence over Fundamental Rights, providing the government the right to deny individual rights for state purposes.

It prohibited 'anti-national activities', defining them as vaguely as those intended to 'disrupt harmony'. Ten duties, including compulsory national service, were assigned to all citizens. One 'fundamental duty' required people 'to develop the scientific temper' and 'the spirit of enquiry'. The courts could no longer handle election disputes. Nor were they to have any jurisdiction over tribunals. The Supreme Court was barred from considering the constitutionality of a state law; the high courts from those of Central laws.

Amendments to the Constitution were removed from the jurisdiction of the courts altogether. The parliament now had an unquestioned right to enact any amendment, including those to the Constitution's basic structure. The term limit of the Lok Sabha and the state assemblies was raised from five to six years. The quorum requirements for legislatures were completely abolished; an empty house with a single government supporter could now pass a bill. If it considered the situation 'grave', the Central government was authorized to send armed forces into a state without consulting the state government. Parliament could make laws for any state if it considered the security of the nation under threat. So much so that even the Preamble of the Constitution was changed; India was now a 'Sovereign Socialist Secular Democratic Republic' instead of a 'Sovereign Democratic Republic'. But above all, the forty-second amendment made the president expressly bound under the Constitution to act as advised. The impact was monumental. 'The shift in the balance of power within the new Constitution made it all but unrecognizable,' wrote Granville Austin.[54]

What fundamentally changed the essence of India's Constitution was that the office of the president was rendered completely impotent. The amendment compelled the president to do as advised. In Article 74, which originally stated that 'there shall be a Council of Ministers with the Prime Minister at the head to aid and advise the President in the exercise of his functions', the words after 'President' were changed to 'who shall, in the exercise of his functions, act in accordance with such advice'.

As the so-called debates on the amendment bill began in parliament, Nani Palkhivala called the amendment 'the most devastating attack upon the Constitution'. In a column in *The Indian Express,* he enumerated how it was aimed at 'destroying the basic structure of the Constitution', by proposing 'to overthrow the supremacy of the Constitution and install Parliament (a creature of the Constitution) as the supreme authority to which the Constitution will be subservient'.[55] 'It is Diwali – the festival of lights,' Palkhivala wrote, 'as the lamps glimmer in and outside millions of homes, inexorable Time will be ticking away the remaining few days before the light goes out of the Constitution.'[56]

However, by now the entire system was packed with yes-men. Just as the amendment was cleared by the Cabinet without any dissent, it passed both Houses of Parliament with little opposition. The Rajya Sabha passed it by 190 votes to nil; the Lok Sabha by 366 to four.

India now had a perfect dictatorship: one person ruled the entire nation under the guise of parliamentary democracy, replete with a written Constitution. That the system was now neither parliamentary nor democratic, and the Constitution not worth the paper it was written on, was nobody's business but Indira Gandhi's. Until, of course, like most dictators she started believing in her immortality, and made a mistake.

RESTORATION OF CONSTITUTION

There was no doubt that it was parliamentary supremacy that had brought India perpetual dictatorship. If Gandhi wanted to continue to rule the country forever, there was no power or provision in India's system that could legally depose her. She had already extended the term of her parliament twice. As it is, with a hold over two-thirds majority in parliament, she could now amend any part of the Constitution. Her Cabinet was full of rubber stamps. A coterie led by her son was running a police state under draconian censorship laws.

So, when all of a sudden Indira Gandhi announced in January 1977 that fresh elections to the Lok Sabha will be held in a couple of months, the nation was shocked. Once again she had not consulted her Cabinet. She had gone against the advice of even Sanjay. By calling elections early, she was once again trying to use to her advantage the parliamentary system's feature that allowed the prime minister to pick a time of her own choosing to go to polls. She thought she could win big again if elections were held with an element of surprise and without giving too much time to the opposition parties. It was a shrewd move, for if it succeeded she would have legitimized her totalitarian rule for a long time to come. After two years of Emergency, the opposition parties were in disarray and deeply divided. Both the Intelligence Bureau and RAW had given her estimates that her party could get more than 350 seats if she were to go to the polls immediately.[57]

But her calculation went wrong. She and her son, and almost everyone else associated with the Emergency lost in the elections in March. Her party won only 153 seats. A coalition of four parties who had joined together under the Janata Party banner grabbed 299 of the 542 seats in the Lok Sabha. The Janata Party led by Jayaprakash Narayan and Morarji Desai had campaigned on the choice between 'democracy and dictatorship'.

The nation heaved a sigh of relief. But it was only Indira Gandhi's own miscalculation that had delivered India from the clutches of a dictator. 'The impossible happened,' said Palkhivala in a speech soon after the election results were announced. 'The first act of the liberated people should be to thank, from the depths of their souls,' he said, 'whatever Higher Forces they believe in – for the deliverance.' To the victors, he had a message: 'It is not the MPs dressed in brief authority who are supreme. It is the Constitution which is supreme.'[58]

This was the first time a coalition of non-Congress political parties had come to power in India. But the parliamentary system was impractical when it came to handling multiple parties. It was designed to work in a political environment in which there were only two national parties, and that too only if both were nearly equal in popularity.[59] The principal reason the Indian system became authoritarian was because there was essentially only one party, the

Congress. The coalition began falling apart within days, and the government lasted only a couple of years. The coalition was wobbly not because of the conflicting ideologies of its constituent parties, but due to the ambition and one-upmanship of its leaders.

In the parliamentary system, who became prime minister was a matter of negotiation and tussle among coalition partners. That too, *after* they had won the elections. This excluded the electorate from having a say in who became the leader of their nation. Even worse, it made the selection of the prime minister dependent not on his capabilities but on his political muscle or on his political vagueness. Since there was no single leader with a majority in parliament, the Janata coalition became embroiled in the fight for the post of prime minister. Jayaprakash Narayan, now famous as Loknayak (People's Leader) and who really brought the Indians out in droves to vote for the Janata Party, decided not to run for the position. Narayan and another elder statesman, J.B. Kripalani, were asked to resolve the impasse among the three contenders – Morarji Desai, Charan Singh and Jagjivan Ram – but they failed. Even as the nation's democracy lay in ruins, a long drama of selecting India's prime minister ensued for the whole world to see.

Besides, a coalition was inherently against one of this system's key principles, the concept of collective responsibility. That all ministers were collectively responsible to the legislature – all for one, and one for all – was an impossible principle to maintain when the prime minister couldn't turn a minister out or control his activities. If he went so far as to remove a minister, the coalition fell apart. A coalition government was, therefore, always on the verge of falling. This is precisely what happened with the Desai government.

While it lasted, the Desai government handled the easily reversible Emergency provisions quickly. Within a day the external emergency, in force since 1971, was revoked. The new Janata government made several announcements: the judges who were transferred or demoted were being reinstated; the remaining curbs on fundamental freedoms and civil rights were being removed; and the rule of law and the right of free expression were being restored. RAW's wings were clipped and control of the CBI was given back to the home ministry.

But when it came to fixing the balance of power in the Constitution, the new government chose to keep some of Indira Gandhi's distortions. It decided to retain the two most fundamental balance-of-power changes she made – compelling the president to act as advised and removing the judiciary's power to safeguard the Constitution's basic structure.

The main reason behind this decision was convenience. Those in power realized very quickly how useful it was to have all the powers. The moment of this realization came when, at the very beginning of its term, the Desai government wanted to do something about the state governments still held by the Congress party. Not only were they going to frustrate the new government in implementing its plans, they were going to keep the Janata Party from gaining a majority in the Rajya Sabha and from controlling the presidency. Elections to both were coming within a year. So, the party politics began. The Janata government decided to dissolve all nine Congress governments and impose President's Rule.

Once again, a parliamentary government had tasted the benefits of holding supreme powers. Even though a bill that sought to reverse many of the forty-second amendment's changes, including the 'anti-national provisions', was introduced in parliament as early as April 1977, Desai decided to let it lapse. A parliamentary affairs committee set up in May to be the forum for considering constitutional changes was also allowed to fade away. Then months later, in August, Desai 'inexplicably established a Cabinet subcommittee to deal with the same issues'.[60] This Cabinet subcommittee decided that the authoritarian provisions of the forty-second amendment should only be repealed selectively.

On the most important balance-of-power issue, that between the president and the prime minister, the subcommittee decided that the president should not be allowed independence. When at the end of 1977 the Desai government finally brought forth its first amendment bill, the Constitution (Forty-third Amendment) Bill, it only repealed a handful of the most obviously mischievous provisions of the forty-second amendment. Law Minister Shanti Bhushan expressed regret that a one-line repeal of the Forty-second Amendment Act was rejected on the grounds that some of its provisions were 'worth keeping'.[61]

On the second most important balance-of-power issue as well – that between parliament and the judiciary on the matter of the basic structure of the Constitution – the thinking of Desai's government was no different than that of Indira Gandhi. It too desired parliamentary supremacy. 'Shanti Bhushan did not wish to leave defining the basic structure entirely to the judiciary.'[62] To at least show some difference from the totalitarian regime of Indira Gandhi, Bhushan thought of going to the people via a referendum if a bill amended the basic features of the Constitution. But after this idea was defeated in the Rajya Sabha, the parliament's power to amend any provision of the Constitution remained exactly as unfettered as Indira Gandhi had left it.

In fact, the real problem with the judiciary's independence, that of appointment of judges, was left entirely unaddressed. Indira Gandhi had shown that under the Indian system the judiciary's independence suffered not because it didn't have the power to protect the basic structure, but because the prime minister had the sole power to appoint or transfer judges. The Desai government did nothing to fix this.

The so-called 'comprehensive' repeal of the authoritarian provisions of the forty-second amendment was finally done by the forty-fourth amendment, but it left both the balance-of-power issues – with the president and with the judiciary – as before. The only change was that the president was given the power to ask for reconsideration of a bill. Article 74 was altered for the final time. It now had a new proviso inserted at the end: 'Provided that the President may require the Council of Ministers to reconsider such advice, either generally or otherwise, and the President shall act in accordance with the advice tendered after such reconsideration.'[63]

Even the way the Janata government fell revealed how nearly all of the Constitution's fundamental shortcomings had escaped reform.

As amended, the Constitution now gave the president only one slight discretion, that of deciding whom to invite to form the government when no single party had a majority in parliament. But since this discretionary power still wasn't explicitly defined and was left to convention, the Indian system lurched into a crisis as soon as the Desai government resigned.

The system failed the very first time a president had to exercise his discretion in deciding who should become prime minister. The Constitution simply stated, 'The Prime Minister shall be appointed by the President.' It turned out that President Reddy invited every single leader except the one who was most viable, simply because of his personal political rivalry. Palkhivala called Reddy's decision, 'unjustified to the point of Constitutional impropriety'. A.G. Noorani, said that 'President Reddy has in one fell blow violated ... a whole set of established conventions of parliamentary democracy'. And Granville Austin wrote: 'Without firm evidence one concludes that the President acted from personal caprice in opposing Jagjivan Ram for Prime Minister. It will be recalled that Reddy and Ram had competed to be the Congress Party's candidate for the presidency in 1969. And it is possible that Jagjivan Ram's scheduled caste background did not please Reddy.'[64] India's Constitution offered Ram no remedy.

Thus, the basic defects in India's Constitution that led to democracy's ruin remained unaddressed. Indira Gandhi was able to ruin democracy because she had used 'the Constitution itself to negate and to subvert the basic principles of democracy', as President Sanjiva Reddy told parliament in February 1978. He urged the nation's lawmakers to remove its 'dark spots'.[65] The Janata government was never able to bring Indira Gandhi to justice because it couldn't build the case that she had done anything illegal or unconstitutional. The only reprimand it was successful in making was political. It was astonishing that within three years after ending her Emergency, Indira Gandhi would come back to power by roundly defeating the Janata Party in the January 1980 elections. Soon after her return, the report of the Shah Commission, instituted to look into the Emergency excesses, would disappear; it is not officially available to this day.

Since the Constitution failed to protect itself, an enumeration of its other failures is perhaps academic. First it failed in resolving and protecting the powers held by the system's topmost official, the president. Then, it failed to stop a prime minister from amassing dictatorial powers. And it did not give the people the means to remove an unwanted leader. Once again, it failed in holding the top officials accountable and in punishing a wrongdoer of the worst kind. Crucially, India's Constitution did not allow its citizens the opportunity to fix the flaws because it couldn't deliver stable governments. It failed in the handling of almost every situation that was different from those at the time of its framing. The first time a president asserted himself, India's Constitution failed. As soon as a consensus was needed to select a prime minister, it failed. The first time there wasn't an overwhelming majority party like Congress, it failed. It failed in protecting the judiciary or the fundamental freedoms of India's citizens. Above all, the Constitution failed the Indian people by not allowing them a decent quality of life, despite the sloganeering enshrined in its Directive Principles and its Preamble.

The Janata episode also exposed one other fact about the Indian system: that it was the Indian people who protected the Constitution, not vice versa. If not for their faith in democracy, their wisdom in discriminating right from wrong and their sense of responsibility in fulfilling their part, the Constitution of India wouldn't have survived at all. 'History will record,' Palkhivala said in a press conference soon after the defeat of Indira Gandhi, 'that the true gains of the Emergency have been the unification of the opposition, the sharp awakening of the political conscience of the nation and the dawn of the realization among the people that they are the only keepers of the Constitution.'[66]

The barely surviving Constitution, however, still had all of the same infections that brought it so near its death in the first place. Perhaps it was worse, because now it was weak even in spirit. Any idealism, however ostensible, was now gone.

NOTES

1   Russell, B. (1961), *The Basic Writings of Bertrand Russell*, New York: Simon & Schuster, p. 665, 'Taming Power'.

2   To Sir Samuel Hoare, 11 March 1932, cited in Shourie (2009), *Worshipping False Gods: Ambedkar, and the Facts Which Have Been Erased*, New Delhi: Rupa & Co., p. 236.

3   Cited in Pandit, H.N. (1974), *The PM's President: A New Concept on Trial*, New Delhi: S. Chand & Co., p. 74.

4   Letter dated, 9 April 1948, cited in Austin, G. (1966), *The Indian Constitution: Cornerstone of a Nation*, (henceforth *IC*), New Delhi: Oxford University Press, p. 135.

5   Letter dated 8 August 1948, cited in Austin, *IC.*, p. 136.

6   Rao, op. cit., Vol. 5, p. 374.

7   Austin, *IC*, p. 133.

8   Ibid., p. 134.

9   Ibid., p. 137.

10   Pandit, op. cit., p. 5.

11   Malhotra, Inder, 'All the Prime Minister's Men,' *The Indian Express*, 17 April 2009.

12   Letter dated 20 February 1950, Durga Das (ed.) (1973), *Sardar Patel's Correspondence 1945-1950*, 10 Vols, Ahmedabad: Navajivan Publishing House, cited in Austin, G. (1999), *WDC*, p. 28.

13   Ibid.

14   Ibid., p. 35.

15   Ibid., p. 36.

16   21 March 1950, cited in Pandit, op. cit., p. 91.

17   Letter dated 27 August 1950; Austin, *WDC*, p. 22.

18   Letter dated 11 September, paraphrased by Austin, *WDC*, p. 83.

19   Austin, *WDC*, p. 84.

20   Letter dated 15 September 1951, Chaudhary, Valmiki (ed.), *Dr. Rajendra Prasad: Correspondence and Select Documents*, 19 Vols,

Bombay: Allied Publishers Ltd., 1984; cited in Austin, *WDC*, p. 23. The letter was classified 'Top Secret'.

21   Austin, *WDC*, p. 23.

22   Malhotra, Inder, 'All the Prime Minister's Men,' *The Indian Express*, 17 April 2009.

23   Pandit, op. cit., pp. 21–23.

24   Jennings, I.W. (1961), *The British Constitution*, London: Cambridge University Press, p. 195.

25   Austin, *WDC*, p. 178.

26   Pandit, op. cit., p. 36.

27   Austin, *WDC*, p. 178.

28   Austin, *WDC*, p. 193.

29   Ibid.

30   Ibid., pp. 269–70.

31   Cited in Shourie, A. (2007), *The Parliamentary System: What We Have Made of It, What We Can Make of It*, New Delhi: ASA Publications, Rupa & Co., p. 176.

32   Austin, *WDC*, p. 282.

33   Pandit, op. cit., pp. 47, 53.

34   *The Illustrated Weekly of India*, 11 August 1974; cited in Palkhivala, N.A. (2009), *We, The People*, New Delhi: UBS Publishers, p. 11.

35   Ibid., pp. 58, 75.

36   Nayar, K. (1977), *The Judgement: Inside Story of the Emergency in India*, New Delhi: Vikas Publishing House Pvt. Ltd (henceforth *TJ*), p. 23.

37   Austin, *WDC*, p. 303. He attributes this information to A. G. Noorani.

38   Nayar, *TJ*, p. 13.

39   Ibid., p. 15.

40   Ibid., p. 24.

41   Ibid., p. 23.

42   Austin, *WDC*, p. 306.

43   Nayar, *TJ*, p. 38.

44   Austin, *WDC*, p. 309.

45   Nayar, *TJ*, pp. 41–43.

46   Austin, *WDC*, p. 312.
47   Nayar, *TJ*, p. 70.
48   Shourie, A. (2007),*The Parliamentary System*, p. 126.
49   Austin, *WDC*, p. 333.
50   Ibid., pp. 340, 343.
51   Ibid., p. 341.
52   Nayar, *TJ*, p. 118.
53   Austin, *WDC*, p. 376.
54   Ibid., pp. 373–74.
55   'The Light of the Constitution,' 22 October 1976, Palkhivala, N.A. (2009), *We, The People*, p. 201.
56   Ibid., p. 202.
57   Nayar, *TJ*, p. 155.
58   Palkhivala, op. cit., pp. 34, 37.
59   See Chapter 2.
60   Austin, *WDC*, p. 411.
61   Ibid., p. 418.
62   Ibid., p. 420.
63   Rao, B. S. (2006*)*, *The Framing of India's Constitution*, Delhi: Universal Law Publishing, Vol. 6, p. 142.
64   Austin, *WDC*, p. 479.
65   Ibid., p. 422.
66   Palkhivala, op. cit., p. 32.

8

India's System Is 'Rotten' to the Core

Ramachandra Guha, historian and commentator, declared in 2010: 'Let us begin by acknowledging that what we now confront is indeed a crisis ... the statistics purporting to capture the political and economic achievements of India conceal, among other things, shocking inequalities in wealth and living standards; a third-rate education system and a fifth-rate healthcare system; a criminal justice system on the verge of collapse; a serious and still growing left-wing insurgency in central India; continuing tensions in the states of the northeast and northwest; a spate of farmer suicides in the countryside; rising crime rates in the cities; rapid and possibly irreversible environmental degradation in both city and countryside; a fragile neighbourhood ... and more.'[1]

The parliamentary system in India was increasingly becoming a 'parliamentary anarchy', but not a single official attempt would be made to develop an alternative. When in 2000, after sustained pressure from civil society the BJP-led Vajpayee government appointed a commission to review the Constitution, the opposition raised cries of a 'hidden agenda'. Only two of the eleven members of the National Commission to Review the Working of the Constitution were politicians; the commission was heavy with retired or current officials of the judiciary or of civil services. However, the terms of reference of the commission would exclude 'any tinkering with the parliamentary system or the basic structure of the Constitution'.[2] On the overall working of the

Constitution, the commission's report would state the matter as diplomatically as possible: 'There are more failures than successes, making the inference inescapable that the fifty years of the working of the Constitution is substantially a saga of missed opportunities.'[3] According to its mission, however, the commission could only recommend reforms of the current system. Successive governments would implement some of those on an ad hoc basis, and only when faced with public outcry, but the commission's overall report would never be placed in parliament.

In a desperate plea, in 2011 a ninety-five-year-old former judge of the Supreme Court, V.R. Krishna Iyer, wrote a strongly worded open letter to Rahul Gandhi. As the scion of the Nehru-Gandhi family, Rahul was not only a high official of the ruling Congress party, he was widely expected to be anointed someday as India's prime minister. Iyer implored: 'Why are you silent? You will become the hero if you take up the great challenge of transformation of India into an egalitarian society.' Rahul Gandhi responded: 'I work because I believe in working to improve a system that is rotten and not to be glorified ... I spend a lot of waking hours thinking and working to improve what I see as a rotten system.'[4]

The problem was that India's system was rotten to the core. Its deficiencies were fundamental, not worthy of repair.

SYSTEM INSTALLS PUPPETS AS PRESIDENT

The office of the president would remain scuttled. Questions would be raised over and over again about what powers the president really has, but no clear answers would emerge. 'Is it appropriate, in a democracy,' A.G. Noorani would ask in an article as he tried to enumerate the president's powers, 'for fundamental elements in that democracy to be left in an uncertain form, understandable only (and then imperfectly) by those trained in law and political science'?[5]

Since his powers were so ill-defined, the main criterion for selecting a president would continue to be party or personal loyalty. Some would take this to a comical extreme, the most famous example of which was President Zail Singh's kowtowing to Indira Gandhi, who had elevated him from a chief minister to Union home minister and then to the highest office in the nation during her second reign. His election was challenged in the Supreme Court on the grounds that he was unfit for office. An unperturbed President Singh declared: 'I am prepared to pick up a broom and sweep any place if Mrs Gandhi asks me to do so.'[6]

His successor, President R. Venkataraman, was also a staunch Congressman. He was Indira Gandhi's minister of finance, and along with Zail Singh, a member of her innermost circle, the Political Affairs Committee of the Cabinet. When in 1987 Indira Gandhi's elder son Rajiv Gandhi needed a president with unquestionable loyalty to the party, he would choose Venkataraman. His successor President Shankar Dayal Sharma's story was similar. He was a legal scholar of some repute, but it was his vigorous support of Indira Gandhi's quest for leadership of the Congress party that brought him to the limelight. He was rewarded first with membership in the party's Working Committee, then with the post of general secretary and then with the vice-presidency. P.V. Narasimha Rao, a Congress prime minister, would select Sharma for president.

The non-Congress prime ministers would fare slightly better. They would be the only ones who would select presidents for their non-political activities. Prime Minister I.K. Gujral, who left the Congress party to join the Janata Dal, selected K.R. Narayanan for president, who was a Congressman, made vice-president by the Congress party, but was better known for his foreign service as ambassador to China and the USA. The only pure non-politician, and a scientist, to become president – A.P.J. Abdul Kalam – would be selected by Prime Minister A.B. Vajpayee of the Bharatiya Janata Party. Kalam, who became famous as the 'People's President', was the only president with whom the people of India found some affinity.

Sonia Gandhi, the new leader of the Congress party, picked a long-time loyalist of the Gandhi family, and a woman, Pratibha Patil, as

India's next president. In an article entitled 'The Gandhis' Girl', *The Economist* magazine reported how the opposition considered Patil 'a stooge of the Gandhi family' and how during the campaign she was 'photographed girlishly hand-in-hand with Sonia Gandhi'.[7] When in 2011 a minister in the Rajasthan government commented that she was 'rewarded' for her loyalty to the Gandhi family, and that 'she used to make tea and cook food at Indira Gandhi's residence', he was asked to resign.[8]

The race to anoint your own man or woman as president would lead to corruption. When in an age of coalition governments no single party alone could get a president elected, party bosses would make deals. The prime minister's party in control of government would offer sops, Cabinet berths, special benefits to certain regions, and sometimes even hard cash to other parties for their support. This came out most openly in the 2012 presidential election. The ruling Congress party once again nominated a party faithful, a man famous as the party's most adept troubleshooter, Pranab Mukherjee. But down in popularity due to its economic performance and corruption scandals, the party had to go the extra mile to gain support for Mukherjee, a sitting minister of finance. *The Economist* reported that 'leaders of two crucial, populous, swing states, Uttar Pradesh and Bihar, fell behind Mr Mukherjee as the central government promised aid worth some $12 billion'.[9]

ENCOURAGES FRAGMENTATION, FEEDS INSTABILITY

Coalition governments under the Indian system would prove to be untenable. In the thirty-five years of working under the altered Constitution (since Indira Gandhi's forty-second amendment in 1976), only one government, of V.P. Singh in 1990, would resign following a defeat in a no-confidence motion. Every other premature end of an Indian government in the post-Indira Gandhi era came because the coalition of various parties fell apart. Even when a coalition lasted the whole term of a government, the leaders of its constituent parties were constantly engaged in politicking rather than governing.

The system itself rewarded fragmentation of political parties. Newer and newer parties would be formed because the leader of each new party could bargain for more powers in exchange for his support in parliament. This problem was made significantly worse by the delinking of national and state elections begun by Indira Gandhi in 1971. That gave rise to hundreds of state-level parties which would also win elections for members of parliament.

In his 2007 exposé of the Indian system, Arun Shourie, author and a former member of parliament and Union minister, described 'fragmenting the electorate' as one of this system's 'key problems'.[10] In the first general election in 1952, there were only fourteen national and fifty-nine state parties; by 2007 there were a total of 909.[11] The BJP-led coalition called the National Democratic Alliance (NDA) in 1998 would consist of eleven parties; five years later, the first government formed by the Congress-led United Progressive Alliance (UPA) would have fourteen. The second UPA government formed in 2009 would be supported by roughly eighteen parties.

There were two gloomy outcomes of this unending division of parties: the legislature would become increasingly unrepresentative, and the governments progressively weaker. One result of this fragmentation, Shourie showed, was that '99 per cent of the members got into the Lok Sabha by getting less than half the electors to vote for them'. Some would become a member of parliament with the support of as few as 17 per cent of the electors.[12] As for the governments, Shourie wrote: 'Not only is a coalition of such disparate groups inherently weak, the singular interest of constituents other than the dominant one is to ensure that the government *remains* weak ... A weak coalition in place, the dominant constituent of the coalition rendered lame, every puny "leader" is king.'[13] Former President R. Venkataraman would admit in 1999 that 'recently the situation had deteriorated so much that the smaller parties had begun to blackmail ... Truly the tail had started wagging the head.'[14]

It was clear that smaller, state-level or regional parties were here to stay. Politics, in the end, was a local sport. And no one could represent local interests better than local parties. After years of being controlled by Central governments, the people in nearly every state were desperate for some autonomy and recognition. As a result, the share of the vote for state-level parties and independents would continually rise, reaching more than 52 per cent in the 2009 Lok Sabha elections. The two national parties, the Congress and the BJP together, would receive less than 48 per cent of the votes.[15] When in the 2011 state elections local leaders had emerged once again as the big winners, Shekhar Gupta, then editor of *The Indian Express,* wrote in his editorial: This election provides further evidence that the days of the very centralized, high command-led parties are now over.'[16]

This was a serious problem because every failed coalition created a constitutional crisis. In the thirty-five years (1977–2012) of functioning under the prime minister-centric system created by Indira Gandhi, India would have a total of thirteen prime ministers. A prime minister would stay in office only for two-and-a-half years on average. One government, of A.B. Vajpayee in 1996, would last only thirteen days. Six would fall before they finished their first year.

Instability of governments would become such a big problem that the Constitution would be amended several times to restrict defections of legislators, party splits and mergers and the size of ministries. Members of parliament would switch parties at the drop of a hat, accepting offers of cash, ministerial position, party candidacy to family members, allotment of property or a licence, passage of favourable laws and other bribes. 'The evil of political defections has been a matter of national concern,' said the Objects and Reasons of the Constitution (Fifty-second Amendment) that came into force in 1985, 'if it is not combated, it is likely to undermine the very foundations of our democracy'.[17] The amendment provided that a member be disqualified from parliament if he voluntarily left the party under whose banner he won the election. Party splits and mergers were allowed but with some restrictions. But the problem would continue. 'The ingenuity of the immoral converted the retail malaise of defections into a wholesale malady,' wrote Manish Tewari, a Supreme Court advocate and a member of parliament.[18] Admitting in 2004 that the Anti-Defection Law 'had not been able to achieve the desired goal of checking defections,' the ninety-first amendment made the provisions stricter by dropping certain exemptions to disqualification of members from parliament. It also restricted the size of the council of ministers; first to 10 per cent and then amend it again to 15 per cent of the size of the legislature. But this restriction was circumvented by making new ministers and calling them 'parliamentary secretaries' instead.

LACK OF OVERSIGHT FUELS CORRUPTION

In a system in which a majority could do whatever it pleased, the lure of a ministry was difficult to resist. Every legislator wanted one, because, as pointed out by Shourie, it was like winning a 'lottery'. A minister would control huge budgets; institute special programmes without much scrutiny; make all appointments and transfers of his ministry's personnel; even control the appointments and transfers of other departments in his constituency. Not only that, if he could build a level of trust with the prime minister or the chief minister, he could manage to pass laws that were personally beneficial to him. 'Persons strive to enter legislatures,' Shourie wrote, 'not because they have any particular competence for legislation ... entering the legislature is the stepping stone to becoming a minister; [it] can help shield one from the law... there are co-curricular windfalls, from voting for or against a government ... Ministers appoint judges, they appoint vice chancellors, they transfer police officers down to the station house officer in your neighbourhood *thana*.'[19]

A system with a single centre of power and no oversight of government gave majorities in legislatures a free-for-all for corruption. Corruption would become endemic. In 1985, Prime Minister Rajiv Gandhi declared that 'the fence has started eating the crop'.[20] Year after year the global indexes would rank India as one of the most corrupt nations in the world; Transparency International's Corruption Index would drop India eleven places in 2011, ranking her ninety-fifth in the world.

'Corruption scandals have rocked practically each parliament session in recent years,' Madhav Godbole, a former home secretary-turned-author wrote in 2011.[21] 'Our system has descended to such a level,' Shourie noted a few years earlier, 'that large parts of the country are now not just under the sway of bandits; they are prey to roving bandits, not just stationary ones.' Shourie was making the point that since governments under the Indian system were here one day and out the next, those who came to power looted without any concern for the future.[22] By 2013, Meghnad Desai, author and columnist, declared, 'Politics is the highest profitability business in India.'[23]

A total lack of any oversight, with sufficient powers to not just raise questions but to be able to stop a government from taking a certain action, was a serious defect. It allowed the same people to function as both lawgivers and law-enforcers. Even worse, those who had the power to raise taxes were the same people who decided how to spend the money. The opposition under the Indian system could ask questions in parliament or in various committees, but didn't have the powers to force a reversal in policy.

The practice of establishing commissions of inquiry to scrutinize specific government activities was also downright impractical. A government was expected to start an inquiry against itself, and then to reprimand itself. Invariably these commissions would become mired in political theatrics, their reports would never be accepted, or they would simply disappear. 'According to [a police officer who was part of the Shah Commission of inquiry against Indira Gandhi] the only people who faced a tough time due to the inquiry report were those people who were part of the Commission ... the government seems to have ordered to destroy all the copies of the inquiry report ... [it] is now a rarely found document,' the *Indian Express* reported in 2000.[24] A retired supreme court justice, B.N. Srikrishna, who headed the commission of inquiry into the Bombay riots of 1992, would write: 'This is the painful and pitiable saga of most reports of commissions of inquiry appointed in this country so far … A tale told by an idiot, full of sound and fury, signifying nothing.'[25] The oversight provided by the Comptroller and Auditor General of India (CAG), a constitutional body, would also be politically motivated and unreliable because its chief official was appointed by the government itself.

IRRESPONSIBLE GOVERNMENTS, SHIELDED BY 'BOSSES'

The basic premise of the parliamentary system – that legislatures controlled the government – was turned on its head by the flagrantly single-centre-of-power Constitution that India now had. 'Far from the Council of Ministers being accountable to and controlled by Parliament,' Shourie would declare, 'it is the Council of Ministers precisely because *it* controls Parliament. And unless you can bring the government down, it cares little for what you say or do on the floor of Parliament.'[26] Godbole would concur; in 2011 he wrote that 'in the United States, the legislature truly makes the laws of the land. It is not a rubber stamp for the executive branch. The position in India is quite the opposite.'[27]

But, there was something even more menacing behind India's rampant corruption. Shielded by their party bosses who were in exclusive control of the entire law and order machinery, a huge number of legislators would either become criminals themselves or have a nexus. Shourie reported that, in 1993, 'The Vohra Committee appointed by the Government … stated in strong terms that the nexus between crime syndicates and political personalities was very deep … [but] the report was shoved into the almirahs of the Home Ministry … No wonder, the cancer has gone on spreading.'[28]

Yet corruption wouldn't be the Indian system's biggest problem.

'RULE' BY OLIGARCHS RESULTS IN BAD LAWS

The biggest single drawback of the Indian system was that it would continue to make lousy laws. In a 'unicentric' system, the majority ran amok. Indira Gandhi had removed the only other authority, the president, to actually have the power – albeit poorly defined – of stopping a majority from taking a certain action. This unrestricted power affected lawmaking in many ways: in establishing the agenda of what laws would be undertaken; in prescribing the provisions of those laws; in their drafting quality; in the handling of their debates; and, in their passing.

'Bills are passed without meaningful discussion,' Shourie wrote, 'indeed, amidst ear-splitting *hulla*. Even budgets are passed amidst chaos. Hours and hours are spent on adjournments over the headline of the day, and then the "legislators" are corralled to constitute a quorum and the Bill is declared to have been passed.'[29]

India's parliament was relegated to simply going through the motions of lawmaking. Bills continued to be passed with speeds similar to those seen during Indira Gandhi's Emergency. In one session in 1990, the Chandra Shekhar government passed eighteen bills in less than two hours; in 1999, parliament met for only twenty sittings but passed twenty-two bills; in 2001, thirty-three bills were passed in thirty-two hours; in a 2007 session the Lok Sabha passed three bills in fifteen minutes; and so on. A member complained to the media in 2002 that 'a crucial bill of bio-diversity was passed in just fifteen minutes'. Another important bill on non-productive assets of banks was passed by the Lok Sabha with only thirty-eight members present. 'The Rajya Sabha, which is supposed to be a revising chamber, passed three Bills in less than five minutes in its sixteen-day session in 2008 ... On the last day of the Lok Sabha in 2008, eight important bills were rushed through in seventeen minutes, with no discussion whatsoever. This must have been a world record.'[30]

There would also be a steep decline in the duration of time the parliament was in session. Since the power of convening parliament lay entirely in the hands of the government, the legislature would be called into session only when it most suited the majority party. While in the 1950s parliament functioned for nearly 130 days in a year, in the

2000s its sittings each year would decline to less than fifty days. The last time parliament sat for more than a hundred days would be 1988. In 2007 the Lok Sabha functioned for only sixty-six days, working only 4.3 hours each day instead of the scheduled six.

The quality of laws also suffered because parliament, consigned merely to being the government's rubber stamp, would be increasingly disorderly. The opposition was totally toothless. It could do no more than ask questions, make speeches, or walk out. So, it tried to grab attention through boisterous behaviour or by forcing an adjournment. In 2004, Kuldip Nayar, author, columnist and a member of parliament, would reveal that 'during the six years I stayed in the Rajya Sabha, I found MPs waiting for instructions for disturbing the House. Whips and other office-bearers of political parties told them how to stall the proceedings.'[31] India's legislators would exchange blows; snatch bills from the minister's hands; attack ministers; refuse to be quiet during their speeches; rush to the well in front of the Speaker's chair; fling furniture, shoes and other items; climb on desks; hurl abuses; expose their undergarments; and so on. In 1989, the Lok Sabha would be adjourned a record eight times on a single day, during the discussion on the Bofors scandal. Both Houses of parliament were paralysed for five days over the Tehelka exposé. In 2007, the parliament would not be allowed to function for more than a week over the Indo-US nuclear deal before being adjourned sine die. The Speakers of India's parliament would admonish – 'this is not a zoo'; 'you should be ashamed of yourself'; 'have some manners'; 'children are more disciplined' – but to no avail. 'Parliamentary democracy can survive only if the House functions,' Meira Kumar, Speaker of the Lok Sabha, said in 2010. 'Frequent disruptions of the House will gradually render this institution irrelevant.'[32]

There was a deeper reason why many laws were poorly conceived or terribly drafted. The attention of India's legislators was solely focused on politics. The legislative agenda was decided by a coterie, and the ministers would simply push a law through. Since they were professional politicians, not experts or skilled professionals in the area of their ministry, ministers would rarely show any pride of authorship in the laws they were pushing. Private members of parliament, i.e., those who were not ministers, were also not interested in lawmaking because they had little hope, to begin with, of passing a law sponsored by them.

Unsurprisingly, embarrassing mistakes began to surface. In the case of the Chemical Weapons Convention Act of 2000, for instance, forty different errors were discovered after the law had already been approved by the president.[33]

The core problem was that the opposition was powerless to stop a government from passing a certain law, unless it could bring the whole government down. So their entire focus had to be on the politics behind government's support, not on specific laws or governmental actions. Their job was to oppose. 'The present system makes adversarial politics inevitable,' Shourie wrote. When members of the opposition spoke, they were 'addressing not the issue but the sectional constituencies outside the House', he said.[34]

When in 2011 Prime Minister Manmohan Singh was asked about the opposition's demands for the resignation of a member of his Cabinet who was accused of condoning a huge scam, he simply retorted: 'The Opposition's role is to oppose and there is nothing unusual in this. My ministers enjoy my confidence.'[35] A couple of months later, the leader of the opposition in the Lok Sabha, Sushma Swaraj, was similarly rhetorical. When asked to explain her opposition to a government plan to allow foreign investment in India's retail sector, when her own party had pitched the same proposal in the past, she merely replied: 'There is no bar against wisdom'.[36]

Admitting that in India 'the role of parliament members in influencing the legislation is peripheral, as compared to that of the United States',[37] Godbole recommended a slew of changes. Chief among them was a call for making private members of parliament more relevant. He reported that only fourteen bills introduced by private members were passed in the history of India's parliament, and none after 1970.

Matters were made worse by the fact that India had turned into a brazen oligarchy. As political parties were fragmented they functioned more and more as personal fiefdoms of party founders or their kin. As such, the legislators would be more interested in serving their party bosses than in legislating. Then, in 1985 and again in 2003, anti-defection amendments to the Constitution limited individual members' ability to go against the wishes of the party. Further, the Representation of the People Act was amended in 2003, which removed the domicile requirement for members of the Rajya Sabha. Now a party could elect a person to represent a state even if he didn't belong to that state. A new form of horse-trading in rewarding party loyalists began with seats in the so-called Council of States.

As a result, when party bosses issued whips, its members in both Houses of parliament wouldn't dare protest. 'Simply put, the executive dominates the legislature in the British system,' Godbole wrote, 'because of the existence of strong party discipline.'[38] In 2010, Bimal Jalan, a former governor of the Reserve Bank of India and a former member of the Rajya Sabha, appealed to the nation 'to revoke all amendments, which are designed to "disempower" elected members'. 'The working of Indian democracy by the people would become less oligarchic and more accountable,' he wrote.[39]

In the task of lawmaking, the parliamentary committees established to consider various opinions in drafting legislation also turned out to be an eyewash. Godbole reported: 'Initial fears and apprehensions of Opposition parties during the Indira Gandhi regime about establishing the committee system that it would become a ploy to skirt parliamentary debate and discussion seem to have come true. Passage of bills without any discussion is invariably justified by the ruling combine ... on the specious plea that they have already been carefully scrutinized by the standing committees. ... One wonders what kind of a democracy have we given to ourselves?'[40]

The opponents of majority-sponsored laws were not just powerless in parliament, now they had no hope from the presidency either. The president's assent to new legislation would be granted almost automatically. In the thirty-five-year period after the Janata Party's forty-fourth amendment, which gave the president the right to ask for reconsideration, there were only three instances when a president's assent was refused after the first passing of a law. In 1986, President Zail Singh decided not to approve Prime Minister Rajiv Gandhi's Indian Post Office (Amendment) Bill, but did not return it for reconsideration. It never became clear whether Singh did so for personal reasons or because he considered the law draconian, which it was. Nevertheless, this was the first 'pocket veto', a situation for which the Constitution had no answer. (The forty-fourth amendment was another example of a poorly drafted law, which failed to provide for such an obvious possibility.) The Post Office Bill was never discussed in parliament again. When, four years later, Singh's successor, President Venkataraman, sent it back to the Rajya Sabha, Rajiv Gandhi's government was no more and the Bill remains pending to this day. In the other two instances – the Representation of the People Act and the Parliament (Prevention of Disqualification) Amendment Bill in 2006 – the bills were passed in their original forms again, and the president was left with no option but to grant assent. In the case of the 2006 Bill, the government would make the senseless decision of appointing a committee to study the president's comments. This was the only impact the 'highest office' of the nation could make in India's laws in more than three decades.

As a result, the authoritarian pattern set by Indira Gandhi returned in the laws passed by successive governments. Harsh laws were passed by both Central and state governments, allowing preventive detentions and suppression of freedom of speech. In many cases, the Central government instituted stern measures by simply having the president issue an ordinance. The National Security Act in 1980 sanctioned preventive detention with such broad powers as the maintenance of 'public order' and 'essential supplies and services', and to combat 'anti-social' elements. In 1984, the prime minister made the president promulgate two ordinances allowing detention orders to be submitted many months after the detention; an individual could now be detained for up to two years without charge. The following year, the Terrorist and Disruptive Activities Act (TADA) passed by Rajiv Gandhi reversed the common law of the land. If an area was declared terrorist affected, a man was now guilty until he himself proved his innocence. In those areas – Kashmir, Punjab, Assam, etc. – 'repression became a substitute for reform'.[41] And the conflicts became deeply rooted and permanent.

MAJORITY RUNS AMOK, LEADS TO LOUSY GOVERNANCE

Not only could a government get any law it wished, it would also be able to ride roughshod over the ones that were already passed. When the time came to put laws in force, the same government that passed the law decided which ones to enforce, when, where, and how aggressively. One such instance was the Delhi Rent Control Act, passed in the early 1990s, which was never enforced. The Act was designed to balance the interests of the landlords with those of the tenants by providing for an annual increase in rents. But faced with violent protests from tenants, the government chose not to 'notify' the Act, thus making it impossible for officials to enforce it.[42]

The use of the Central Bureau of Investigation (CBI) and other enforcement agencies for political purposes also stands out as malicious and blatant abuses of power. 'The record of CBI has repeatedly shocked the conscience of the country,' Godbole noted, 'with its partisan investigations and toeing the line of its political masters. ... The time has, therefore, come to revive the proposal for creation of the office of special or independent counsel as in the USA.'[43]

The abuses of executive privileges are countless. Members of parliament were declared immune from legal proceedings even for such serious allegations as taking a bribe for voting in parliament. That was the case in 1998 when members of a political party voted for

Narasimha Rao's government in a no-confidence motion. Fugitives from justice would be allowed in India's parliament to sit as members. Members with criminal backgrounds would be allowed to become ministers. In 2007 the Central government made a sworn statement to the Supreme Court 'that "convicted" members of legislatures must be allowed to stay in the legislatures otherwise government might fall because they survive on slender majorities'.[44] Godbole reported that more that 20 per cent of India's legislators had a criminal background. It was clear that law enforcement agencies were a plaything for India's politicians.

Then there would be sops. Once in majority, a party could give itself or anybody else whatever it pleased. Populist programmes would be launched without any scrutiny or restraint. In December 1993, the Narasimha Rao government, 'to placate MPs and provide a prop to his minority government',[45] launched a scheme for the members of parliament themselves. The Members of Parliament Local Area Development Scheme (MPLADS) gave each member a grant of Rs 50 lakh to be spent for 'small development works in his constituency' entirely at his own discretion. The amount was raised by successive governments to Rs 5 crore. The scheme 'seriously compromised' the separation of powers between the executive and the legislative branches, as well as the federal principles, and became a source of unprecedented corruption.

The elevation of Manmohan Singh to prime ministership in 2004 was another example of the problems endemic to the Indian system. He was not even a member of the Lok Sabha, nor would he ever become one. Sonia Gandhi, the leader of the party, decided single-handedly to make him prime minister. Singh was a member of the Rajya Sabha, a position to which he was elected by the party's legislators. But Singh didn't even belong to the state, Assam, whose legislators elected him. He had filed a false affidavit of being a resident of that state.[46] Singh would never face a popular election, thus breaking one of the hallmark features of the parliamentary system that the government should be run by the people's direct representatives. This arrangement created a situation in which one leader, Sonia Gandhi, ran the nation but was not accountable to its legislature. Kuldip Nayar wrote that Singh only governed; it was Sonia Gandhi who ruled.[47]

Political parties would be able to do as they pleased because India's Constitution required parties for its successful functioning, but there was no law providing that political parties themselves have a Constitution or be publicly accountable. 'It is unfortunate that the Founding Fathers of the Constitution failed to enact a legal framework for political parties, on the basis of which they can be held accountable,' wrote Godbole.[48]

SMALL, INDIRECT ELECTIONS PRODUCE INCOMPETENT LEADERS

The parliamentary system was based upon the concept of people's representatives, elected in their separate constituencies, coming together in the nation's legislature. No representative represented the entire nation or even a state. Small elections were won on very local issues and by caste and other manipulations. It was possible for local politicians to win these elections by buying votes and by outspending their opponents. Representatives thus elected would be limited in their outlook, capabilities and agenda.

India's system was not bringing forth good men. This was evident from the very first general election, and to no less a person than Jawaharlal Nehru himself. Reminiscing about his coverage of the 1951 elections, Inder Malhotra reported how Nehru became depressed as soon as he went out to campaign in the nation's first parliamentary elections. 'What "filled him with dismay" was the selection of Congress candidates that he described as "disgusting". What got his goat were the "cliques", "bossism", the "scramble" and "lack of organization".' Nehru told his colleagues that 'third-rate individuals were being chosen on grounds of caste and sub-caste. I have felt recently as if I was in a den of wild animals.'[49]

FALSE FEDERALISM AND POOR GOVERNANCE THREATEN SECURITY

Federalism of the type in which state governments had real independence was incompatible with the parliamentary system.[50] India's effort to build both strong Central and independent state governments was, therefore, bound to falter. In 1951, 'the first use of President's Rule was a far cry from the Constituent Assembly's intentions, growing as it did from an internal Congress dispute', reported Granville Austin. 'Nehru, against Prasad's remonstrances, ordered [Punjab] Chief Minister Gopichand Bhargava to resign despite his having a majority ... Nehru had set the country a bad example.'[51] During Indira Gandhi's insecure years (1967–73), President's Rule was imposed twenty-two times. In 1977, as soon as it came to power, the Janata government imposed President's Rule in all Congress-ruled states even though they were in majority. Governments of all hues would continue the practice, imposing the President's Rule some forty more times after 1980.

The problem was deeper than just politics. The forceful and extreme centralization of power denied expression to deep-seated regionalism across the nation. Nearly all regionalism in India was based on linguistic or communal grounds; it could not be wished away, nor ignored. 'Federalism is normally a necessary condition for the protection of territorially specific diversities,' Ashutosh Varshney, a professor of international studies and social sciences at America's Brown University wrote, 'and having two or more political identities is not subversive to the nation. One can be a Bengali and an Indian'.[52] Gandhi had recognized this a century ago. 'As the basis of my pride as an Indian,' he wrote in 1909, 'I must have pride in myself as a Gujarati. Otherwise, we shall be left without any moorings.'[53]

All a system of government in India needed to ensure was that no group or region could infringe on the rights of others or of minorities. Each region merely, but desperately, desired that it genuinely controlled its local governance and that it also had a real say in national matters.

In 1957, C. Rajagopalachari 'thought that the solution to "centrifugal interests" was to concede greater autonomy to the states; to centralize was "both ridiculous and alarming"'.[54] In 1961, the National Integration Council, appointed by Nehru himself, noted: 'National integration cannot be built by brick and mortar, by chisel and hammer. It has to grow silently in the minds and hearts of men.'[55]

But no one challenged the compatibility of federalism and the parliamentary system, although some theoreticians outside India had done so,' writes Granville Austin.[56] As a result, the arbitrary dissolution of state governments, and other similar unilateral decisions against them, would continue unabated. Of the fifty-seven instances of President's Rule in the period from 1951 to 1987 analysed by the Sarkaria Commission, 'nearly 50 per cent had resulted from central government wishes'.[57]

Sudden dissolutions of state governments, combined with the fact that a parliamentary government could fall at any time due to a loss of majority, would substantially reduce the average number of years an Indian state government was in office. The average tenure of a chief minister elected for a five-year term, would decline from 3.9 years in Nehru's time, to only 2.6 years in recent times.

What really made a travesty of federalism in India was the way in which the office of governor devolved under this system. Governors would be accused of acting as 'agents of the Central government, and not as holders of an independent constitutional office', in the words of L.P. Singh, a former governor. The Sarkaria Commission noted that the people were dissatisfied by the lack of 'impartiality and sagacity' shown by the office of governor and for being used by the Central government 'for its own political ends'. As early as the mid-1960s, the Administrative Reforms Commission had reported that it was 'as likely as not' that a governor was appointed for considerations other than his ability. But the fact would remain that governors were appointed by the majority party at the Centre, as arbitrarily as everything else. In 1990, another former governor made it plain, once and for all, that the office had 'become a party appointment' serving the party rather than 'the interest of the nation'.[58] The party in power would appoint or remove governors with callous disregard for any constitutional provision or convention. Commenting on yet another inexplicable removal of a governor in 2004, Soli J. Sorabjee, a former attorney general of India, wrote: '...the pleasure of the President ... cannot be equated with that of Henry the VIII, the much married monarch, who cast away his wives at his own whim and fancy. Exercise of any power ... cannot be arbitrary or capricious.'[59]

This pseudo-federalism would cause many secessionist and separatist movements, and insurgencies, to fester in India's states. 'The central and state governments' unwillingness to heed pleas and to redress genuine grievances, and also to increase participation in governance through decentralization,' wrote Granville Austin, 'worsened many situations.'[60]

Secessionist movements that erupted in the early years of the republic – Tamil, Sikh, Kashmiri and Naga – continue in one form or another to this day. Violence would compel Central governments to make special and separate constitutional provisions for states seeking more autonomy or groups seeking separate states. Kashmir was given special constitutional status under Article 370; Nagaland was established as a separate state within India by the thirteenth amendment. No Act of parliament would apply to Nagaland unless the state legislative assembly agreed.[61] Many states were divided to meet people's demands for more local control, and on communal or linguistic grounds. Several more 'linguistic states' had to be formed, even after the wholesale reorganization of 1956.

Without a set of truly federal principles to guide them, Central governments would accept new states or grant autonomy only after bitter and prolonged violence. Since such decisions were taken mostly on an ad hoc basis, no one was satisfied. The violence continued. A communist (Maoist) insurgency that originated in West Bengal in 1967 festered for decades, only to become increasingly violent. It has spread to Bihar, Jharkhand and other areas. In 2010, Maoists had a 'presence in 20 of the 28 states, and control large tracts of tribal forest land in eight of those states'.[62] Punjab, West Bengal, Assam and Kashmir continued to face bitter communal violence decades after the Partition. Punjab had to be divided into four areas, by carving out Haryana, Himachal Pradesh and Chandigarh from its territories, based primarily on language and ethnicity. And Sikh demands for more autonomy in Punjab was a major source of bloodshed in the country. Similarly, in Assam, ethnic violence erupted over and over again even though the state had been divided many times. After a 2003 accord with the Central government, Bodo insurgent groups had agreed to end their armed rebellion in exchange for an autonomous region, in 'a formula long used by Indian leaders to subdue regional rebellions', reported the *New York Times*.[63] The separatist movement in Kashmir also continued, becoming India's most prolonged and bloody conflict. Demands for new states would keep coming, and more often than not they would get attention only when they flare up. In 2009, violence broke out in the south in support of a separate state, Telangana, to be carved out of Andhra Pradesh, a 'linguistic' state established in 1956 despite the opposition of Telangana people. As soon as the government showed some readiness, more protests broke out: for Gorkhaland in West Bengal, for Maru Pradesh in Rajasthan, and so on.

'More lives have been lost due to internal insecurity than in the five wars India has fought since independence in 1947,' Ashok Mehta, a retired major general of the Indian army reported in 2010.[64] The total number of states and Union territories in India would more than double, to a total of thirty-six (twenty-nine states and seven UTs).

The people, however, would still hunger for true federalism. In 1985, the Shiromani Akali Dal promised in the Anandpur Sahib Resolution that it would 'try that the Indian Constitution becomes federal in the real sense and all states are equally represented at the Centre'.[65] When, in 2012, the Central government announced the formation of another policing authority, National Counter Terrorism Centre, without consulting state governments first, there was an uproar. Subhash Kashyap, a well-known constitutional expert, would call it a 'sad hangover from the colonial period', caused by 'constitutional illiteracy or a willful distortion of the Constitution'.[66]

'The country could not prosper unless it adopted a "genuine" federal system,' Punjab chief minister, Parkash Singh Badal, declared in his state assembly in 2012. The Constitution was framed keeping this in mind, he said, but 'federalism had not been adopted'. He appealed that the House pass a resolution demanding the setting up of a new Constituent Assembly to rewrite the Constitution along 'genuinely federal lines'.[67]

This lack of genuine federalism caused governance in India to suffer at the local level. Not just because of the instability of state governments, but also because of the centralized control over money and economic policy. The two most important institutions set up for managing financial relations between the Centre and the states – the Finance Commission and the Planning Commission – would both turn out to be heavily biased in favour of the Centre. The reason was simple: members of both were appointed by the Central government. The Sarkaria Commission took note of 'the states' complaints that they were not allowed to 'participate in the selection of Finance Commission members, nor in setting its terms of reference'.[68] The Planning Commission was even more centralized and bureaucratic. Its activities would especially hurt local governance, because 'the degree of centralization bred in the planners an undue confidence in their ability to comprehend and manage diversity'.[69]

As it did everywhere else in the world, centralized planning in India has failed. It was too far removed from the ground realities, and it killed initiative. Besides, 'the state rabbits, as it were, never combined against the central wolf,' Austin commented. The state governments, as a result, were reduced to 'utter dependence' on the Centre.[70]

Central governments of all hues played dirty tricks with states ruled by opposition parties. By holding or withdrawing Central programmes, or by diverting investments, or by imposing new taxes, or by instituting harsh regulations, or by stalling certain decisions, the majority party at the Centre would attempt to destabilize state governments run by its opponents. Here too, the Indian system provided the Central government a tool: the presidency. The president's assent would be delayed or denied to the laws passed by states run by opposition parties. For instance, in 2012, more than twenty bills passed by opposition-led states were stalled by the government at the Centre.

STATE GOVERNMENTS SUFFER THE SAME AILMENTS

The state governments were also based on the same parliamentary model. In reality, the chief minister was king, the legislature his rubber stamp, and the governor totally irrelevant. The state police, investigative bureaus and enforcement agencies were all under the chief minister's direct control. The appointment of every executive official was approved by him, down to the lowest-level staff. He made all laws. He decided which ones to enforce and how aggressively. He handed out all government contracts and approved every department policy.

In most states, the entire polity was in the hands of state-specific 'regional' parties who took turns in coming to power. The leaders of these parties were popular leaders who would compete with each other by making more and more populist promises to the electorate, ranging from sops to new districts, even to separate states. These parties were truly their personal fiefdoms. Cronyism and nepotism were rampant. The tickets for candidacies to the legislative assembly, the Lok Sabha and the Rajya Sabha were decided by party bosses, leading to a bidding war among the seekers. Elections would be won by doling out cash, in one form or another, from public funds: free laptops, television sets, cycles, school uniforms, food items, liquor, utensils, insurance, travel, wedding assistance, cows – you name it. Every state government has been accused of high corruption. Laws were passed to personally benefit the coterie that typically gathered around a chief minister. The members of the opposition were bought through favours or promises to not prosecute for corruption when they were in power. Corruption scandals were exposed or alleged almost on a daily basis. And so on.

By the time the Central government attempted to bring some independence to village panchayats and local municipal bodies through constitutional amendments in the early 1990s, it was too late. The local polity, essential services like water and electricity, police and enforcement agencies, government contractors, health and education facilities, transport services, roads and every other public resource were by now under the control of the leader of the ruling party. And so were the politicians of every village and every town.

'PARLIAMENTARY SUPREMACY' AND THE JUDICIAL SYSTEM

The judiciary would be the only institution that would recover, however precariously, in the post-Indira Gandhi era. Functioning within the limits of the amended Constitution, it managed over time to moderately restore its balance of power vis-à-vis the executive. It moved proactively to reassert its independence in the two areas that were under attack: protection of the basic structure of the Constitution, and the prime minister's powers to appoint judges.

In the Minerva Mills Case in 1980, the Supreme Court once again limited the powers of parliament to alter the basic structure of the Constitution. The government had taken over the textile mill and had nationalized it in 1974. The owners had challenged the nationalization by questioning the constitutionality of the forty-second amendment. Nani Palkhivala represented the mill's owners and argued that it was the court's 'last chance … to choose between a free and an authoritarian society in India'. He urged the court to repeal the forty-second amendment, a task left unfinished by the forty-fourth, and 'stop the rot in the Constitution'. The court agreed. The majority held as unconstitutional the forty-second amendment's provision that 'there shall be no limitation whatever on the constituent power of Parliament' on the ground that the power to amend is not the power to destroy'.[71]

However, nothing in the Constitution had really changed. Judges had gone back and forth from the beginning of the republic on the issue of parliamentary supremacy over the Constitution. They could do so again. Also, there was no guarantee that another overwhelming majority in Parliament, led by an energetic prime minister, wouldn't once again seek parliamentary sovereignty. After all, that was the basis of the parliamentary system.

In 2007, after yet another debate in Parliament over the judiciary's independence, Inder Malhotra, a leading columnist, let it all out: 'Although it is incontestable that none of the democratic institutions can claim to be "supreme" – only the Constitution is – an amazingly large number of parliamentarians and politicians go on repeating, parrot-like, that whatever parliament decides must prevail because duly elected MPs represent the "sovereign will of the people". With all due respect to all concerned, in existing Indian circumstances, this standpoint is not only outlandish but also bombastic and indeed bogus.' He then described how unrepresentative India's parliament really was: 'Even at the best of times since the commencement of the Constitution, members of parliament, individually and collectively, have represented only a substantial minority of the votes actually polled, never a majority ... more and more MPs get in with only a minority of the votes polled, often with no more than 25 per cent ... to claim that he or she is "embodiment" of the "will of the people of India" is nothing short of effrontery.'[72]

The prime minister's exclusive powers to appoint and transfer judges were be restricted, but not without a decade-long fight from successive governments. During her second stint in power, Indira Gandhi began with the transfer of judges again. The pattern was familiar. The government, it was believed, was attacking the judiciary in retaliation for its defeat in the Minerva Case. Nine petitions against the transfers were filed in the Supreme Court, which became famous as Judges Case I. The court upheld the government's position. It ruled that a judge's consent was not necessary for his transfer, nor was it necessary that the Chief Justice concur. The two sides remained in an uneasy truce, but not for long. In 1993 the issue erupted again during Narasimha Rao's government. This time, in the Judges Case II, the court ruled that in appointments and transfers of judges 'the opinion of the Chief Justice of India ... is entitled to have the right of primacy'.[73] Rao and Chief Justice Venkatachaliah set up a 'peer committee' to establish norms for appointments and transfers.

This ended the prime minister's exclusive control over the judiciary's appointments, but it caused a new problem. Now, there were concerns about the judiciary's accountability, because now there were 'judges appointing judges behind a veil of secrecy', as columnist M.J. Antony noted in 2009.[74]

Thus the fundamental problem in the Indian system – that a single authority held exclusive control over judges' appointments – remained. In fact, when judges themselves held near-total control over the appointments, transfer and promotions of judges, the accountability of the judiciary worsened. With no elected representative now in control, there was no mechanism to bring the judiciary to account. In 2011, during the debate on yet another failed impeachment of a judge, the leader of the opposition in the Rajya Sabha, Arun Jaitley, described the new ailments the collegium system had created: 'The best in this country are not willing to become judges. We have to seriously consider why ... The criteria for appointment today does not exist ... Collegium is also a system of sharing the spoils ... Secondly ... the matter of judges judging judges and nobody else participating in this is also an issue which requires a serious review. ... The third issue is this... when appointments are made we have to seriously consider how the institution functions, whether it functions without any pressures ... Separation of powers requires that every institution works in its own spheres. And if every institution works in its own spheres, it has to lay down the *lakshman rekha* of its own jurisdiction.'[75]

As a result of all this, India has one of the worst judicial systems in the world. The courts are clogged with pending lawsuits. There are stories upon stories of how long it took to reach a verdict, shamefully exemplifying the adage 'justice delayed is justice denied'. In 1999, Austin reported that 'some seventy per cent of jail inmates in the country – who number over 150,000 persons – are awaiting trial', calling it 'the blackest blot on the nation's record'.[76] In 2009, Prime Minister Manmohan Singh's government disclosed that more than 26 million cases were pending in India's courts, the largest such backlog in the world. He called on the judiciary 'to wipe every tear of every waiting litigant', as he placed the blame squarely on the Supreme Court.[77] But the backlog continued to grow. Two years later, the government admitted that of the roughly 32 million cases that were pending in India's high courts and subordinate courts, 26 per cent were more than five years old. The situation in the Supreme Court was even more alarming; of the more than 56,000 cases pending, 64 per cent had been under consideration for more than a year.

Then there was the matter of the quality of justice. There were serious allegations, some even proven, of misconduct and high corruption. But no judge in India would ever be removed from office. A former law minister told the Supreme Court in an affidavit that according to his knowledge eight of the sixteen chief justices of India were 'definitely corrupt'.[78] 'There is no provision for the speedy removal of an errant judge,' P.P. Rao, a senior advocate of the Supreme Court and an expert in constitutional law lamented.[79]

Despite all this, the courts in India were quick to overstep their function. The Supreme Court invented the concept of Public Interest Litigation (PIL) giving courts unprecedented powers over executive functions. Judges became activists, issuing orders for government departments to make or implement policies in areas as diverse as sewage systems to transport facilities to environment clean-up. This was a serious breach of the principle of separation of powers, and as such raised questions about who was really accountable – the judge or the government.

'EVEN GOD WILL NOT BE ABLE TO HELP THIS COUNTRY'

'The judiciary is busy with executive functions, the legislature with investigations and the executive with everything other than governance,' Somnath Chatterjee, a former Speaker of the Lok Sabha, declared in public.[80] A Supreme Court justice had this to say in court: 'The whole government machinery is corrupt, whether at the Centre or in the States. ... Even God will not be able to help this country.'[81]

Overall, India's system had become so corrupt and so unresponsive that in 2011 the people came out on the streets. Protests erupted across the nation in support of a movement called India Against Corruption, with Anna Hazare, a seventy-four-year-old social activist as its figurehead. Hazare announced in April that he would go on an indefinite hunger strike unless and until the government agreed to pass a Jan Lokpal (People's Ombudsman) Bill, establishing an independent body with powers to deal with corruption. Thousands of protests erupted across the nation in support. Hundreds joined Hazare in his fast. The movement drew such large crowds, and so rapidly, that it became international news. *Time* magazine called it 'the most striking act of dissent' in the world, and placed it in its Top 10 list of all developments that year.[82] Four days later, the government announced that it would bring a Lokpal Bill in the monsoon session of Parliament, and agreed to set up a commission with 50 per cent of its members from civil society to draft the legislation. Hazare ended his hunger strike.

Prime Minister Manmohan Singh explained why the bill was being delayed: 'Corruption must be combated, but not by upending or disregarding democratic processes and institutions. The Constitution is our founding document ... its procedures cannot be flicked away to make way for supra-institutions.'[83] Hazare went on a hunger strike again and again, but recognizing the hopelessness of his cause the crowds waned. In August 2012, Hazare withdrew his movement.

Remarkably though, like an ostrich, most Indians continued to look at their parliamentary system and their failed Constitution with reverence. In 2007, Shourie was compelled to ask: 'Is there a bottom, on reaching which, we will conclude, "Yes, this arrangement is not working, it has to be replaced"?'[84]

What made the situation especially astonishing was that a system to replace this rotten one was not hard to find. It had been available to the world for centuries, as widely as sunshine.

NOTES

1   *Outlook*, 1 February 2010.

2   Rao, B.S. (2006*), The Framing of India's Constitution,* Vol. 5, Delhi: Universal Law Publishing, p. 848.

3   Ibid., p. 855.

4   *The Indian Express (IE)*, 17 April 2011.

5   'Powers That May Be', *Hindustan Times*, 17 September 2007.

6   Austin, G. (1999), *Working a Democratic Constitution: A History of the Indian Experience*, New Delhi: Oxford University Press, (*WDC*), p. 513, quoting Satinder Singh's *Giani the Great*.

7   *The Economist* online (*Economist*), 26 July 2007.

8   *Hindustan Times*, 11 February 2011.

9   'Booted Upstairs', *Economist*, 21 June 2012.

10   Shourie, A. (2007), *The Parliamentary System: What We Have Made of It, What We Can Make of It*, New Delhi: ASA Publications, Rupa & Co., (*PS*), p. 11.

11   Godbole, M. (2011), *India's Parliamentary Democracy on Trial*, New Delhi: Rupa & Co., p. 3.

12   Shourie, *PS*, p. 29.

13   Ibid., p. 36; italics in original.

14   Lecture at India International Centre, New Delhi, on 16 October 1999. Accessed on 11 September 2013 from http://www.indiastar.com/Venkataraman1.html

15   'Indians Deserve Better Governance', *The Wall Street Journal (WSJ)*, 18 June 2009.

16   'Delhi Disconnect', *IE*, 21 May 2011.
17   Kashyap, S. C. (2004), *Constitution Making Since 1950*, Delhi: Universal Law Publishing Co., p. 163.
18   'Setting our MPs Free', *IE*, 9 December 2009.
19   Shourie, *PS*, pp. 76, 85.
20   Austin, *WDC*, p. 645.
21   Godbole, op. cit., p.13.
22   Shourie, *PS*, p. 23.
23   'Bharat versus Hindustan', *IE,* 27 January 2013.
24   'How They Buried Shah Commission Report Even Without an Epitaph', *IE*, 3 July 2000.
25   'And Then Action Not Taken', *IE*, 30 November 2009.
26   Shourie, *PS*, p. 25.
27   Godbole, op. cit., p. 101.
28   Shourie, *PS*, pp. 78–79.
29   Shourie, *PS*, p. 26.
30   Godbole, op. cit., pp. 101–03.
31   Cited in Godbole, op. cit., p. 112.
32   Godbole, op. cit., p. 380.
33   Godbole, op. cit., p. 102, quoting *The Telegraph*, Kolkata, 21 June 2001.
34   Shourie, *PS*, pp. 66–67.
35   *IE*, 25 September 2011.
36   *IE*, 30 November 2011.
37   Godbole, op. cit., p. 316.
38   Ibid., p. 200.
39   'The Working of India's Democracy,' *Business Standard,* 27 March 2010.
40   Godbole, op. cit., p. 125.
41   Austin, *WDC*, p. 515.
42   Godbole, op. cit., pp. 102–03.
43   Ibid., p. 280.
44   Ibid.,p. 21.
45   Ibid, p. 216.

46   Ibid., p. 364.

47   *Asian Age*, 17 March 2008, cited in ibid.

48   Godbole, op. cit., p. 251.

49   'The First Vote Cast', *IE*, 20 March 2009.

50   See Chapter 2.

51   Austin, *WDC*, p. 607.

52   'Are the States Too Strong?,' *WSJ*, 24 May 2012.

53   Chandra, B., A. Mukherji and M. Mukherji (2008), *India Since Independence*, New Delhi: Penguin Books, p. 151.

54   Austin, *WDC*, p. 561.

55   Ibid., p. 553.

56   Ibid., p. 568, note 39.

57   Ibid., p. 608.

58   C. Subramaniam, cited in Austin, *WDS,* p. 574.

59   *IE,* 19 July 2004.

60   Austin, *WDC*, p. 562.

61   Ibid., p. 152

62   'Enemy Within', *WSJ*, 25 February 2010.

63   *The New York Times*, 17 August 2012.

64   'Enemy Within', *WSJ*, 25 February 2010.

65   Austin, *WDC*, p. 539, note 18,

66   'The Heart of the Matter', *The Times of India,* 4 May 2012.

67   *The Tribune,* 28 March 2012.

68   Austin, *WDC*, p. 618.

69   Ibid.

70   Ibid., p. 616.

71   Austin, *WDC*, p. 503.

72   'Will of 25 Per Cent of People', *IE*, 6 May 2007.

73   Austin, *WDC*, p.532.

74   'Time to Let in Some Sunshine', *Business Standard*, 15 October 2009.

75   Proceedings of the Rajya Sabha, 17 August 2011.

76   Austin, *WDC*, p. 664.

77   *The Times of India (TOI)*, 17 August 2009.

78   Ibid., 17 September 2010.
79   'Why is it so Hard to Budge a Judge', *IE*, 19 August 2011.
80   *IE*, 10 March 2011.
81   Justice B.N. Agarwal, quoted in Noorani, A.G., 'Talking Judges', *Frontline*, 25 February 2011.
82   *Time*, 7 December 2011.
83   'By the Book', *IE*, 1 July 2011.
84   Shourie, *PS*, p. 1.

9

Americans Reinvented Government

American Constitution makers had learnt from Europe that an evil and oppressive government was the source of almost all social ills. And the source of evil in government was unfettered power. An uncontrolled government, history had shown, could inflict any sort of pain upon its people. Americans had experienced first-hand the evils of a government with no manacles and no morals. Great Britain's oppression of the American colonies had brought the colonists to their knees. One after another, the Acts of the British Parliament – the Sugar Act of 1764, Stamp Act of 1765, Townsend Duties in 1767, and the Tea Act in 1773 – had either imposed back-breaking taxes on the colonists, or created British monopolies. American colonies were being plundered by the monarch in England. 'The object of England,' Thomas Jefferson, the author of America's Declaration of Independence, noted, 'is the permanent domination of the Ocean and the monopoly of the trade of the world ... The resources of other nations, then, must be impressed to supply the deficiency of her own.'[1]

Jefferson and his fellow Americans rebelled. 'No taxation without representation', became the rallying cry. The thirteen colonies came together in their opposition to the British. In 1775 a war was declared against England. Next year the Continental Congress asked Jefferson to write the now-famous Declaration of Independence. Arguing that 'all men are created equal; that they are endowed by their Creator with certain unalienable (sic) rights; that among these are life, liberty, and the pursuit of happiness; that, to secure these rights, governments are instituted among men, deriving their just powers from the consent of the governed; that whenever any form of government becomes destructive of these ends, it is the right of the people to alter or to abolish it', Jefferson and fifty-five others signed the Declaration on 4 July 1776. As the war for independence raged, the colonists formalized their 'league of friendship' by adopting a set of rules. An independent America's first Constitution, the Articles of Confederation, was ratified and adopted by the colonies in 1781.

AMERICA'S FIRST CONSTITUTION

Within a decade, America's first Constitution began showing signs of its unsuitability. The loose union the Articles of Confederation established created a rather weak federal government in the National Congress. The Congress was inherently unfair to boot. Each state, the erstwhile colonies, had one vote regardless of its population; a majority of nine out of thirteen was needed for decisions. The union government had no executive power to enforce the Acts of Congress. The Congress was empowered to make war, borrow money and settle disputes between states, but couldn't levy taxes or regulate commerce. Amending the Constitution required unanimity.

America's first Constitution was really a peace treaty, not a Constitution in the traditional sense. It didn't describe a government for the thirteen sovereign states, but the terms of a union of necessity, in order to gain independence from the British. Its purpose was to form an alliance in which 'each state retains its sovereignty, freedom and independence, and every power, jurisdiction and right' which was not 'expressly delegated' to the United States.[2]

It was a miracle that the Americans won the revolutionary war – owing in no small part to the inspired leadership of George Washington and to the indecisiveness of the British – because the states hadn't really united. Within months of signing the Articles, the Confederation officials were out begging for the signatories to contribute to the war effort. 'The biggest problem was that the national government was too weak to function effectively.'[3] The inadequacies of the Continental government led to a bankrupt treasury and disgruntled soldiers even through it had won the war in 1783. By 1787 it was clear that the national government under the Articles could not conduct the affairs of the nation. A call went out to the only person in America who had the necessary credibility to pull the nation together, to 'exercise his influence'. Washington responded, 'Influence was not government. Let us have one by which our lives, liberties, and properties will be secured, or let us know the worst at once.'[4]

A thirty-six-year-old legislator from Virginia, James Madison, protégé of Jefferson, decided to do something to prevent his nation from falling apart. He took a scientific approach. The method he chose was to first analyse all the incidents when governments failed to deliver, and deduce from them the causes of the ailments. He decided to compile the vices of the political system that the Articles of Confederation had created.

Twelve shortcomings, published in April 1787 under the title 'Vices of the Political System of the United States', fell into two broad categories: the inadequacies of the federal authority and the defects in the laws of states. Among the weaknesses of the federal government were the 'failure of the states to comply with the constitutional requisitions; encroachments by the states on the federal authority; trespasses of the states on the rights of each other; want of concert in matters where common interest requires it; want of sanction to the laws, and of coercion in the Government of the Confederacy'. The laws being passed by the thirteen state governments were failing the people too, due to the 'multiplicity of laws in the several states; mutability of the laws; injustice of the laws; impotence of the laws'.[5] The message was clear. The flaws Madison highlighted in the political system called out for greater coercive power over the newly independent states. In short, the United States needed a stronger Central government.

Madison was, however, troubled by something even more menacing than a weak Central government. He had noticed that many of the laws made by state governments were unjust. He figured out the reason, that whenever 'a common passion unites a majority what is to restrain them from unjust violations of the rights and interests of the minority'? To him, unjust laws were the most worrisome evil. It was 'more alarming', he said, 'because it brings more into question the fundamental principle of republican government, that the majority who rule ... are the safest guardians both of public good and of private rights'. In short, according to Madison, a majority-only government was doomed to failure because it was inherently unjust.

Madison had seen the destructive results of unjust governments before. A year before this research of his own confederacy and the thirteen legislatures, he had made an even more exhaustive study. He had analysed confederacies, modern and ancient, spread over a period of 3,000 years, including the likes of the Lycian, Amphyctionic, Achaean, Helvetic and Germanic confederacies. All these confederacies had failed. Madison was deeply concerned about the fundamental question raised by their failures: Is the principle of majority rule sound? His answer was a resounding no.

'To what causes is this evil to be ascribed,' Madison asked. He noted that there were two causes: representative bodies and the people themselves. In representative bodies, he found that 'a majority in the legislative councils, with interested views, contrary to the interest and views of their constituents' often 'join in a perfidious sacrifice of the latter to the former'. 'A succeeding election it might be supposed would displace the offenders and repair the mischief,' Madison said, 'but how easily are base and selfish measures masked by pretexts of public good and apparent expediency?' As for the people, he thought the seeds of factionalism were deeply sown. 'Place three individuals in a situation ... and give to two of them an interest opposed to the rights of the third. Will the latter be secure? The prudence of every man would shun the danger,' he wrote.[6]

For the evil of unjust governments, Madison didn't have any quick fixes but prescribed two principles. One, he thought that some 'modification of the sovereignty' of the states was necessary because in a larger republic it was more difficult for the common interests and passions to form majorities. And two, he wanted to devise a process of elections that drew the 'purest and noblest' to come forward as leaders.

This was only a teaser. As Madison wrote this, Americans were about to begin such an existential debate on the principles of government as no people had attempted before. A debate so profound that it would result in the invention of a whole new form of government.

LESSONS FROM THE AMERICAN EXPERIENCE

No other people in history had more experience with Constitutions than America's founding fathers. They had lived under fifteen different Constitutions. After living for generations under the British, they had now experienced for a whole decade fourteen Constitutions of their own – one confederate and thirteen states. They had experienced these Constitutions under both war and peace. A whole body of political thought and a large number of experienced leaders were now at hand to steer the Americans in the development of their second Constitution.

To formulate a more perfect Constitution, the American leaders required an entirely new set of principles. The principles of government that had been in the minds of Americans for a generation, and on which their Declaration of Independence was based, were no longer sufficient. The natural rights of man as a law of nature, the theory that governments enjoy their power over citizens by contract only, that this power is delegated for the sake of securing the rights of citizens, that all men are equally free and independent, that the people have the right to abolish an inadequate government – all these provided a definition of liberty for generations past. But the dog of liberty, unleashed from tyranny, now needed a leash again.

To succeed in their second revolution, the American leaders would draw on every bit of their vast experience, re-examine every tenet of good government and re-engineer every institution. They began by asking why they should have a government in the first place.

GOVERNMENT, A NECESSARY EVIL

'If men were angels, no government would be necessary,' said Madison. 'If angels were to govern men neither external nor internal controls on government would be necessary,' he noted, but 'in framing a government which is to be administered by men over men … you must first enable the government to control the governed, and in the next place oblige it to control itself'.[7]

The Americans thought that the force of 'reason', rather than that of a government, was really what governed men. They believed that man's real nature was moral and decent, and suitable for self-government. The Americans were fortified in this belief by the arguments presented by British philosopher John Locke. Frequently credited as the 'intellectual godfather' of the American Revolution, Locke was also the theorist behind the English Revolution of 1688. He was not necessarily original in his ideas, but he gave clear and reasonable expressions to beliefs held for centuries by lovers of liberty. 'Men living together according to reason,' Locke wrote, 'without a common superior on earth with authority to judge between them, is properly the state of nature.'[8] In Locke's formulation the government was based on an agreement between free individuals, not between rulers and ruled.

Man's happiness, therefore, didn't require government. If he needed one at all, it was to stop others from hindering his pursuit of happiness. This was contrary to the prevalent belief at the time, especially in Europe, where governments behaved as rulers over men incapable of providing for themselves.

POWERFUL BUT NON-OPPRESSIVE GOVERNMENT

Balancing liberty with obedience was thus the principal challenge the Americans faced. Central to Madison's analysis also was the same dilemma: Americans both *feared* and *needed* a powerful government. They had revolted against a government that was too powerful and oppressive, but had landed themselves with one that was too weak and indecisive.

The American leaders had seen that a government that could only ask was as bad as the one that could only force; that 'mere advice was a sad substitute for laws'.[9] In short, the coercive powers in a government endangered, as well as promised, liberty.

This conflict was apparent throughout the revolutionary war, which brought to the forefront the fact that coercive powers in a government were vitally important. In this sense, the war was fortuitous for, without it, the contrast between the two opposing principles of government would not have come into focus so easily, nor would a fix have been needed so urgently.

LESS GOVERNMENT THE BETTER

'The best government is that which governs least,' a maxim made famous by Henry David Thoreau, resounded well with American constitution makers. The lessons they had learnt were always that self-government and small government were better. A limited government was essential in order to keep a servant from growing into a master.

Rights retained by citizens were crucial, even to the point of risking anarchy. Some rights were inalienable, like 'life, liberty, and pursuit of happiness'. Others were 'useless to surrender to the government, and which governments have yet always been found to invade', wrote Jefferson, 'these are the rights of thinking, and publishing our thoughts by speaking or writing; the right of free commerce; the right of personal freedom'.[10]

Realizing, however, that an extensive government was necessary to build an empire, the Americans began to worry about the threat of the two tyrannies – of the majority, and of the government itself. Finding the methods to protect themselves from these two forms of oppression became their chief aim.

DIVIDE POWERS FOR A 'GOOD' AND 'SAFE' GOVERNMENT

Jefferson described the emerging consensus: 'The way to have good and safe government is not to trust it all to one, but to divide it among the many.'[11] Dividing powers reduced the risk of both the tyranny of majority and of government.

Yet, it could also improve government's effectiveness. The quality of governance depended upon the degree and technique of dividing powers. The American experience had shown that dividing powers too extensively risked people's liberties too. 'It is a melancholy reflection that liberty should be equally exposed to danger whether the Government have too much or too little power,' Madison said.[12]

But the best way to achieve such a balance was not apparent. None of the existing governments, especially the British, was a good model. Jefferson noted: 'It is not in the history of modern England or among the advocates of the principles or practices of her government that the friend of freedom, or of political morality, is to seek instruction ... The vital principle of the English constitution is corruption'.[13]

The Americans turned to political philosophers to see if they had any instruction in separating powers. In 1690 in his *Second Treatise of Government*, Locke had described a principle for limiting the powers of rulers. If 'the same persons who have the power of making laws to have also in their hands power to execute them ... they may exempt themselves from obedience to the laws they make', he had written. Similarly, a famous French political philosopher, Charles-Louis de Secondat, Baron de Montesquieu, had said that 'in well-ordered commonwealths ... the legislative and executive power come often to be separated'.

It was in the writings of Montesquieu that the Americans found a practical basis of separating powers. In his 1748 work *The Spirit of the Laws'* Montesquieu had refined his concepts. He had presented arguments for the three 'separate and equal' branches of government. The best way to prevent tyranny, he had said, was to entrust to the legislature the task of enacting laws, executive to enforce laws and judiciary to punish violators of law. Montesquieu had a word of warning: 'When legislative power is united with executive power in a single person, in a single body of the magistracy, there is no liberty, because one can fear that the same monarch or senate that makes tyrannical laws will execute them tyrannically.'

WANT OF A PROPER EXECUTIVE

In the American experience with both the British and their own governments, the solution to a strong yet non-oppressive government revolved around the executive, because both energy and oppressiveness were qualities inherent to that branch.

For the American leaders of the time, quintessential libertarians all, the conclusion that a good government must have coercive powers was not an easy one to reach. But want of energy in government was so apparent that executive power was seen as the ingredient necessary to secure a strong government. As the emphasis in American polity changed from liberty to authority, there was a corresponding change of weight in government from the legislative to the executive.

Madison had noticed the problem in his studies as well. 'Experience had proved a tendency in our governments to throw all power into the legislative vortex,' he wrote, 'the Executives are in general little more than ciphers.' He warned that 'if no effective check be devised for restraining the instability and encroachment of the latter, a revolution of some kind ... would be inevitable'.[14]

In state after state, executive officers pleaded against legislative dominance. Complaints were registered for political interference in government, for corruption, for reducing the salaries of judges, for legislators drawing money directly from the treasury, for unreasonable removal of officials, and so on. Jefferson described the conditions in his state of Virginia: 'The judiciary and executive members were left dependent on the legislative for their subsistence in office, and some of them for their continuance in it. If therefore the legislature assumes executive and judiciary powers, no opposition is likely to be made; nor, if made, can it be effectual.'[15]

Even worse, the states made bad laws as a result of omnipotent legislative powers. Madison reported in his *Vices* that the newly independent states overreacted to the abuses of power by British governors, and denied the executive branch powers to veto legislation. This caused many problems with laws. Legislatures made too many laws; or unjust laws; they frequently repealed or superseded; or they couldn't be or wouldn't be enforced.[16]

The vital necessity of a strong executive was apparent not just from the vices, but also from some virtues. One such deeply influential case was the experience Americans had in the state of New York. The Constitution of that state provided for a singular governor who had 'the supreme executive power and authority', complete with veto power so that laws may not be 'hastily or unadvisedly passed'. This was the first Constitution in history which applied the theory of separation of powers in earnest. For the first time a legislature was actually limited by the Constitution. The Constitution of New York and its executive department in particular were functioning well, and served as a healthy example for the new nation to follow.[17]

That experience had also shown that a one-man executive, as opposed to a committee, was the best. Executive efficiency and responsibility varied inversely in proportion to the size of the executive body. The chief source of this instruction was the state of Virginia, and Jefferson himself was the principal student. It was under his governorship that the state, desirous of freeing the legislature from details of administration, had appointed an executive committee. The experiment failed miserably. He would later recall that plurality in the executive was the main reason behind the failure; 'the form of a plurality, however promising in theory, is impracticable with men constituted with the ordinary passions', he wrote.[18]

PITFALLS OF SMALL ELECTIONS

The first line of defence against tyranny of the majority, the Americans had learnt, was the republican character of their government. If protection against an oppressive government was in the division of powers, the protection against an oppressive majority lay in the division of people's representatives. The more varied the distribution the better. That is, more number of representatives per citizen, from a greater variety of constituencies, and divided among the largest number of branches of government. To do this effectively, the size of the constituency in which elections were held mattered. The smaller the constituency, the greater the chance that the election would be stolen and a majority would take hold.

But how were they to stop a majority from taking hold without restricting people's liberties? In an essay entitled 'The Union as a Safeguard against Domestic Faction and Insurrection', Madison noted that the 'causes of faction' are 'sown in the nature of man' and cannot be cured. Nor should there be an attempt to cure them because the 'spirit of party and faction' was necessary.[19] The idea was to control the 'mischiefs of faction', and that could be done by one of two methods: either by preventing the same passions or interests to exist in society at the same time, or by restricting those factions from carrying out their 'schemes of oppression'. The latter remedy was the only possibility, Madison argued, and it could be done by controlling the 'number and local situation' of people's representatives.

'The question resulting is whether small or extensive republics are more favourable to the election of proper guardians of the public weal,' Madison noted, 'and it is clearly decided in favour of the latter.' Madison went on to show that if the constituencies were too small, one had to guard against the 'cabals of a few', but if they were too large, one had to worry about 'the confusion of a multitude'. In a large constituency, however, 'it will be more difficult for unworthy candidates to practice with success the vicious arts by which elections are too often carried'.[20]

FRAMERS OF THE US CONSTITUTION REINVENT GOVERNMENT

The Continental Congress was in no mood to alter its own basic structure. But the pressures of the multiple crises America faced – a bankrupt national treasury, commercial discord among the states and a rebellion – weighed heavily. In February 1787, five months after the call for a Constitutional Convention, it authorized that a convention be held 'for the sole and express purpose of revising the Articles of Confederation'. Madison and certain other leaders, however, knew

that a whole new Constitution was needed and that simply tinkering
with the Articles wasn't going to solve the great dilemma of devising a
government with both energy and safety.

Madison worked these five months not just on his list of vices or
the basic outline of a new Constitution, but on another very important
assignment: cajoling George Washington to attend the Convention.
The fifty-five-year-old Washington, America's most popular and
respected leader, had retired after a lifetime of service. Madison and
others slowly flattered and sweet-talked Washington. They all knew his
participation was vital for establishing the credibility of the Convention,
and to enhance the 'magnitude of the occasion', as Madison put it. A
follower wrote to the general: should 'an energetic and judicial system
... be proposed with your signature, it would ... doubly entitle you
to the glorious republican epithet – The Father of Your Country'.[21]
Equally crucial at the Convention was another contemporary father
figure, eighty-one-year-old Benjamin Franklin. Founder of one of the
country's finest universities, a successful businessman and an inventor,
Franklin was also a former president of Pennsylvania and ambassador
to France. He had become America's leading voice of unity.

Fifty-five delegates – together with Washington and Franklin – all
selected for the purpose by their state's legislature came together in
May 1787 in Franklin's hometown, Philadelphia. Only twelve of
the thirteen states participated; Rhode Island chose not to send any
delegates. Most state legislatures authorized the delegates to vote only
when a majority of the state's delegates were present. Some couldn't
pay for their delegates; some delegates kept refusing to serve. The
Convention, as a result, had trouble achieving a quorum. After an
eleven-day delay, the convention finally began, with the inevitable first
act – the selection of Washington as its president. Forty-two of the fifty-
five men had served in the Continental Congress, thirty-five had served
in the military, nearly all were wealthy and unusually well educated,
a majority of them were trained to practice law. All had earned their
place due to their recognized public service.

The Convention began with the adoption of two unusual rules. First, each state was awarded one vote, giving each equal weight, regardless of its size. And second, any member was allowed to request reconsideration of any motion previously voted upon. The first rule, given the rules of the confederacy calling the convention, was inevitable. But the second had far-reaching consequences. It allowed the Convention to function not like a legislative body, but rather as an informal committee. This parliamentary device, commonly used in legislative bodies in America, allowed the delegates to convert the assembly into a committee of the whole. The delegates could then freely discuss or take 'straw votes' on issues without making them binding. The committee's decisions were only recommendations, and hence allowed the delegates to revisit the issues till the final votes were taken by the convention.[22]

In utmost secrecy – to the chagrin of many, including Jefferson, who was in Paris at the time as the American ambassador – the Constitutional Convention of America deliberated through the summer, for four months.

A REVOLUTIONARY APPROACH TO GOVERNMENT

The first thing the Convention did was to break the very directive by which they were authorized to convene. Approved 'for the sole and express purpose of revising the Articles of Confederation', the Convention adopted the Virginia Plan, named after the state delegation that presented it. This was no *revision*. It was a *revolution*.

Largely the handiwork of Madison, and drawing upon his *Vices*, the Virginia Plan was 'a total alteration of the present federal system'. It proposed a strong national government, change from a single-house to a two-house legislature 'with full legislative powers upon all subjects', including veto over any state law, a change from equal representation of states to apportionment according to the population and wealth of each state; and the creation of a national executive. The seventh of the fifteen resolutions sketched the 'national executive' to be indirectly elected by the national legislature; it however left open the questions of whether it would be one man or a committee, and the term of office. In another revolutionary proposal, the plan suggested a council of revision, to be composed of the chief executive and a number of judiciary, with the authority to examine every Act passed.

Many delegates were stunned by the revolutionary character of the Plan, but it set the tone. As soon as it was introduced, the American leaders found themselves debating a whole new set of principles of government that required leaps of imagination among America's founding fathers.

However, the Plan drew a blank in describing the executive power. Not because Madison hadn't done his homework, but because the principles involved stretched the imagination. In fact, executive power would become the chief problem for all delegates. Every aspect of this branch of government – its form, powers, mode of selection, term in office, re-eligibility – would sharply divide them until the very end.

CREATION OF AMERICAN PRESIDENCY – TAKE ONE

James Wilson would become the Father of the American presidency. Wilson, like Madison, lacked the gifts of charm and oratory but was known to be very sharp and knowledgeable in political theories. Two days after the Virginia Plan was introduced, Wilson, a Pennsylvanian, presented a very different idea for the executive power. 'If we are to establish a national Government,' he said, 'that Government ought to flow from the people at large … [and] the executive consist of a single person.'[23]

A hush fell, 'a considerable pause' in the words of Madison, who was the self-appointed minute taker of the Convention. The sage, Franklin, who spoke very little due to illness so severe that he was carried to the Convention by prisoners from a local jail, broke the ice: 'it was a point of great importance', he said, and invited the delegates to 'deliver their sentiments on it before the question was put'.

Wilson's proposal had raised two earth-shattering prospects: an executive who would be independent of the legislature, and one that would also end the representation of states in the executive branch.

He proposed 'to derive not only both branches of the legislature from the people, without the intervention of the state legislatures, but the executive also; in order to make them as independent as possible of each other, as well as of the states'. His executive would rest on the support of the whole people not just state legislatures.

There was more. The chief executive would be one man, 'giving most energy, dispatch, and responsibility'. There would be no council 'which oftener serves to cover than prevent malpractices'. Wilson's executive would not just be independent of the legislature, he would have an absolute veto over it. Also, this executive would have unlimited re-eligibility and a relatively short term in office. Wilson noted that 'he was not governed by the British model which was inapplicable to the situation of this country, the extent of which was so great, and the manners so republican, that nothing but a great confederated republic would do for it'.[24]

Charles Pinckney, a young delegate from South Carolina, whose own plan submitted earlier had proposed a single executive, immediately seconded Wilson's plan. But Roger Sherman of Connecticut rose to oppose. Executive magistrate should be 'nothing more than an institution for carrying the will of the Legislature into effect', he said, because legislature was 'the depositary of the supreme will of the society'. Edmund Randolph, governor of Virginia, who would ultimately refuse to sign the final document, was dead against a singular executive. He saw in it 'the foetus of monarchy' and feared 'executive tyranny'. Many arguments were voiced against: that the people at large were incapable of making a wise selection of their chief magistrate, that the ordinary citizens were too gullible, that their votes could be easily manipulated, that they were simply too ignorant, that the sheer expanse of the nation would make it impossible to inform all Americans.

Wilson continued to argue that it was exactly due to the vast extent of the country that a single executive was required, and that America's 'republican manners' made it impossible that an American president could turn into a monarch. After two days of debates, the delegates wouldn't have anything to do with the direct election of the executive. Wilson won a big victory, however; by seven votes to three, the Convention approved a single executive.

If the delegates were not willing to accept a completely independent executive, they were equally unwilling to accept its complete subordination to the legislature. Many alternatives were proposed, from letting only the Upper House of the legislature to select the president to allowing the state legislatures to do so. Wilson himself proposed an alternative, that the states be divided into districts and that 'electors' from those districts then select the chief magistrate. Over a period of four days, the delegates would vote them all down. The Virginia Plan's original scheme for electing the president by national legislature had the votes in its favour – eight to two. But the delegates knew the issue was far from settled. Every issue concerning executive power made the delegates uneasy. The executive's ineligibility for a second term was voted in, but only temporarily, before being changed again. The Virginia Plan's proposal for a council of revision was opposed by Wilson, of all people, for it mingled the executive with the judiciary. He insisted that executive powers must be 'distinct and independent'.

The next break in organizing the executive came with regard to the power of veto. Wilson insisted that the executive's independence made it imperative that he possess an 'absolute negative', otherwise 'without such defence the legislature can at any moment sink it into non-existence'. Franklin opposed the call for executive's veto power, fearing that 'no good law could be passed without a private bargain'. Sherman was opposed to 'enabling any one man to stop the will of the whole'. Madison found the middle ground, which ultimately passed, that granted the executive the veto but also allowed the national legislature to overrule any veto with a two-thirds majority.

But the most important issues about the executive power remained undecided when the Convention adjourned on 4 June. And then America's Constitutional Convention almost failed.

REINVENTING GOVERNMENT

Madison and his men had come very far, their concept of a 'national government' was agreed to. But now they faced a counter-attack from the smaller states in the Convention which almost derailed the entire effort of devising a new Constitution. The small states feared, with some justification, that 'stripped of their equal right of suffrage' in the national legislature, they would be at the mercy of the large states. A coalition of small states, represented by William Paterson of New Jersey, vehemently opposed the Virginia Plan. They suggested instead a government strictly 'federal', in which the sovereignty resided with states, and the individual states would elect a plural 'federal executive', a committee.

A long debate on the issue of representation ensued. Complicating the debate was the elephant in the room – the issue of slavery. Americans wanted representative government, but not all Americans wanted the black slaves to be treated equally. Madison had couched the issue of slaves in his proposal by providing for their representation in the 'wealth' of a state. But sooner or later, it had to be addressed. Faced with a complete unravelling of the national government plan, the delegates were forced to find a formula for the representation of all the people in a state. A formula was found in 'whole number of whites' and 'three-fifths of all other persons'. The three-fifths were the rough approximation of the measure of wealth that each slave contributed to the economy. But the impasse on the issue of representation persisted.

In the middle of this stand-off, the man known most for his intellect, Hamilton, took a stab at the problems. They eluded him as well, in part because his plan proposed that the states should be done away with altogether, replaced by one strong national government on the British model. Calling the British government 'the best in the world', and its House of Lords 'a most noble institution', Hamilton argued that 'the hereditary interest of the King was so interwoven with that of the nation' that he was unlikely to be corrupt. Hamilton wasn't proposing a hereditary model for the United States; his point in fact was that 'stability and permanency demanded that at least one branch of the legislature, as well as the chief executive, should hold their office for life'. In a speech that lasted more than five hours, Hamilton suggested a strong executive with powers of absolute veto, sort of an elected monarch, dependent upon neither the people nor the legislature for his election. The proposal met with a 'deafening silence'. Not a single delegate rose in support.[25]

The stalemate over the issue of representation of big versus small states continued. The delegates however persevered, and it was the delegation from Connecticut, led by William Samuel Johnson, that most consistently spoke about a compromise. The so-called Connecticut Compromise was found fortuitously, in an already proposed provision: the legislature's second house. Johnson suggested that 'in some respects the states are to be considered in their political capacity and in others as districts of individual citizens'. He proposed that the states, 'instead of being opposed to each other, ought to be combined: that in one branch the people ought to be represented, in the other, the states'.

A Grand Committee formed for the purpose adopted the suggestion and proposed an 'equality of votes in the second branch', called the Senate. This ingenious provision – the concept of 'divided sovereignty' – created a government part national and part federal, and became one of the most notable inventions of the American political system.

CREATION OF AMERICAN PRESIDENCY – TAKE TWO

With the bitter conflict about the representation of states resolved, delegates returned to organizing the presidency, which proved to be much tougher. This was mostly due to a still hazy understanding of the concept of separation of powers. As a principle, separation of powers was easy to see, but to put it into practice was an entirely different challenge. America's founding fathers knew *why* they wanted to keep powers separate, but they didn't know *how* to make the three powerful branches work together for a strong and safe government.

The revised Virginia Plan was still the basis of debate on the provisions of the executive power. The debates, though less contentious, were going around in circles, especially on the method of election, re-eligibility and length of term. Seven distinct methods of selection were suggested, but still the Convention reverted to the original plan of choice by the legislature, a seven-year term, and no second term.

The decision about a single executive was, however, now unanimous. The selection of the president by the legislature – already voted in twice – was tested again. And once again Wilson's proposal that the president be directly elected was defeated, nine to one. But this time the debates made it clear that the vast number of votes against were from those who worried that local rather than national considerations would impact the voters. Sensing an opening, Luther Martin, who would later leave the Convention in a huff, floated a variation of Wilson's earlier idea allowing the state legislatures to appoint electors, thus answering the provincial concerns of the delegates. The result, however, was another defeat. Out of weariness, the delegates once again endorsed the original Virginia Plan, this time unanimously.

It was the debate on re-eligibility of the president that finally turned the tables. First the delegates voted to limit the president to one term, then in July, due simply to confusion and fatigue they reversed that decision and allowed re-election. James McClurg, Madison's fellow Virginian, argued that in a system in which the legislature would select a president, running for re-election would simply make him even more dependent on the legislature. Instead, he proposed that the president be appointed for life, that is, 'during good behavior'.

This proposal horrified those who feared executive tyranny, but others liked the independence it bestowed upon the executive. It forced all delegates to reconsider their thoughts on the independence of each branch of government. Madison suddenly realized the error in his approach. He opposed McClurg on the grounds that it would be difficult to find a tribunal to determine 'good behavior', but he now knew that the 'union between the executive and legislative powers' that he had proposed was dangerous, and that it was 'absolutely necessary to a well-constituted republic that the two should be kept distinct and independent of one another'.[26]

The idea of electing the chief executive by a source other than the legislature began to gain strength as soon as Madison gave it his nod of approval. When it came, Madison's support was unequivocal. He declared that 'the appointment of the Executive should either be drawn from a source, or held by some tenure, that will give him a free agency with regard to the Legislature'. He argued that the appointment of an executive by the legislature 'would be attended with intrigues and contentions that ought not to be unnecessarily admitted'. For these reasons Madison was now disposed to have the executive appointed by some other source.' The people at large was in itself the fittest,' he said. 'It would be as likely as any that could be devised, to produce an Executive Magistrate of distinguished Character.'[27]

The debates on the organization of the executive branch had no pattern. Like Madison himself, most delegates changed their minds after hearing arguments. There were no interests or groupings like on the issue of state representation, no fixed positions. A late but forceful advocate of the idea of an executive independent of the legislature came in the form of Gouverneur Morris. Morris, a bombastic and eloquent speaker – who would later say of the Constitution that 'while some have boasted it as a work from Heaven ... I have many reasons to believe that it is the work of plain, honest men' – became a forceful voice for this cause.

'Of all the possible modes of appointment,' he warned, 'that by the Legislature is the worst.' A union was impossible unless an executive 'provided with sufficient vigor pervade every part of it', he declared. The executive must be 'the guardian of the people ... against legislative tyranny'. The people need protection from the 'great and wealthy who in the course of things will necessarily compose the legislative body', and therefore 'one great object of the Executive is to control the Legislature'. Pointing to the British system, Morris said: 'In all public bodies there are two parties. The Executive will necessarily be more connected with one than the other.'

He declared that the American executive would be different: 'This Magistrate is not the King, but the prime-minister. The people are the King.'[28]

Despite this now famous 'the people are the king' oratory, Morris wasn't able to convert many. On 23 July, when the Committee of the Detail was formed, so little progress had been made on issues pertaining to the presidency that that matter was excluded from the committee's charge.

Facing the delegates' rapidly diminishing capacity to evaluate proposals, Madison rose to summarize. He saw only two alternatives: direct election by either the people, or electors chosen by the people. Of the two, he preferred the former, but he worried that this would put the small states at a disadvantage. He also feared that the north would always be at an advantage since it would have more 'qualified' voters. Hence some form of indirect election was the only alternative left. But such a proposal didn't have the votes, and Madison didn't want to push his luck.

The delegates, tired of the issue, decided to refer it as well to the five-member Committee of Detail. But before the matter was closed, another vote was taken – the seventh – and once again the original plan of election by the legislature passed, seven to three. However, this time Madison voted against his own Virginia Plan.

The Committee of Detail, headed by Randolph with Wilson as a member, wasn't authorized to change any principles. Wilson, whose draft was presented as the Committee's report, spelled out some minor issues. (The chief executive was now known as the 'president'; procedures were laid out for appointments of officials, for the exercise of veto powers, and for the overriding of the veto.) But it was stuck with the election of president by the national legislature and for one term of seven years only. The provisions concerning the presidency would not be discussed by the Convention as a whole again. They were then referred to an eleven-member Committee on Postponed Parts.

The US presidency was still sorely incomplete. The only powers expressly vested in the executive, even at this late stage, were veto powers. There were powers to make appointments, which would allow the president to have his Cabinet, but not of appointing judges. There were four attempts by Madison and Wilson to join the Supreme Court to the president, but they had all failed. 'Consequently, on this date the Convention had recourse to the increasingly popular expedient of creating a committee to expedite matters.'[29]

The eleven-member Committee on Postponed Parts included Morris and Madison. It was this Committee that ultimately organized the executive.

CREATION OF AMERICAN PRESIDENCY — FINAL TAKE

If Wilson was the Father of the American presidency, the Committee on Postponed Parts was the midwife aiding in its birth. The moment of birth was described by one of the members of the committee, John Dickinson, a delegate from the state of Delaware, in testimony written by him fifteen years later. The Committee was having a tough time organizing the presidency, he reported, and just about approved once again that the Congress elect the president.

Dickinson raised an alarm. The 'powers which we have agreed to vest in the President were so many and so great', he warned, that the people will never approve a constitution 'unless they themselves would be more immediately concerned in [the President's] election'. Gouverneur Morris urged the members of the committee to 'sit down again, and converse further on this subject'. Madison, according to Dickinson's recollection, 'took out a pen and paper, and sketched out a Mode of Electing the President' that might provide a more direct role for the people. Madison had described the electoral college. 'This intervention by Dickinson and the subsequent responses by Morris and Madison probably constitute the most decisive moment in the creation of the American electoral college.'[30]

Wilson's plan had two imperatives: that the chief executive be singular and that he be chosen directly by the people. A mode of selection approaching a popular election had finally entered the Constitution, but not without cost. The price was a mind-numbingly complex procedure, the electoral college, which kept the legislatures involved in the selection.

The electoral college that Madison sketched served many purposes. First, it addressed the concern that people in general were gullible and could be easily manipulated. Second, it quelled fears of parochialism by requiring that at least one of the two candidates come from another state. Third, the electors would vote within their states, thus satisfying those who worried about the cost and practicality of reaching an expansive nation. Fourth, by providing for voting in the same proportion as each state's entitlement in the national legislature, the college made the election procedure representative in a proportion that both large and small states found acceptable. Fifth, it finessed the question of who would select the electors by leaving the state legislatures the power to 'appoint'. Sixth, it made the selection palatable to the smaller states by leaving the final decision, in case no candidate wins the majority, up to the Senate, where each state has equal representation. (This would however change; the power would later be given to the House of Representatives instead.) Seventh, for those who worried that no candidate would receive a majority in a country as large and as provincial as America, the procedure provided that each elector cast two votes. Eighth, allowing each state the proportion of votes as agreed before, the procedure also satisfied the southern states since it extended the three-fifths compromise to the selection of the president without unnecessarily parading the fact. Thus, an ingenious way was found to meet 'the indispensable necessity of making the Executive independent of the Legislature', as Morris commended.

Before this gruelling back-and-forth ended, the Americans came within a hair's breadth of adopting a parliamentary system. The proposals that the president be chosen by the people was defeated, or that he be appointed by the legislators was approved, eight different times before finally being reversed.

In the same give-and-take fashion, the Committee on Postponed Parts filled in the details regarding the president's relationship with the Senate. The president gained control of foreign affairs, and of appointment of judges, but was required to get the Senate's consent over executive appointments. Neither the Senate nor the president was given exclusive control over appointments or treaties. The Committee's report also specified other provisions, regarding vice-presidency and impeachment. But one provision was entirely new, that the president must be a natural born citizen of the United States. While this seemed to be driven primarily by the delegates' concern over foreigners getting into administration, it also added a patriotic sentiment to the office of the presidency.

Despite the presidency being the most debated branch in the Convention, it was the Congress that constituted the heart and soul of America's new government. While fine-tuning the Constitution, a telling and profoundly consequential change was the decision regarding the appointment of the nation's treasurer. The Congress controlled the purse of the nation, but the power of appointing the treasurer went to the president. This further ensured that the president had a wide range of powers.

RALLYING THE PEOPLE

Fifty-five 'plain, honest men' had laboured for four months to create America's Constitution. But the American people didn't know what had transpired. The pact of secrecy of the deliberations inside the Convention had worked. The journals of the proceedings were prohibited from publication until 1818. Madison's notes too were published only after his death, in 1836.

The new Constitution needed ratification from the states before adoption, and the American people needed to be rallied. Campaigning began as soon as the new Constitution was presented to the public. Supporters of the Constitution, led by Madison, began calling themselves Federalists – a misnomer, for they supported a strong national government contrary to the traditional meaning of the term.

The opponents – led by Patrick Henry, an acknowledged popular leader known as the Son of Thunder – became, by default, the Antifederalists.

The American people took more than a year to ratify their new Constitution. From September 1787, when the final draft was signed until the ratification by ten states and adoption in March 1789, the tallest leaders of America were engaged in the fight of their lives. Henry, for instance, spoke non-stop for seven hours against the Constitution in the state legislature in Madison's home state, Virginia, the most populous state at the time. Anticipating the shrill public discourse, America's founding fathers set out to educate and inform the people. Madison and Hamilton published a series of essays, eighty-five in all, which became known as *The Federalist Papers*, and were the finest articulation of the arguments behind the decisions taken by the Convention.

When in March 1789 a new government took the oath of office under the new Constitution, George Washington – who had received every single one of the sixty-nine votes cast by the electors – set out to create the world's first presidential government. He still marvelled at the mammoth effort, 'little short of a miracle', that the men gathered in Philadelphia could 'unite in forming a system of government so little liable to well-founded objections'.[31] Jefferson would become the third president of the United States; Madison, the fourth, in 1809. When referred to as the 'Father of the Constitution', Madison protested that the document was not 'the offspring of a single brain', but 'the work of many heads and many hands'.

Madison and his colleagues had indeed brought about a revolution in man's thinking about self-government.

'A BEAUTIFUL EQUILIBRIUM'

The most striking feature of America's Constitution was its balance. Since it was an outcome of a series of compromises and genuine debate, it created a near-perfect equipoise of powers.

By design, this marvel of balances was difficult for those in power because it required them to share powers. Working under the new

Constitution wasn't easy, yet its balancing of powers was admired by all. Jefferson called its balancing of state and federal governments a 'beautiful equilibrium'. Similarly, John Adams, who succeeded Washington as America's second president would write in awe and admiration of American Constitution's many balances:

> Is there a constitution upon record more complicated with balances than ours? In the first place, eighteen states and some territories are balanced against the national government. ... In the second place, the House of Representatives is balanced against the Senate, the Senate against the House. In the third place, the executive authority is, in some degree, balanced against the legislative. In the fourth place, the judicial power is balanced against the House, the Senate, the executive power, and the state governments. In the fifth place, the Senate is balanced against the President in all appointments to office, and in all treaties. In the sixth place, the people hold in their hands the balance against their own representatives, by biennial ... elections. In the seventh place, the legislatures of the several states are balanced against the Senate by sexennial elections. In the eighth place, the electors are balanced against the people in the choice of the President. Here is a complicated refinement of balances, which, for anything I recollect, is an invention of our own and peculiar to us.[32]

Separation of powers remains the best-known feature of the US system. But there were a few other principles that were equally important.

LIMITING GOVERNMENT PROTECTS RIGHTS, FOSTERS SELF-RELIANCE

Americans took the concept of self-government seriously, and quite literally. Jefferson's famous remark – 'Sometimes it is said that man cannot be trusted with the government of himself. Can he, then, be trusted with the government of others?' – said it all.

Americans gave their government a limited role, to manage only those affairs of the people for which government was absolutely necessary. They also ensured that these affairs were dealt with at an appropriate level – national or state – and without infringing on people's personal freedoms. Madison described the principle, that 'in all cases where power is to be conferred, the point first to be decided is, whether such a power be necessary to the public good'.[33]

Still, when the framers of America's Constitution first released the document without specific restrictions placed on government, there was a hue and cry. A livid Jefferson wrote to Madison soon after learning about the details of the proposed constitution: 'Let me tell you what I do not like … the omission of a bill of rights, providing clearly, and without the aid of sophism, for freedom of religion, freedom of the press, protection against standing armies, restriction of monopolies, the eternal and unremitting force of the *habeas corpus* law, and trials by jury'. He said: 'I have a right to nothing, which another has a right to take away.' A Bill of Rights was quickly added to America's Constitution, placing what may be the severest limitations on the powers of any government in history.

To ensure that the government stayed limited, specific powers were assigned to each branch to suit its unique purpose. However, to the Congress, the Constitution gave two unspecified broad powers. A clause authorized it 'to make all laws which shall be necessary and proper for carrying into execution the foregoing Powers'; and another which gave Congress a leeway to collect taxes for the 'general welfare of the U.S.' Although these two provisions gave Congress the tendency to expand government's role beyond the original powers, they were no carte blanche. The presidency was empowered to resist any such moves through its power of veto. Besides, the Supreme Court was authorized to stop a government from overreaching.

In fact, the presidential system was invented for the primary purpose of limiting the powers of government. 'The nature of the executive department which the [Constitution] created,' wrote Charles Thach in his original work, *The Creation of the Presidency*, 'was essentially an integral part of that wider concept of limited government which is the most distinctive contribution of American political thought and experience to the art of government.'[34]

Americans' desire to keep their national government limited in powers was so intense that it wasn't given the power to levy an income tax until the sixteenth amendment in 1913.

SEPARATION OF POWERS MAKES GOVERNMENT FREE

The US Constitution's most famous principle – separation of powers – was based on a very simple but profound thought. Hamilton said it best during the debates: 'Give all power to the many, they will oppress the few. Give all power to the few, they will oppress the many. Both therefore ought to have power, that each may defend itself against the other.'[35]

The US Constitution divided powers as extensively and smartly as possible. First it ensured that the fount of all powers, the people themselves, had a direct say in as many branches of government as possible. It did so in two ways: one, by raising the number of elected representatives per capita; and two, by extending the sphere of elections to the entire nation. Small elections had advantages but, as Madison noted, they risked people acting in 'concert' in their 'plans of oppression'. This system had the legislature derive its powers from smaller constituencies, while the executive power, in order to give it a national character, was derived from the republic as a whole.

Secondly, the American federal structure ensured that powers were divided between two genuinely independent separate governments, national and state. This enhanced each government's focus and hence its effectiveness. But more importantly, it kept one out of the other's area. There were some concurrent powers – conduct elections, establish local governments, protect public health, etc. – but the framers chose not to list the powers left to the states. Hence all those powers not specifically delegated were implied to be held by the states. Certain amendments to the Constitution further strengthened state governments: the tenth amendment removed all doubt that powers not delegated are reserved to the states; and the eleventh gave states immunity from certain legal actions. Then, of course, the Supreme Court was there to decide if one government trampled the other, or the people.

Both national and state governments were mutually independent. 'It is a fatal heresy,' Jefferson wrote in an attempt to clear a common misconception, 'to suppose that either our State governments are superior to the federal, or the federal to the States. The people, to whom all authority belongs, have divided the powers of government into two distinct departments, the leading characters of which are foreign and domestic; and they have appointed for each a distinct set of functionaries.'[36]

Thirdly, and most consequentially, the Americans gave each branch of government, at both national and state levels, a distinct function. This separation of legislative, executive and judicial powers was most significant because a government's effectiveness depended on how well these departments were administered. Here too, government's performance and safety were interlinked. To secure each branch from encroachments by any other, it was necessary that each performed its assigned role well. Each branch's performance was thus directly related with its independence; the better the performance, the greater the independence.

The separation of powers fortified each branch in several ways. First, each branch was made directly accountable to the people by having its officials as directly elected as possible. Second, each was given the utmost independence by assigning specific responsibilities. Third, all the elements – size, term in office, qualifications of officials, re-eligibility – were designed to strengthen each branch's ability to perform its designated role. Fourth, each was given powers to defend itself from encroachments. And last, the officials of each were prohibited from becoming members of any other branch.

'We think, in America,' wrote Jefferson, 'that it is necessary to introduce the people into every department of government, as far as they are capable of exercising it; and that this is the only way to insure a long-continued and honest administration of its powers.'[37] The direct election of the president was, of course, the most notable and innovative application of this principle.

COORDINATED DEPARTMENTS ESSENTIAL

As we have seen, the chief aim of the framers of the US Constitution was to create an 'energetic' government. As Madison said, 'Energy in government is essential to that security against external and internal danger, and to that prompt and salutary execution of the laws which enter into the very definition of good government.'[38] However, an energetic government was unsafe. Jefferson wrote to Madison: 'I am not a friend to a very energetic government. It is always oppressive.'[39] So, the Americans balanced the two requirements of energy and safety by inventing this doctrine of coordinated departments.

This principle of coordinated departments was at least as important a constitutional principle as that of separation of powers. It gave the process of separating powers a purpose. Through a set of innovative checks and balances, the US Constitution gave each branch a say in the others' functioning, but without entangling them in perpetual tension. The aim was to engage each branch in delivering good governance, rather than in creating deadlocks. Each was empowered to offer rival plans to those proposed by another branch, so as to improve the overall quality of laws and their implementation.

These famous checks and balances were not designed to 'produce conflict to stay evil, but to produce unity in effectuating decent measures', says Ann Stuart Anderson, in an essay entitled 'A 1787 Perspective on Separation of Powers.'[40] They provided the American system with constitutionally legitimate methods to resolve conflicts.

Madison described how the twin principles of separation of powers and coordinated departments were both necessary: 'Unless these departments be so far connected and blended as to give to each a constitutional control over the others,' he wrote, 'the degree of separation which the maxim requires, as essential to a free government, can never in practice be duly maintained.'

When it came to coordination among branches, legislative power was the primary concern. The Americans desired their legislature to be pre-eminent but not domineering. 'Legislative usurpations,' Madison wrote, 'which, by assembling all power in the same hands, must lead to the same tyranny as is threatened by executive usurpations.' Therefore, almost all checks and balances restricted the legislative branch from overwhelming the others. The US Constitution didn't establish a government of three equal powers – legislative, executive and judiciary – nor in which the executive was dominant, as is commonly held, but one in which a prominent legislature was balanced by bicameralism, and then checked by the executive.[41]

The powers provided to the presidency were therefore the crux of the matter. The energy Americans required of their government made it necessary to have a strong executive, and the strength they required of their executive made it necessary that he was provided with potent constitutional controls over the other branches.

DUAL DEMOCRATIC LEGITIMACY

America's Constitution makers rejected the notion that a nation's sovereignty and legislative power were identical. Sovereignty belonged to the whole government, not just the branch that made laws. The legislature's power to make laws was simply that, and nothing more. So, instead of the doctrine of parliamentary sovereignty, America's Constitution was based on the principle of dual democratic legitimacy. Both the executive and the legislative branches represented the people, and both were accountable to them directly.

This was in essence the principle of representation, applied properly. The rejection of the idea of supremacy of any single power in government made it necessary that each centre of power represented the will of the people. Hence, officials of each branch of government were elected as directly by the people as possible. As Thach noted, 'With the abandonment of the idea of the supreme legislature went the concept of executive responsibility to the legislature, and in its place came that of the executive as representative of and responsible to the people. ... This solution was, after all, but an adaptation of the principle of representation, properly safeguarded, to the problem in hand.'[42]

The most profound application of this principle was the presidency. The president of America stood for and spoke for the entire nation. 'No one else represents the people as a whole, exercising a national choice,' wrote Woodrow Wilson about the American president, before he himself became one. 'He is the representative of no constituency, but of the whole people. When he speaks in his true character, he speaks for no special interest.'[43]

FEDERAL SOVEREIGNTY IMPROVES GOVERNANCE

America's federalism was about local governance. 'Our country is too large,' wrote Jefferson, 'to have all its affairs directed by a single government.' The preference for local governance was based on the familiar argument of better accountability. But it had drawbacks; of not having a unified force for handling foreign affairs, or strong defences, or a robust monetary policy, and so on. Hence America's founding fathers invented a bi-level government, or dual sovereignty.

An American was a citizen of both his nation and his state. When he voted in the national election, he voted as a citizen of his nation, not his constituency; and he voted on a national agenda, not a local programme.

But the Constitution was careful not to delegate any more powers than necessary to the national government. The state governments had significant responsibilities, in the areas of education, public health, criminal justice, etc. Even more consequentially, the states were left to empower and determine the organization of their local governments. All local governments – counties, municipalities, townships, school districts, etc, (now numbering around 90,000) were created by the actions of the state legislatures.

The doctrine of dual sovereignty gave Americans the best of both worlds. Madison noted in his *Vices*, 'As a limited monarchy tempers the evils of an absolute one, so an extensive republic meliorates the administration of a small republic'. In a larger unified nation, there were two benefits: it was more difficult for the factions to form a majority, and there was a greater likelihood of finding great leaders.

'The smaller the society,' Madison wrote, 'the fewer probably will be the distinct parties and interests composing it … [and] more easily will they concert and execute their plans of oppression.' Further, Madison noted that 'the influence of factious leaders may kindle a flame within their particular states, but will be unable to spread a general conflagration through the other states'. Similarly, a large nation was beneficial because it helped find good leaders. Madison argued that 'as each representative will be chosen by a greater number of citizens in the large than in the small republic, it will be more difficult for unworthy candidates to practice with success the vicious arts by which elections are too often carried'.[44]

JUDICIAL REVIEW MAKES GOVERNMENT ABIDE BY THE LAW

Hamilton described the principle: 'No legislative act … contrary to the Constitution can be valid.' He explained why; because 'every act of a delegated authority, contrary to the tenor of the commission under which it is exercised, is void'.[45] This principle of judicial review granted the courts in America, particularly the Supreme Court, a power to declare whether an act of government was constitutional or not. Instead of legislative supremacy, this established the supremacy of the Constitution. No branch of the US government would be above the law.

This established that the will of the people, as expressed in the Constitution, is above the will of people's representatives. 'The courts were designed,' Hamilton wrote, 'to be an intermediate body between the people and the legislature … to keep the latter within the limits assigned to their authority.'

The concept of judicial review was essential in the structure of government the Americans adopted. In a system with multiple centres of power, and none supreme, conflicts could only be resolved by a code of law. Under this principle, that supreme code of law became the Constitution, and courts the impartial judge.

NON-PARTISAN GOVERNMENT AVOIDS TYRANNY OF THE MAJORITY

The US Constitution made no mention of political parties. The system of government it established was not one in which parties formed governments. In fact, a party, even if it had the majority in all its branches, couldn't take complete hold of government. A minority must be protected from the tyranny of the majority – and the many centres of power ensured that passing important laws was not possible without the minority's support. Broad coalitions needed to be built around issues, which took time. The Constitution placed acting according to the general will of the people, rather than that of one faction, over efficiency in government.

This principle of impeding majority rule was most crucial, for in its core the American system was majoritarian. Representatives were elected in single-member districts by the first-past-the-post system. Each election chose only one victor; the candidate receiving the most votes won regardless of the margin of victory. This quickly led to the development of a two-party system at the local level. But since the system required a national election to select the president, the parties also acquired a national character.

Political parties were useful, if only they could be engaged in improving governance rather than in constantly jockeying for power. For a party to hold a majority in the various centres of power in the American system, enough to overcome the checks and balances, at all levels of government, all at the same time, was nearly impossible. A divided control of government, where one party controlled the executive branch and the other the legislative, blocked either from running amok with power. A deadlocked government was a fair hazard if it prevented bad lows. A minority party could not be tyrannized, nor was it forced into playing the role of an opposition for every proposal, but instead it was given real powers to actively participate in creating policy and overseeing its implementation.

'It is of great importance in a republic,' Madison wrote, 'not only to guard the society against the oppression of its rulers, but to guard one part of the society against the injustice of the other part.' He thought it was 'evil' when in a society 'a stronger faction can readily unite and oppress the weaker'; and it was nothing but 'anarchy'.[46]

STABLE GOVERNMENT GIVES NATION CHARACTER AND CONFIDENCE

Another key principle of America's Constitution was to balance the principle of stability with the vital principle of liberty. It did so by providing that each branch depended upon the people, rather than on each other; and by giving officials unalterable fixed terms in office.

'Stability in government,' Madison wrote, 'is essential to national character … as well as to that repose and confidence in the minds of the people, which are among the chief blessings of civil society'.[47] Similarly, Hamilton concluded that without stable governments 'no great improvement or laudable enterprise can go forward which requires the auspices of a steady system of national policy'.[48]

The Constitution makers had noted that the chief cause of instability was that the entire government depended upon the legislative body. Political rivalries and infighting brought governments down, only to be replaced with similarly fragile governments.

So, to bring stability to their structure, the makers of the US Constitution turned once again to the people. The people selected each branch of their government, separately, and as far as possible, directly. Madison declared that 'the great fabric to be raised would be more stable and durable if it should rest on the solid foundation of the people themselves, than if it should stand merely on the pillars of the Legislatures'.[49] This served the dual purpose of providing stability with the requisite liberty. Since a branch didn't depend on any other for its survival, it paid attention to people's desires.

LESS BURDENSOME GOVERNMENT ENHANCES PEOPLE'S DRIVE

Another important balance that the US Constitution struck was with regard to money. It gave government legitimate powers to raise taxes but also ensured that governments didn't become overly onerous or intrusive. Hamilton noted that money was 'the vital principle of the body politic', but he also realized that 'the most productive system of finance will always be the least burdensome'.[50]

The provisions that kept governments off people's money and property gave the US Constitution its capitalist underpinnings (although the word 'capitalism' was yet to be coined). It protected the people's right to private property, and it limited government's tendency to be extravagant. It ensured that markets were kept free and that government's attempts to regulate businesses were checked.

'The diversity in the faculties of men, from which the rights of property originate,' Madison wrote, 'is not less an insuperable obstacle to a uniformity of interests.' But he urged that 'the protection of these faculties is the first object of government'. He advised against 'a rage … for an equal division of property'.[51] 'That is not a just government,' he said, 'nor is property secure under it, where arbitrary restrictions, exemptions, and monopolies deny to part of its citizens that free use of their faculties, and free choice of their occupations.'[52]

Acquiring and maintaining private property was an interest that gave people the drive. It needed to be nurtured rather than hindered. 'Life and liberty were generally said to be of more value than property,' said Gouverneur Morris in the Constitutional Convention, 'an accurate view of the matter would nevertheless prove that property was the main object of society.'[53] In the Bill of Rights, the American Constitution granted that no one shall be 'deprived of life, liberty, or property, without due process of law; nor shall private property be taken for public use without just compensation'. In 1868, the fourteenth amendment extended this restriction to the state governments.

Similarly, the US Constitution limited government's powers of taxation by enumerating them for the national government, and by giving coequal powers to the states. This allowed each government to levy taxes only for the areas of their respective responsibilities. However, the greatest check on government's extravagance was the separation of powers. By separating the executive and legislative powers, the Constitution was able to keep the spenders of money separate from the approvers. The presidency was given the powers to spend while the legislative bodies retained the powers over the purse. Jefferson wrote that 'a constant hold by the nation of the strings of the public purse is a salutary restraint'.[54]

The government was also meant to be non-intrusive in people's economic matters. The Constitution didn't give it any authority to establish or operate any business or service, except the post offices. The government was empowered only 'to regulate commerce with foreign nations, and among the several states', requiring that 'no preference shall be given by any regulation of commerce or revenue to the ports of one state over those of another'. Hamilton noted that 'the prosperity of commerce' was 'the most useful as well as the most productive source of national wealth'.[55] Thus, capitalism was at the core of the US system. 'The US Constitution provides for and secures a capitalist economy,' writes Bernard Siegan. 'The existence of capitalism requires that private enterprise and private markets be legally safeguarded and allowed to function freely. Government intervention in the economy is permissible, but only when very special circumstances demand it.'[56]

RESPONSIBLE GOVERNMENT GIVES PEOPLE DIRECT CONTROL

The US Constitution reinvented the principles of responsible government because the prevalent tenets of the British variety were either unacceptable or inapplicable. Under the American system each branch was directly accountable to the people. The separation of powers, and its checks and balances, made the arrangement practical and effective. The most important of these was the oversight authority given to the legislative bodies over the executive. This gave an

American government both a potent day-to-day check and a frequent electoral check, making it truly responsible to the people.

So, both representative branches were held directly accountable, but by different methods. 'In order to control the Legislative authority, you must divide it,' Wilson said. 'In order to control the Executive you must unite it. One man will be more responsible than three.'[57]

Since governance was mostly in the hands of the executive, the president was assigned the heaviest responsibility. 'If divided, the responsibility of the Executive is destroyed,' Wilson noted. Similarly, Jefferson wrote that it was crucial for a good executive to 'leave no screen of a council behind which to skulk from responsibility'.[58]

To further ensure that the executive branch remained responsible, it was given watchdogs. The separation of powers under the US Constitution allowed both the legislature and the judiciary to interfere with the powers of the president. Legislative bodies, with their powers of oversight, and the judiciary, with those of judicial review, could investigate or pass judgement on the functioning of any executive department. In turn, the legislature was kept responsible by giving the president the powers of veto.

In the more than 220 years since its adoption, the US Constitution has been amended only seventeen times. The separation of powers impedes unwise changes. A two-thirds majority of the entire legislative body, and three-fourths of the state legislatures, must approve each amendment. Legally, the president's role in the amendment process is meaningless.

Jefferson once wrote to a friend how he thought his nation's Constitution was 'unquestionably the wisest ever yet presented to men'.[59] It is hard to disagree.

NOTES

1   Padover, S.K. (1939), *Thomas Jefferson on Democracy*, New York: Mentor Book, New American Library, Hawthorn Books, p. 36.

2   Beeman, R. (2009), *Plain, Honest Men,* New York: Random House, p. 89.

3   Manuel, Paul C. and Anne M. Cammisa, (1999), *Checks & Balances? How a Parliamentary System Could Change American Politics,* Boulder, CO, USA: Westview Press/Perseus Books, p. 60.

4   Beeman, op. cit., p. 17.

5   Madison, J. (1787), *Vices of the Political System of the United States,* retrieved 2010, from TeachingAmericanHistory.org: http://teachingamericanhistory.org/library/document/vices-of-the-political-system/

6   Ibid.

7   Madison, J., Alexander Hamulton and John Jay, (1787-88), *The Federalist Papers 51,* retrieved February 13, 2011, from The Avalon Project, Yale Law School: http://avalon.law.yale.edu/subject_menus/fed.asp

8   Locke, J. (1952*),The Second Treatise of Government,* (Thomas P. Peardon, Ed.,) New York: The Liberal Arts Press, The Bobbs-Merrill Company, p. 13.

9   John Jay's address to the people of the state of New York on the subject of the Constitution, cited in Thach, C.C. (2007), *The Creation of the Presidency, 1775-1789,* Indianapolis, IN, USA: Amagi Books, Liberty Fund, p. 4.

10   Padover, op. cit., p. 5.

11   Ibid., p. 62.

12   To Jefferson, 10 October 1788, Madison, J. (1900), *The Writings of James Madison*, Vol. 5; retrieved, 2012, from The Online Library of Liberty: http://oll.libertyfund.org/title/1933.

13   Padover, op. cit., p. 36.

14   Madison, J. (1900). *The Writings of James Madison*, Vol. 3, retrieved, 2012, from The Online Library of Liberty: http://oll.libertyfund.org/title/1933

15   Notes on Virginia, Jefferson, T. (1904), *The Works of Thomas Jefferson*, Putnam's Sons (libertyfund.org)

16   Madison, J. (1787), *Vices of the Political System of the United States,* retrieved 2010, from TeachingAmericanHistory.org: http://teachingamericanhistory.org/library/document/vices-of-the-political-system/

17 Thach, op. cit., p. 23.

18 Padover, op. cit., p. 59.

19 Madison, J. et al, *Federalist 9.*

20 Ibid., *Federalist* 10.

21 Beeman, op. cit., p. 31.

22 Ibid., p. 82.

23 Quotes in this section are from Farrand, M. (1911), *The Records of the Federal Convention of 1787*, retrieved 2012, from The Online Library of Liberty: http://olllibertyfund.org/title/1057 and from Beeman, R. (2009), *Plain, Honest Men,* New York: Random House.

24 Thach, op. cit., pp. 70–76.

25 Farrand, Max (Ed.), The Records of the Federal Convention of 1787, Uale University Press, New Heaven, 1911. Vol. 2 pp. 168–170. Accessed on 17 May 2014 from http://oll.liberty fund.org/titles/1786#farrand_0554-02_188

26 Farrand, *Convention Records*, Vol. 2, pp. 33–35.

27 Ibid., pp. 56–57;Thach, op. cit., p. 86.

28 Ibid., op. cit., p. 69.

29 Thach, op. cit., p. 116.

30 Beeman, op. cit., p. 299.

31 Ibid., Preface.

32 To John Taylor, 1814, Wilson, W. (1973), *Congressional Government*, Cleveland, OH, USA: The World Publishing Company, p. 32.

33 Madison, J. et al, *Federalist 41.*

34 *Thach,* op. cit., p. 150.

35 Farrand, op. cit., Vol. 1, p. 288.

36 Padover, op. cit., p. 39.

37 Ibid., p. 62.

38 Madison, J. et al, *Federalist 37.*

39 Padover, op. cit., p. 161.

40 Goldwin, Robert. A. and Art Kaufman (eds) (1986), *Separation of Powers: Does It Still Work?*, Washington DC, USA: American Enterprise Institute for Public Policy Research, p. 141.

41 Ibid., p. 143.

42   Thach, op. cit., p. 151.

43   Wilson, W. (1973), *Congressional Government*, Cleveland, OH, USA: The World Publishing Company, p. 68.

44   Madison, J. et al, *Federalist 10.*

45   Ibid., *Federalist 78.*

46   Ibid., *Federalist 51.*

47   Ibid., *Federalist 37.*

48   Ibid., *Federalist 62.*

49   Farrand, op. cit. Vol. 1.

50   Madison, *Federalist 35.*

51   Ibid., *Federalist 10.*

52   Madison, J. (1900), 'Property' in National Gazette, 1792, *The Writings of James Madison*, retrieved 2012, from The Online Library of Liberty: http://oll.libertyfund.org/title/1933

53   Goldwin, Robert. A. and William A. Schambra, (eds) (1981*), How Capitalistic is the Constitution?*, Washington DC: American Enterprise Institute for Public Policy Research, p. 108.

54   Padover, op. cit., p. 75.

55   Madison, J. et al, *Federalist 12.*

56   Siegan, B. (1981). 'The Constitution and the Protection of Capitalism', in Goldwin, Robert. A. and William A. Schambra, (eds) op. cit., p. 107.

57   Farrand, op. cit., Vol. 1.

58   Padover, op. cit., p. 35.

59   To Humphreys, 1789, Padover, op. cit., p. 66.

10

A Different Approach to Government

In its structure as well as functioning, the American presidential system is starkly different from the British parliamentary variety. This is to be expected, for their fundamental principles are poles apart.

However, there are some noteworthy similarities. Both systems are based on the principles of representative democracy and rule of law. Governments under both are run by people's representatives elected through open and fair elections. The basic electoral system is the same: a single representative is selected from each constituency, the one who goes 'first past the post'. The American system is also based on the traditions of British common law, that there is a higher law against which legislative actions should be measured. In America, the Constitution became that higher standard. Also, the rich British constitutional heritage of protecting people's freedoms, enshrined in their Magna Carta and Bill of Rights, inspired the Americans to add similar protections in their Constitution.

But this is where the similarities end. The Americans had to invent an entirely different system because they purposefully rejected the British.

WHY AMERICANS REJECTED THE BRITISH PARLIAMENTARY SYSTEM

At the heart of the matter behind the American rejection of the British system was that they saw government as a servant of the people, not as their guardian. They wanted a limited government that only performed functions that were suitable and specifically delegated. In their 1999 book *Checks and Balances*, Paul C. Manuel and Anne M. Cammisa described the two mindsets: 'A core difference between the British and American system may be identified in their views of the purpose of government. Britain relies on a flexible legislative body to respond to societal needs; the United States advocates limiting government to guarantee individual freedoms and avoid tyranny.'[1]

The first British feature that the Americans discarded was the notion of legislative supremacy. They wanted to ensure that in their system no power was supreme. Even the presidency, painstakingly developed as a centre of power, was not to be an uppermost sovereign. Madison described exactly why: 'The accumulation of all powers, legislative, executive, and judiciary, in the same hands ... may justly be pronounced the very definition of tyranny.'[2]

Similarly, they rejected outright the concept of monarchy. 'Many of the fathers of the Constitution ... rejected the English example in its entirety,' wrote Klaus Von Beyme in *America as a Model*, 'since they did not believe that a "republican" imitation of England's monarchist constitution was possible.'[3] As a consequence 'the British system was abandoned for the representative chief magistrate', wrote Thach. 'The [American] framers ... had a new theory of executive responsibility, based on unity, integration, choice by, and complete responsibility to, the people.'[4]

Unequivocal also was the American rejection of the British concept of a council of ministers. They were against commingling the executive with legislative bodies. Then there was the matter of corruption – the British ministerial form had a propensity to be corrupt. No doubt, there were other reasons – instability, legislative intrigue, executive weakness. But the venality of the legislators in England was well known. The Americans also decided against a system that gave power to political parties in order to avoid concentration of powers.

Above all, the Americans rejected the British notion of majority rule. The form of government Americans chose, therefore, was quite the opposite of the British; it gave minority views real power. As Beyme wrote, 'The British party system ... includes such a strong inclination towards majoritization that it would be barely compatible with the American Constitution and the deep concern to protect minority interests.'[5]

IMPACT OF WASHINGTON IN AVOIDING PARLIAMENTARY SYSTEM

America's adoption of a groundbreaking new system, was also serendipitous. Had the American leaders not had among them one man so far beyond reproach and as unquestionably presidential as George Washington, the framers of the US Constitution would most likely have floundered. Americans could imagine in Washington a president who would make the new Constitution work.

'The example of Washington was host in itself,' wrote Thach. 'Energy, probity, disinterestedness, and a magnificent tactfulness in avoiding even the semblance of advancing his personal interests are written large on almost every one of his official acts ... Washington afforded the country an example of the national leader par excellence.'[6]

During the debate on whether the executive should be one person or many, Edmund Randolph, the governor of Virginia, worried about handing all executive power to one man. 'Randolph's remarks about the dangers of "executive tyranny" may well have been more vehement had Washington not been present,' writes Beeman in his superb account of the making of America's Constitution. 'Without Washington in the Assembly ... America might well have a parliamentary, and not a presidential, system of government,' he wrote.[7]

TWO REAL LEVELS, THREE DISTINCT DEPARTMENTS

While the principal aim of the British system was to empower the people's representatives, the main purpose of the American system was to bring good governance.

For good governance, it was necessary to have local governments. Naturally, it was essential that they had some degree of sovereignty. To sustain a system of many sovereign governments, it was necessary that there be a strong national government. And for the national government to be strong, it was indispensable that it had a nationally elected leader. Finally, for a strong government to be safe, it was necessary to have separation of powers. The coming together of all these necessities mothered the invention of the presidential system.

TWO GOVERNMENTS: FEDERAL AND STATE

America's Constitution gave state governments significant powers, by creating a hybrid system. (See chart at the end of the section.) It combined features of a confederation, where member states held sovereignty, with those of a unitary system, where one Central government was given the entire sovereignty.

However, in its foundation the US Constitution was solidly federal – its most fundamental point of variance from the British system. To those who worried that the union would fall apart or become a mere consolidation of states, Madison pointed to a litany of features. He reminded the people that the Constitution was ratified by state governments. And that two out of the three branches of government (the presidency and the council of states) were to be elected by them as well. And that state governments were given genuine powers. Also, the Constitution provided no provision for cessation. 'The proposed Constitution,' he wrote, 'is, in strictness, neither a national nor a federal Constitution, but a composition of both. In its foundation it is federal, not national; in the sources from which the ordinary powers of the government are drawn, it is partly federal and partly national; in the operation of these powers, it is national, not federal.'[8]

State governments were given significant authority in the areas of education, public health and criminal justice. Even more consequentially, the state governments determined the powers and the organization of local, city and county governments. As for the powers given to the national government, Madison had to justify each one of them. He argued they were necessary for America's 'security against foreign danger'; or for 'regulation of the intercourse with foreign nations'; or for 'maintenance of harmony ... among the States'; and so on. He then described the whole approach:

The powers delegated by the proposed Constitution to the federal government are few and defined. Those which are to remain in the State governments are numerous and indefinite. The former will be exercised principally on external objects, as war, peace, negotiation, and foreign commerce … The powers reserved to the several States will extend to all the objects which, in the ordinary course of affairs, concern the lives, liberties, and properties of the people, and the internal order, improvement, and prosperity of the State. The operations of the federal government will be most extensive and important in times of war and danger; those of the State governments, in times of peace and security.[9]

The key to making this dual sovereignty work was that residual powers were left with the states. However, the framers left a door open for the national government to assume power over states when necessary. The Constitution allowed Congress 'to make all Laws which shall be necessary and proper for carrying into Execution the foregoing Powers'. So, when conflict arose between the national and state governments, the Supreme Court ruled that the national government had certain implied powers for ends consistent with 'the letter and spirit of the Constitution'.

The glue that kept the national and state governments together was provided by the principle of national supremacy. America's Constitution made the Constitution and the laws passed under it the 'supreme Law of the Land'. Madison feared that without a principle that kept disagreements among member states from erupting, they might create a 'monster' in which 'the head was under the control of its member parts'.

The federal structure had a deeply profound role in making American government safe. It allowed sects to be active locally but without forming nationwide majorities. This was especially significant for religious freedom.

Powers Granted by the American Constitution

To the national government	To both national and state governments	To the state governments
• To 'lay and collect taxes, duties imposts, and excises'	• To levy and collect taxes	• To conduct elections
• To regulate interstate and foreign commerce	• To borrow money	• To establish local governments
• To borrow and coin money	• To charter banks and corporations	• To regulate commerce within the state
• To declare war	• To make and enforce laws	• To protect public health, safety and morals
• To raise and support an army	• To establish courts	• To ratify amendments to the Constitution
• To maintain a navy	• To take property for public purposes	• And all other powers not delegated to the national government nor denied to the states
• To provide for a militia		
• To govern territories and national property		
• To define and punish piracies and other high-sea felonies		
• To establish post offices and roads		
• To grant patents and copyrights		
• To set standards of weights and measures		
• To 'make all laws necessary and proper to carry out the foregoing powers'		

Powers Denied by the American Constitution

To the national government	To both national and state governments	To the state governments
• To tax commerce within a state	• To grant titles of nobility	• To tax imports and exports
• To give preference to one state over another in matters of commerce	• To tax exports	• To coin money
• To change state boundaries without state permission	• To permit slavery	• To make treaties
• To violate the Bill of Rights	• To deny citizens the right to vote because of race, colour, sex	• To wage war
		• To deny due process and equal protection of the laws

Adapted from American Government by Gitelson, Dudley and Dubnick, Eighth Edition, 2008, page 41

THREE COORDINATED DEPARTMENTS

America's Constitution established three distinct departments at the national level. Congress, the legislative branch, was given the power to make laws; the president, the responsibility to execute or enforce those laws; and the judiciary, the Supreme Court, was given the task of settling disputes arising from the application of laws. The same structure was replicated in each state government as well.

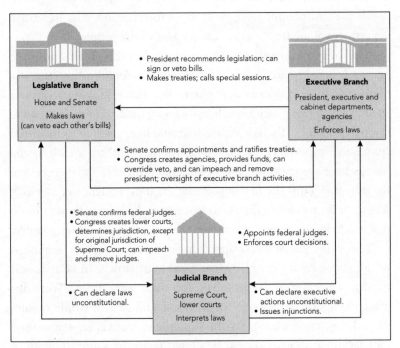

Separation of Powers and Checks and Balances (Adapted from *American Government*, Gitelson et al., [2008], Boston, MA, USA: Houghton Mifflin Company, p. 58.)

The beauty of the US system was not in how these departments were separated but in how they were blended (see diagram above). Following Madison's principle, each was given some 'constitutional control over the others'. A complete separation of the three departments would be about as counterproductive as was a complete unification. If the purpose was to ensure a safe government, simply separating the departments was unlikely to work unless each was empowered to watch over the others.

In short, the purpose of the blending was to create watchdogs. But devising methods by which each branch could control the others, without being overpowering, was a challenge. The branch that worried the Americans the most was legislative. Madison thought that legislative usurpations were most dangerous because 'the legislative department alone has access to the pockets of the people'.[10]

The only practical way to protect a branch from complete encroachment was to ensure its independence. And the only sure way of securing independence was to give each an inherent ability to protect itself. To empower each branch in this way, Madison proclaimed the cardinal principle: 'Each department should have a will of its own; and consequently should be so constituted that the members of each should have as little agency as possible in the appointment of the members of the others.'[11] Thus the key to securing the independence of a branch was to make its chief officials independent. And the only way to do that was to let the people select them directly, or as directly as possible.

This principle of direct appointment by the people was applied to the very extent possible. Most notable of which, of course, was the direct election of the president. But there were limits. 'Were this principle rigorously adhered to,' Madison admitted, 'it would require that all the appointments for the supreme executive, legislative, and judiciary magistracies should be drawn from the same fountain of authority, the people, through channels having no communication whatever with one another.' He argued that it was justifiable to have some deviations from the principle, particularly in the case of the judiciary, as this branch required 'peculiar qualifications' in its members. Since judges were appointed for life, Madison believed the disadvantages of their appointment by other departments would soon disappear.

However, complete independence of branches, although necessary, was also dangerous. Three disparate branches, each directly accountable to the people, had no impetus to work together as a whole. A branch could continually encroach upon the others without any fear, or function in isolation without any concern. 'A dependence on the people is, no doubt, the primary control on the government,' Madison noted, 'but experience has taught mankind the necessity of auxiliary precautions.'

A 'DEFECT' IN THE SYSTEM

To ensure that the three branches of their government worked together as a cohesive unit, the Americans took a remarkable step. They introduced a defect in their system. 'The defect of better motives', as Madison called it, was a deliberate introduction of conflict in the system with the purpose of improving the aims and methods of each branch.

Every branch was given some authority to incite or ruffle the others. Defending this system of antagonism by design, Madison wrote: 'This policy of supplying, by opposite and rival interests, the defect of better motives, might be traced through the whole system of human affairs … We see it particularly displayed in all the subordinate distributions of power, where the constant aim is to divide and arrange the several offices in such a manner as that each may be a check on the other'.

The principal purpose of these checks and balances was to create conflict when the plans were poor, but unity when they had improved. As such, each representative branch was given the authority to engage proactively in improving other branches' actions. These powers allowed a branch to not just obstruct, but to initiate rival proposals. Proactive opposition within government was possible only when the system encouraged rivalries. 'Ambition must be made to counteract ambition,' Madison noted as he explained why it was necessary to create competition among the various branches.

Accordingly, each branch was given powers that it didn't normally possess for its assigned function, but were additional authorities by which a branch could oppose or question the others. Also, each representative was personally empowered. Not only could he stand in opposition to a proposed plan, he could also come up with an alternative.

'But it is not possible to give to each department an equal power of self-defence,' Madison said. He had a different remedy for each representative branch. 'In republican government, the legislative authority necessarily predominates. The remedy for this inconveniency is to divide the legislature into different branches.' For the executive, Madison wrote: 'As the weight of the legislative authority requires that it should be thus divided, the weakness of the executive may require, on the other hand, that it should be fortified.'[12]

A LEGISLATURE WITH TWO EQUALLY POWERFUL HOUSES

America's legislative body, the United States Congress, had two equally powerful chambers, the House of Representatives and the Senate. Mainly, this was done to divide powers. But the Senate was also essential for a truly federal system. It provided equal representation to each state.

The House of Representatives was designed to be the voice of current public opinion, while the Senate was to curb the radical tendencies and the passions of the day. In a famous description of the purpose of the Senate, when Jefferson questioned the need for a bicameral legislature, Washington replied, 'Why do you pour that coffee into your saucer?' 'To cool it,' responded Jefferson. 'Even so,' said Washington, 'we pour legislation into the senatorial saucer to cool it.'[13]

Accordingly, each chamber drew representation from different elements of the American society. The House was larger, its members faced frequent popular elections, and they represented their constituency in a fixed proportion to its population. The senators on the other hand, served longer terms, were appointed by their state legislatures, and represented the citizens of their states in equal numbers – two senators per state. In 1913, the Americans decided that senators should also be elected by popular elections rather than by their state legislatures.

Congress was an assembly of equals. Each representative or senator had equal legitimacy. There were no aristocratic or hereditary or nominated members. Each member was equally authorized to introduce legislation. For a bill to become law it had to pass in identical form in both the House and the Senate. Both chambers were elected for a fixed term. Neither legislative body could pick its own timing to go to polls. Madison thought the British practice of allowing the period of a legislature to be altered by the 'ordinary power of the government' was 'dangerous'.

As the principal indicator of the people's will, the House was frequently refreshed. Every two years the entire House of Representatives had to go to polls. Madison acknowledged that while the Americans thought that 'where annual elections end, tyranny begins', a two-year term was necessary for a representative to become a 'competent legislator'.[14] He argued that a member needed more experience on the job than just a year.

The Senate was a different matter altogether. It became much more than just a typical second chamber with powers of review over legislation. The Americans utilized this institution in so many creative ways that it became crucial to the basic structure of their Constitution. First, by giving it powers of introducing and passing legislation equal to the House, they ensured that a majority in the House didn't have carte blanche. Second, the Senate's usefulness went beyond just stopping a majority in the House from running amok, it also improved the quality of the laws passed. The Senate was purposefully designed to take a more mature and deliberate view of the laws than the House. Third, the edifice of American federalism was built upon the Senate acting as the assembly in which the states had equal representation. This was a radical new way of utilizing the second chamber of a nation's legislature to balance the powers between the national and local governments. Fourth, the Senate was given a vital role in balancing executive powers. It was given powers of oversight over the executive: confirming the appointments of officials nominated by the president and ratifying treaties. Fifth, the Senate was also given a judicial role. It confirmed the justices appointed to the Supreme Court; and it shared along with the House the power of impeachment of officials, including a judge or a president. Lastly, the Senate was also given the role of providing stability.

Senators were expected to have 'greater extent of information' and 'stability of character'. Hence they were required to be older than the members of the House (thirty years as compared to twenty-five), and more entrenched in the American way (a citizen for nine years compared to seven). Since the requisite superior competence and character could 'never be sufficiently possessed by a numerous and changeable body', as Madison noted, the Senate was smaller (two senators for each state; now a total of 100), and had greater stability. A higher degree of permanency was accomplished in two ways. The senators were given a longer term in office (six years as compared to two for the House), and only a third of the senators were refreshed every two years.

The Senate was the true balancing force in the American system. The other balancing techniques – veto power of the executive, confirmation power of the legislative, legislature's power of impeachment, etc. – are better characterized as checks rather than balances.

The balancing of the legislative body was extremely important because Congress actually made laws. The only role the executive could play in lawmaking was to respond to congressional inquiries, or help formulate public opinion. The president was empowered to veto a bill passed by Congress but it was only a conditional veto. The Congress could override by passing the law again by a two-thirds majority.

Congress's most powerful authority was, however, not lawmaking, it was oversight. Legislative oversight in the American system, unlike the British, had real teeth. Not only could Congress starve the executive branch of funds, it could also subpoena public officials. This added weight to the questions that the members of Congress asked executive officials. Congress could require an executive officer to prepare periodic and detailed reports about any aspect of his department. Through its control of appropriations, Congress could require the executive branch to come back again and again to justify its requests for funds. This wasn't all. Congress was also authorized to conduct special investigations. Either chamber of the US Congress could compel a government official or even a private citizen to give testimony or provide evidence. Members of Congress were prohibited from being appointed by any other branch, and vice versa.

THE PRESIDENT — AN EXECUTIVE FOR THE ENTIRE NATION

The American presidency was designed as a symbol of government, as well as an embodiment of the nation. A president was both the head of state and the head of government. When he spoke, he spoke for the entire nation.

The term 'representative government' was thus given a new meaning. Since both Congress and the president were directly elected, both represented the people equally. It was Wilson who pointed out that neither was to be trusted alone. 'The prejudices against the Executive,' he said, 'resulted from a misapplication of the adage that the Parliament was the palladium of liberty ... Where the Executive was really formidable, King and Tyrant were naturally associated ... not legislature and tyranny. But where the Executive was not formidable, the two last were properly associated,' he noted.[15]

First and foremost, the Americans saw in their presidency a chance to find exceptional leaders through a nationwide election. Hamilton noted, that 'the process of election affords a moral certainty, that the office of President will never fall to the lot of any man who is not in an eminent degree endowed ... Talents for low intrigue, and the little arts of popularity, may alone suffice to elevate a man to the first honors in a single State,' he said, 'but it will require other talents, and a different kind of merit, to establish him in the esteem and confidence of the whole Union.'[16]

The presidency was the US system's most important office. 'Energy in the Executive is a leading character in the definition of good government,' Hamilton wrote. Accordingly, the presidency was designed to act robustly and vigorously. 'A feeble Executive implies a feeble execution of the government,' Hamilton declared, 'and a government ill executed, whatever it may be in theory, must be, in practice, a bad government.'[17]

'Unity', the vesting of all executive power in a single individual, had the greatest impact on an executive's energy. 'That unity is conducive to energy will not be disputed,' Hamilton argued. 'Decision, activity, secrecy and despatch will generally characterize the proceedings of one man in a much more eminent degree than the proceedings of any greater number.'

An executive council was the worst form of an executive. Of the two ways of destroying executive's unity – vesting it in more than one, and vesting it ostensibly in one – the latter received Hamilton's vitriol the most. 'One of the weightiest objections to a plurality in the Executive is that it tends to conceal faults and destroy responsibility,' he said. Accordingly, the US Constitution did not provide for a Cabinet or a council of advisors. The so-called Cabinet was created by President Washington, when he frequently met his attorney general and his secretaries of state, treasury, and war. But since the Cabinet was not a creature of the Constitution, the president remained solely responsible.

As for duration, America's Constitution provided the president with a fixed term of four years. He could be removed only on 'impeachment for, and conviction of, treason, bribery, or other high crimes and misdemeanors'. The power of impeachment was granted to Congress but was divided between the two chambers. It was very difficult to remove a president, and for good reason. 'It is certainly desirable,' Hamilton noted, 'that the Executive should be in a situation to dare to act his own opinion with vigor and decision.'[18]

In terms of presidential powers, the power of veto was obviously one of the most important. There were two motives, according to Hamilton, 'to enable him to defend himself', and 'to increase the chances ... against the passing of bad laws, through haste, inadvertence, or design'. To the objection that a single man could not be presumed to be more virtuous than the entire legislative body, Hamilton noted that 'the propriety of the thing does not turn upon the supposition of superior wisdom or virtue in the Executive, but upon the supposition that the legislature will not be infallible'. He argued that 'the injury which may possibly be done by defeating a few good laws will be amply compensated by the advantage of preventing a number of bad ones'.

Other than the power of veto, the Constitution gave the president very little role in the making of laws. He was given four rather narrow legislative duties: to convene both or either house in special session; to adjourn Congress if the two houses cannot agree on adjournment; to give Congress information from time to time; and to recommend measures that 'he shall judge necessary and expedient'.

But in appointing government officials, the president was given significant powers. The US Constitution provided that the president 'shall nominate, and by and with the advice and consent of the Senate, shall appoint ambassadors, other public ministers and consuls, judges of the Supreme Court, and all other officers of the United States'. The president's power to nominate the justices of the Supreme Court was profoundly meaningful. Under this authority, the president proposed a candidate to the Senate and if a majority of the Senate approved, the nominee was appointed a justice. Similar procedure was followed in appointing the judges of all federal courts. This allowed the two representative branches to give expression to people's wishes in the nation's judiciary.

The president was also given broad sweeping powers in the area of foreign affairs. Here the president was made the central figure. The US Constitution declared that 'the President shall be commander in chief of the army and navy of the United States'. However, this was no carte blanche. The power to declare war was specifically assigned to Congress; the president was to command troops once Congress decided to wage war. If necessary, the president could commit troops to action without asking Congress first, but since the funding was controlled by Congress, he had to seek its sanction sooner or later. Similarly, the president was authorized to make treaties, but the Senate was given the power to ratify.

As for support, Congress had no role in fixing the president's emoluments. The Constitution provided that he was to receive compensation 'which shall neither be increased or diminished during the period for which he shall have been elected'. Hamilton asked, 'To what purpose separate the executive or the judiciary from the legislative, if both ... are so constituted as to be at the absolute devotion of the legislative?'[19]

US JUDICIARY — INDEPENDENT, DECENTRALIZED, ACCOUNTABLE

America's founding fathers took the design of the US judiciary very seriously because they knew that the entire system depended upon it. 'The dignity and stability of government in all its branches, the morals of the people, and every blessing of society, depend so much upon an upright and skilful administration of justice,' wrote Jefferson. He described the core principle behind the design: 'The judicial power ought to be distinct from both the legislative and executive, and independent upon both, so that it may be a check upon both, as both should be checks upon that.'[20]

The Constitution established a judiciary completely distinct from the presidency and Congress. Article III declared: 'The judicial power of the United States shall be vested in one Supreme Court and in such inferior courts as the Congress may from time to time ordain and establish.' Congress was given this authority to set up lower courts so that the national and state governments could establish a coordinated system of justice. Each state government thus continued to have its own judiciary. This established a decentralized system in which all local disputes were handled in local courts under the state judiciary.

Since guarding against legislative overreach was the judiciary's principal role, the national legislative body was given no judicial powers. The Americans set out to establish the concept of constitutional supremacy that no branch of government could supersede. Hamilton made it explicit: 'Where the will of the legislature, declared in its statutes, stands in opposition to that of the people, declared in the Constitution, the judges ought to be governed by the latter rather than the former.'[21]

To secure the independence of the judiciary was difficult, however, because it was the weakest of the three branches of government. It had 'no influence over either the sword or the purse,' Hamilton noted.

A genuinely independent judiciary was possible only when the judges were free. And the only way to ensure judges' freedom was to make their appointment free from undue control. As to who was best at appointing judges, Hamilton noted the difficulty: 'If the power of making them was committed either to the Executive or legislature, there would be danger of an improper complaisance,' he noted. '... If to both, there would be an unwillingness to hazard the displeasure of either; if to the people ... there would be too great a disposition to consult popularity.' The makers of the American Constitution decided to divide the power of appointing judges between the president and the Senate. The president nominated, and the Senate approved. The state governments, however, continued to appoint judges in a variety of ways. Some followed the same procedure, by dividing authority between the executive and the legislature. Others allowed the legislature to make appointments, or utilized a merit system. Some states even allowed people to appoint judges through direct elections.

To further ensure judiciary's independence, the US Constitution declared that 'the judges, both of the Supreme and inferior courts, shall hold their offices during good behavior'. It also provided that the judges' compensation could not be diminished by the legislature.

The natural consequence of a truly independent judiciary, empowered by the concept of constitutional supremacy, was the power of judicial review. The courts in America, in particular the Supreme Court, could declare an act of government constitutional or unconstitutional. This authority was not specifically granted by the Constitution. It evolved as a corollary of the presidential system and federalism, since it was possible in this system that different branches or governments could have conflicts. The Supreme Court of America became the ultimate arbiter of constitutional disputes. The court's decision could be changed only by an amendment to the Constitution or by its own reversal.

America's judiciary was thus made accountable by design. It was established as a genuinely independent institution. No power controlled it exclusively, for it had two political masters. It expressed the general will of the people because both representative branches had a say in appointing judges. It was decentralized, local and flexible because each state's laws and judicial systems were vastly more responsive to people's needs than a unitary system could ever be.

NOTES

1   Manuel, Paul C. and Anne M. Cammisa, (1999). *Checks & Balances? How a Parliamentary System Could Change American Politics,* Boulder, CO, USA: Westview Press/Perseus Books, p. 72.

2   Madison, J., Alexander Hamilton and John Jay, (1787–88), *The Federalist Papers*, 47, retrieved 13 February 2011, from The Avalon Project, Yale Law School: http://avalon.law.yale.edu/subject_menus/fed.asp

3   Beyme, K. V. (1987), *America as a Model,* New York: St. Martin's Press, p. 36.

4   Thach, C. C. (2007), *The Creation of the Presidency, 1775-1789,* Indianapolis, IN, USA: Amagi Books, Liberty Fund, p. 159.

5   Beyme, op. cit., p. 102.

6   Thach, op. cit., p. 55.

7   Beeman, R. (2009), *Plain, Honest Men,* New York: Random House, p. 128.
8   Madison, J. et al, *Federalist 39.*
9   Ibid., *Federalist 45.*
10   Ibid., *48.*
11   Ibid., *51.*
12   Ibid.
13   Gitelson, Alan R., Robert L. Dudley and Melvin J. Dubnick, (2008), *American Government,* Boston, MA, USA: Houghton Mifflin Company, p. 279.
14   Madison, J. et al, *Federalist 53.*
15   Farrand, op. cit., Vol. 2, p. 300.
16   Madison, J. et al, *Federalist 68.*
17   Ibid., *70.*
18   Ibid., *71.*
19   Ibid.
20   Padover, op. cit., p. 52.
21   Madison, J. et al, *Federalist 78.*

11

Towards Better Governance

There is no denying that India needs a strong government. But what exactly does a 'strong' government mean? An Indian government may be autocratic, but when it comes to governance, it is feeble. The strength of a government doesn't flow from its hoarding of powers, but from how well it exercises them, and whether it has willing participants.

The truth is that neither of the two justifications for India's parliamentary system – better efficiency and greater responsibility of government – was really valid. These arguments were simply guises for establishing a centralized and unfettered government (Chapters 3 and 4). Reason and history has shown that governments are more efficient when they have a division of labour, and they are more responsible when they can be stopped from acting alone. Neither trait exists in the Indian system. Instead of dividing functions, it fuses all powers into one institution and thus becomes inefficient and ineffective. And since it has no overseeing institutions to allow or disallow government's actions, it behaves irresponsibly.

The US government is much more robust. Not just because it is more efficient and responsible, but because, by design, it is focused on being effective. The US Constitution was built on the understanding that gaining efficiency at the expense of effectiveness was not a smart trade-off, especially when it makes government unsafe. A government quick to respond is not necessarily a good government. A deliberated response to social needs, with wide support of the people behind it, makes for better governance.

Here is a look at what India needs, and why a US-type system will deliver immensely superior governance, and a much healthier polity in this nation.

INDIA NEEDS MORE RELIANCE ON LOCAL GOVERNANCE

As a large and diverse nation, India needs local governments that are sensitive to its diversity, and that are accountable. It also needs a strong national government that can keep the union strong and together. The US system is known to deliver both.

It was most significant that America's Constitution was adopted only after it was ratified by the states. The Indians didn't see the need for this step. This different view of federalism set the two nations on entirely different paths of governance. India made the wrong choice. Not only because it was impossible to enforce accountability on a government that was far away but also because it denied the national government real strength, which could only come when participation was willing, not forced. As a result, India ended up with pseudo-federalism.

The sovereignty granted to state governments under the American system delivers much better governance, because it makes them accountable. The state governments in the United States of America are authorized to have their own constitution. They are completely independent of the Centre. To the Central government the US system assigns only a limited role. It grants only those powers to the Centre which are necessary for the Union to act as such; most consequentially, the residuary powers are specifically granted to the states.

The Indian system does the opposite. It grants limited powers to the states, but gives the Centre a wide field and an extraordinary leeway. The Seventh Schedule of India's Constitution which divides powers, assigns more than 140 specific powers to the Centre. In addition, the Centre also receives all residuary powers (under Article 248 and Entry 91 of List I). And, when powers conflict, the Central government gets supremacy (under Article 254). As if this wasn't enough, Central governments have continually encroached powers. One such example was in the area of primary education. The Constitution was amended to take powers in this area away from the exclusive control of the states. Similarly, the Centre found ways around the states' absolute power over the police. Even in the economic structure, successive governments brought more and more control to the Centre. The Finance Commission, a constitutional body set up for the purpose of dealing with the distribution of Central revenues, was bypassed. Instead, a statutory body, the Planning Commission, was placed directly under the control of Central government. All this has led to cries for genuine federalism, and in many cases, to violent protests and insurgencies (Chapter 8).

The decentralized structure of US federalism is advantageous not just in improving local governance, but also in the conduct of elections. The exclusive power to conduct elections allows each state to have its own voting criteria. In America, it did slow down the extension of franchise to many groups – to black Americans and women, for instance – but it did create a more responsive system. One of its main benefits is that political parties are regulated at the state level. They get organized from the bottom up; from county committees to the state federation, and then to the national federation. Each state's party organization is separate. And each is led by a committee of elected officials. The main purpose of these state level parties is to recruit candidates as the party's official nominees for every local, state or national election. This makes for a much healthier polity, because local candidates have a chance to run in primaries and get selected based on their competence and platform. People select candidates for elections, not a party high command.

In such a system, people look to their local and state governments first. They expect them to deal with local issues – education, roads, transport, health, safety, environment, justice, public utilities, etc. – and they hold them accountable. The structure of government and the mode of elections make it all possible. Every government official – from the governor down to the mayor, to the city legislative councilman – is elected directly by the people.

INDIA NEEDS LESS BURDENSOME GOVERNMENT

The creativity, initiative and drive of the Indian people are being suppressed by a system that is burdensome and intrusive. In India, there are no limits to government's authority. As a result, it has become people's guardian instead of their servant. The US system, on the other hand, is built on the principle of limited government; on Henry David Thoreau's famous belief 'that government is best which governs least'.[1] The two Constitutions reflect this too: while the American seeks to 'promote' general welfare, the Indian wants to 'secure' equality, justice, liberty, etc.

The US Constitution grants only nineteen specific powers to the federal government. This leads to a vigorous debate before a new law is passed on whether government is authorized to have a role. This debate describes the single biggest difference between America's two main political parties, the Republican and the Democratic. While the members of the former believe in small government, those of the latter push for more government programmes. Normally, a balance is struck by the two after a healthy give-and-take. The size of the American government is also limited by the Supreme Court's power of judicial review. It can declare a governmental action or a law unconstitutional if it delves in areas not authorized under the Constitution. 'A major advantage of presidential government is said to be that separation of powers means limited government – an indispensable protection of individual liberty against government "tyranny",' wrote Arend Lijphart, the editor of *Parliamentary Versus Presidential Government*.[2]

Limiting government doesn't just make it less oppressive but also less taxing. Since all those who covet power in a democracy want to appear altruistic, populist urges are rampant. Whenever a government can stay in power by doling out public funds, and there is no one to stop it, it taxes and spends. Invariably, this lands every nation into fiscal trouble.

The US system protects against populist urges by the simple device of restricting the majority from acting alone. When government attempts to take on a new role, even when it is constitutionally authorized, a debate ensues. The president cannot spend without authorization from Congress, and the Congress cannot spend directly. All sides – lawmakers and law enforcers, Democrats and Republicans, federal and state officials, government departments and private enterprises, government and civil society leaders, state and church – fight it out in a very public manner.

Even Bagehot, the biggest proponent of the parliamentary form, acknowledged the American system's superior ability to resist populist urges. In view of America's ability to maintain budget surpluses over many years during the 1800s, Bagehot commented: 'No one who knows anything of the working of parliamentary government will for a moment imagine that any parliament would have allowed any executive to keep a surplus of this magnitude.'[3]

The US system gives people the ability to question government's populist programmes. One of the reasons Ronald Reagan became one of America's most popular presidents was that he spoke against big government. Coming to power as he did in the midst of a long period of economic stagnation, he declared that 'government is not the solution to our problem … government *is* the problem'.[4] 'Government is like a baby,' he once said, 'an alimentary canal with a big appetite at one end and no responsibility at the other.'[5]

When Hamilton said that 'the most productive system of finance will always be the least burdensome', he described a truism. Private enterprise thrives when governments are not burdensome, through licensing, regulation, or taxes.

By contrast, the big government in India has created an inefficient public sector, and made India famous for things like 'licence raj' and 'crony capitalism'. Governments in India freely engage in business activities and in over-regulating private enterprise.

America has become famous as a 'land of opportunity' because her system aims at creating equality of opportunity, instead of equality of wealth. By limiting the role of government it allows private enterprise and individual effort to flourish based on merit.

INDIA MUST RELY ON INSTITUTIONS

The Indian system relies on elections to improve governance. But elections don't make governments better, institutions do. Electing a new government without fixing government institutions only replaces one rotten government with another.

The parliamentary system has only one institution, the parliament. As such, internal checks on government are impossible, whereas that is the entire basis of the presidential system. 'Proponents of the parliamentary system ... rely on an *electoral check*, rather than on *institutional checks*, to guarantee against abuses of power,' writes Professor James Ceaser in *In Defence of Separation of Powers*.[6]

Relying exclusively on an electoral check, especially when elections are scheduled after a long gap of five years, is no check at all. As far as the threat of an early election is concerned, that really works only when there are just two parties in Parliament. Even when the number gets up to three, the parliamentary system's ability to control a government fails (Chapter 2). The fact is that instead of curbing poor governance, the Indian system's so-called electoral check makes it worse.

In contrast, the US system keeps governments on their toes by relying on both electoral and institutional checks. Not only are there many more elections, held much more frequently, but it has institutions checking other institutions on a daily basis. When a system only has an electoral check, you can throw a government out. But that doesn't fix problems or make the most of opportunities. That only happens when the institutions are empowered to stop an action or come forward with better plans.

The US system's institutions are simple and easy to understand. They have clear lines of control which fit neatly into the three branches of government (see diagram, Chapter 14, section headed 'The reality of the Indian System'). Their famous checks and balances work because the normal functions of each institution are clearly and simply defined.

When an institution exercises its constitutionally authorized check on the others, there is no hue and cry. All players understand and respect the process.

By contrast, the Indian people are never sure which so-called institution is accountable for what. A government falls, but the president in whose name the government functioned, stays in office. A prime minister loses but he dissolves the very house that oversees him. A Cabinet member fails but he brings down the whole coalition government. The judiciary is not considered a part of government at all. It is not accountable to any elected official or democratic institution of government.

The truth is separation of powers can work only when institutions are separate. 'Where presidential and parliamentary governments *do* differ,' wrote Douglas Verney, a professor of political science, 'is over the separation not of powers but of institutions and persons.'[7] By establishing institutions that have independent legitimacy with the people, and by keeping them secure from other institutions, the American system delivers a mechanism for governing. It works like a machine with designated parts and processes, offering greater stability and deliberation. 'The theoretical foundation of the American presidential system is the soundest,' wrote James Ceaser, 'it is the only one that, by virtue of its formal mechanism alone, provides a workable solution to the great problem of modern government.' He concluded that 'the parliamentary system leaves much more to chance or circumstance than the American system'.[8]

INDIANS NEED SYSTEM OF PARTICIPATION, NOT OF 'RULE'

People in India commonly lament that their democracy is limited to voting. And that there is very little participation at the grass-roots level in actual governance. There is no denying that the Indian system's oligarchic structure fosters elitism (Chapter 8). Those who come to power begin to think they are above the rest. This discourages others from coming forward. It kills wider initiative and hinders hope and inhibits participation.

Verney studied the political systems of nearly a hundred nations to see how they affected people's participation. Comparing the two basic models presented by Britain and America, he commented: 'Whereas in both countries attention has been given to popular participation, this has been taken to greater lengths in America where on occasion efficient government has been sacrificed to what is considered to be a more democratic system ... From the point of view of popular participation,' he concluded, '... American government may be judged more favourably.'[9]

The fact is that the parliamentary system does provide a government the wherewithal to *rule* people, while the presidential system compels it to *follow* them. This is not by chance. Parliament's evolution was all about creating a body to replace the rule of the monarch. In the late 1800s, Bagehot announced that 'the Parliament of today is a ruling body'.[10] Madison and his colleagues, on the other hand, set out to enable the government to control the governed, but also to 'oblige it to control itself'.

The presidential system is designed to foster egalitarianism. Anyone can run for election without a political godfather. Anyone can win without the support of a political party. Here is a report from the authors of *American Government*: 'Presidential, congressional, gubernatorial, and mayoral candidates are now no longer dependent on party volunteers or party campaign-funding events to jump-start their campaigns. That change has shifted the focus from party-centered campaigns to candidate-centred campaigns.'[11] Once in office, any legislator can introduce or support any law. A lawmaker can confront an executive official, and vice versa, because neither is controlled by the other.

INDIANS NEED A 'TRULY' REPRESENTATIVE GOVERNMENT

To call India's parliamentary government 'representative' is a misnomer. First of all, people's representatives in this system are not free to vote. Almost all of them are at the mercy of their party bosses. They select them as candidates, they dole out party and government offices to them and they penalize them for disobeying party whips. For fear of not getting the party ticket in the next election or losing out on an office of profit, Indian legislators vote exactly as they are told. The anti-defection law has only made the situation worse. It 'reduces legislators to bondsmen', says A.G. Noorani, a leading constitutional expert.[12]

Secondly, an Indian citizen has far fewer directly elected representatives in government than does an American. In the federal government alone, every American citizen has four direct representatives: the president, two senators, and a member of the House. Then, in the state government there are at least another three: the governor and the two members of the state assembly. In addition, in his town or city government, each American has three more representatives. Against this total of at least ten direct representatives per American citizen, an Indian has only three: one in parliament, one in the state assembly, and since 1993, one in the local panchayat or municipal body.

Then, there is the fundamental issue of whom an Indian representative really represents. The Indian system requires a representative from a small constituency to think and act in the larger interest of the nation. This is not in accordance with the basic principle of representative democracy, which requires that each representative must represent no more and no less than his constituency. In a parliamentary democracy, says Verney, 'The question is often raised: To whom is a representative responsible? To his constituents? To his conscience? To his country?' Under the American system, there is no confusion about whom he represents. For instance, the president represents the entire country, but not *also* his state or his district. 'Delegate democracy results in much of the burden of responsibility for decisions being left in the hands of people,' Verney writes. He says that 'there does seem to be a heightened sense of responsibility for political action ... in a country like the United States which in some respects tends to favour delegate democracy. ... [In Britain] we have accepted the view of our leaders that firm government is more important than the radical notion that the will of the people must prevail.'[13]

This also raises the issue of what people's representatives actually do in each system. Since in the presidential system they are assigned to a specific branch – president to the executive, senator to the legislative, etc. – they perform the actual tasks for which they were sent. But that is not the case under the parliamentary system. Lijphart notes that 'legislatures in parliamentary systems have two incompatible functions: making laws and supporting a cabinet in office. ... Only in presidential systems can legislatures perform the main task for which they are democratically elected, namely, to legislate.'[14]

The American system thus places a higher number of representatives per capita, at a higher level of performance. Since each representative has a unique role, he is expected to fulfil it well. Each speaks for a different geography and for a distinct set of interests. A representative in the city council watches the interests of a neighbourhood, but the mayor, who is elected directly by *all* residents, looks after the interests of the entire city. He has no particular area that is *his* constituency, so he shows no favouritism to any part of the city. Same thing applies to the governors and to the president.

By contrast, no one in the Indian parliamentary system can truly speak for the nation, because the prime minister is not directly elected by the whole nation. No one can even speak for a state, since the state's chief minister isn't directly elected by the whole state; nor is there a voice in the Central government that represents a state as a whole.

Besides, there is a world of difference between direct and indirect representation. The American system's direct election of the president, governors and other representatives is definitely more democratic than behind-the-scenes selections under the parliamentary system. Lijphart writes that 'the argument that heads of governments, who are the most important and powerful office-holders in democracies, should be directly elected by the people has great validity'.[15]

MAJORITY 'RULE' MUST END IN INDIA

The deepest problem in the Indian system is that political minorities, or minority views, are allowed no say in governance. The opposition can make speeches or walk out of parliament, but the system offers it no powers. It cannot stop a governmental action nor can it take government to account. It has only one remedy: bring the government down. But that doesn't improve governance. The foremost purpose of the American system, on the other hand, is to not let a majority do as it pleases. This improves the quality of governance and creates a healthier polity.

'Ultimately, the people must rule, but no one – no person, no class – is virtuous enough to rule alone,' writes Donald Robinson, the editor of *Reforming American Government*. 'The trick in incorporating these values into a constitutional scheme,' he says, 'is to see that the will of the people ... does not become tyrannical.' He then described how the American system manages to accomplish this: 'Madison ... offers two solutions to this problem. One is to "expand the sphere" to include a large, varied population, so that there will be many interests but no simple majorities. The other is to make the structure and processes of government complex (by the separation of powers, bicameralism, judicial review and federalism), so that foolish and wicked schemes will be exposed and popular majorities can be rallied to oppose them.'[16]

There are several features of the American system that compel a broad consensus to emerge. First, the executive in this system cannot introduce legislation. The president can only persuade Congress, but cannot force it. Secondly, and conversely, the president can veto legislation passed by Congress. It can be overridden but only when Congress can pass it again with at least two-thirds majority. Thirdly, strong bicameralism – the Senate and the House of Representatives have equal legislative powers – also fosters broad consensus. Since both houses have to pass the exact same version, if either is held by the opposite party, the support of both parties becomes necessary. Also, the US Senate has a special power to delay legislation. At least 60 per cent of its members have to agree before a vote can be cast. Fourthly, America's strong federalism makes it very difficult for a national law to pass or be executed if it encroaches upon states' powers. Since states are also governed under the presidential system, they have their own pressures to seek minority support. Last but not the least, under the US system there is no such thing as parliamentary supremacy; a law can be declared unconstitutional. All of this ensures that important measures are passed only when they have wide support.

GENUINE SEPARATION OF POWERS NEEDED TO PROTECT LIBERTY

The main cause of the Indian system's ailments is the non-existence of real separation of powers. Whatever little separation of powers existed in theory became meaningless within a few early years of the republic (Chapters 7 and 8).

Everyone agrees that by separating powers the American system ensures liberty, but what is not as commonly understood is that it also delivers efficient government. William Gwyn, a professor of political science, noted five arguments – 'four concerned with achieving liberty, one with efficiency' – why the presidential system was better at both governance and safety. First, Gwyn presented the four principles by which separation of powers ensured liberty: 1) 'those who make the law should not also judge or punish violations of it'; 2) 'if the legislature was to perform its function of calling delinquent governmental officials to account, those officials should not dominate the legislature'; 3) 'if civil and military officers were allowed to be members of the legislative assembly, they would form a faction there that would pursue its own rather than the common interest'; and 4) 'the legislative, executive, and the judicial branches of government are each empowered to check the exercise of the primary function of the others'.[17]

For efficiency, Gwyn noted that 'ironically, the separation of powers, which has so often been criticized during the past century for reducing governmental effectiveness was often advocated during the seventeenth and eighteenth centuries for increasing it. ... It was then argued that [a large] assembly because of its very size could not execute the laws with necessary "secrecy and dispatch" and that a much smaller organization was therefore required to perform the executive function.' The US system provides this quick-acting executive. But the greater contribution to efficiency comes from the fact that under the US system there is division of labour. Each branch and each government focuses in its own area and is therefore able to fulfil its role with dispatch.

STRONG GOVERNMENT NEEDS EFFICIENCY AND EFFECTIVENESS

Indian government is slow to respond and its responses are usually not up to the mark – a particular irony given that efficiency was one of the main reasons behind adopting this form of government. The fact is that unifying powers has backfired. This is because neither of the two operative branches of government has tasks suitable to its structure. The Indian system expects a numerous deliberative body, the legislature, to take prompt decisions and provide administration. And it asks a council of ministers, made up of politicians, to draft legislation. By combining two disparate functions into one institution, it allows neither branch to show what it can do, but gives them both opportunity to shirk responsibility.

A government must aim not for efficiency but effectiveness. A dictatorship can be very efficient but that doesn't make it a desirable form of government. A proper system of government must aim at not just speed but deliberation as well. Doing the right thing involves paying attention to as many views as possible, especially of those who don't currently hold power. This is precisely what the US system obliges the government to do.

But that doesn't make the US government weak. Douglas Verney confirms that 'it should not be assumed … that the presidential form, because it is divided, is necessarily one of weak government'.[18] The various aspects of separation of powers provide the US government strength. Since each department is empowered, if it has a good leader it can shine. Similarly, since each branch is assigned tasks that are most suitable to its abilities, it has the advantage of focus and hence can deliver quality in its work. Within their own sphere, the top officials of each branch are free to guide and direct policies as they deem fit. And if they are sufficiently persuasive, they can influence the policies of other branches as well. This leads to governing by the force of argument, not by the force of office.

The concept of federalism and limited government also adds strength to American governments, by ensuring that they are not stretched too thin. A federal government department can be created only if Congress authorizes the president. As a result, in the 225 years of its functioning, the federal government in the US has established only fifteen Cabinet departments. The Indian government today has more than fifty-five ministries. The 2009 Administrative Reforms Commission recommended that the number should be reduced to twenty-five.[19]

The division of functions thus delivers both efficiency and effectiveness and makes the US government strong. Peter Schultz, a professor of politics, has written that the 'separation of powers constitutes an attempt to solve one of the major problems of government, that of providing for *both* reasonable government and forceful government without sacrificing either'.[20]

INDIA NEEDS CONSTITUTIONAL MECHANISM TO AVOID DEADLOCK

Constitutional crises are commonplace in India. A government falls because it reaches a deadlock with its coalition partners. The Indian system offers no remedy other than calling for a general election, or to engage in corruption to buy support in parliament. By the very structure of the parliamentary system, governments are always on the verge of falling. After all, the opposition's main purpose is to engineer just such an outcome. This is how, as the theory goes, governments stay responsible. In practice, though, it only leads to deal making to stay in power.

The US system avoids both instability and unfettered deal making by providing a constitutional mechanism to solve deadlock. When a measure is defeated it doesn't mean that its proponent is to be immediately thrown out of office; it only means he has to work harder to persuade others. Some measures never pass. But when after repeated attempts one does, it is usually a much improved version.

'Ultimately, checks are to prevent deadlock,' writes Ann Stuart Anderson, a director of the American Enterprise Institute.[21] The key checks – president's power of veto; the Senate's powers of ratifying treaties and confirming executive appointments; and the Congress's power of impeachment of a president – ensure that each branch has a say. This usually gives each interest group or political party a strong voice. Similarly, the principal balancing factor – the Senate – guarantees that a proposal has the support of at least 60 per cent of its members. If there is a presidential veto, it goes even further, by ensuring the support of two-thirds of the people's representatives before a law can be adopted.

The process of developing such wide support is usually long and messy. This is when separation of powers in the US is often criticized for causing deadlock and paralysis in government. However, Anderson writes that 'many of these criticisms rest on a misunderstanding of separation of powers as it is embodied in the US Constitution'. 'The device is mistakenly thought of as an arrangement of three branches of government of equal power, locked in perpetual tension and balance; hence "checks and balances". Yet, when we examine ... we find that the only example of balance is bicameralism, dividing the legislative body into two to check its excesses. When we examine checks, we find that they do not create tension but provide a constitutionally legitimate method to resolve it.'[22]

First of all, deadlock in government is no vice. Bagehot is the man most guilty of propagating the fallacy that governments ought to know immediately the solution to every problem. He argued that a government is good only when 'the executive gets the laws it wants'. 'In

England a strong Cabinet can obtain the concurrence of the legislature in all acts which facilitate its administration ... but a President may be hampered by [Congress],' he said.[23] The same theme has been picked up by some modern-day critics of the presidential system. Juan Linz, one of such leading detractors, argues that 'since both [president and Congress] derive their power from the vote of the people ... a conflict is always latent and sometimes likely to erupt dramatically; there is no democratic principle to resolve it'. Linz concedes, however, 'the uniqueness of American political institutions and practices that have limited the impact of such conflicts'.[24] But the view has taken hold. In a recent online debate held by *The Economist*, 77 per cent of the voters agreed with the motion that 'America's political system is broken'.[25]

Both assertions – that deadlocks are bad and that American governments suffer from paralysis – are inaccurate. After all, what right does a government have to take an action when the people are not willing? Should a government be allowed to 'obtain the concurrence ... in all acts', as Bagehot commends? Is it not the primary function of democratic governments to act only according to the general will of the people, or not at all?

The answer is that as long as that general will doesn't emerge, it is only appropriate that the government be deadlocked. 'Our modern sensibilities have a hard time accepting that "paralysis" is preferable if the alternative is movement in the wrong direction, but it is,' wrote Peter Wehner opposing the motion in the aforementioned debate for *The Economist*. Similarly, Schultz asked why 'today a premium should be placed on governmental action ... whereas in 1787 a premium was put on governmental inaction'?

As to whether America can, in fact, become paralysed, the evidence speaks to the contrary. David Mayhew, a professor of government at Yale University, debunked this commonly held myth once and for all in his 1991 work, *Divided We Govern*. After an exhaustive analysis of laws passed and investigations conducted by Congress over a period of forty-four years (1946–90), Mayhew concluded that the

US government functions effectively even when different political parties control the elective branches. Of the 267 important laws passed during this period, various US governments 'acquired landmark acts about as frequently per year in "divided" as in "unified" times'.[26] The results were even more astonishing in the case of what are considered deeply partisan activities of Congress, its oversight investigations of the executive. These 'high-publicity investigations in which congressional committees expose alleged misbehavior in the executive branch: such extravaganzas seem to go on regardless of conditions of party control', Mayhew reported. 'Surprisingly,' he wrote, 'it does not seem to make all that much difference whether party control of the American government happens to be unified or divided.'[27]

The ability of the US system to deliver effective governance even in the face of so-called partisan deadlock surprises many. 'Far from being broken,' wrote the author of *The Economist* article 'America's Democracy: A Study in Paralysis', 'it could be argued, American democracy is working with exquisite sensitivity, allowing the administration to advance where it has the people's support but checking it when it overreaches.'[28]

INDIA IN DIRE NEED OF BETTER LAWMAKING

Lawmaking in India, on the other hand, is an entirely partisan exercise. Hence, laws are of poor quality (Chapter 8). Since only government can introduce laws – those brought by private members have hardly any chance of passage – no other member of parliament takes initiative. Party bosses in power decide which laws will be proposed and those in opposition decide which will be opposed. The legislators vote as instructed by their bosses. No one has any interest in the quality of laws. The government is unconcerned because the law is usually assured passage. And the opposition has no interest in the quality because it benefits only if the law is defeated, not if it is improved.

Consider now the remarkable fact that historically, notable laws tend to pass in America with two-to-one margins, and by bipartisan majorities.[29] The answer lies in building a consensus in the society first through a process of purposeful deliberation.

Except in selecting their leaders, members support their party's position in only about two out of every three votes. Although a member's party is a strong indicator of his voting preference, party cohesion in the US system is not very strong.[30]

What brings about these broad bipartisan majorities? It is the structure of the US system. First, a member of Congress is not dependent on his party to win elections. Each member of Congress can initiate and hope to pass legislation regardless of whether his party controls the House or not. This allows a Congressman to make a name for himself through his own actions. As such, members try to associate themselves with important legislation and work hard at getting them passed. Second, the laws proposed are sensitive to the views of the minority. In a system that allows a minority to obstruct the passing of a law, it is only sensible to pursue those laws that have broad agreement. Third, all channels of building public opinion are never in control of one party. The US system offers many institutions, at local as well as national level, to enlist people's participation in support or opposition. The most forceful such institution is, of course, the president. He becomes the leading voice in shaping public opinion, and frequently it is his chief contribution to the legislative process.

Fourth, bipartisan majorities are the norm because one party cannot pass anything alone, especially in divided governments. In order for a government to do anything at all, seeking the other party's support becomes necessary. Fifth, because each political party has some power, people expect it to be exercised proactively, instead of just in opposition to the other party's initiatives.

Sixth, and perhaps most fundamentally, since both parties can do something, problem solving becomes the culture of governance. In a system focused on solving problems, agreement can be reached across party lines relatively quickly. Seventh, in a system in which a law could be derailed easily, the promoters not only propose laws that are sensible, they aim at more than a simple majority to begin with. To cut down the size and intensity of opposition, it becomes necessary for lawmakers to cajole members of the other party earnestly.[31]

As a result, issues rather than politics become more important. Broad support can only be built on issues, not on politics. Coalitions, therefore, are built around policy and issues-based agenda. The larger the coalition the better, because that provides the best insurance against a long series of majoritarian tests that legislation has to pass. Individuals from organizations outside the government – interest groups, individual citizens, former officials, experts in the area – are frequently invited to the public hearings held by congressional committees and subcommittees. Large majorities are sought to overcome threats of a Senate filibuster or a presidential veto. In the end, only well-crafted proposals that enlist both allies and opponents, and are built around issues that are important to the people, work.

The upshot is that when laws are based on broad support they are more reasonable. In this regard, even divided government becomes an important contributor in making laws that are sensible and practical. This is so because parties have to shed their extreme positions. 'The only way to achieve sustainable bipartisanship,' wrote the author of an article entitled "The Merits of Divided Government", 'is to divide control of the government, forcing the parties to negotiate in order to get anything done. That pulls policy toward the centre, which encourages reasonableness. And the very fact that both parties sign off on any given policy makes the public *perceive* that policy as more reasonable, which makes it less controversial and more sustainable.'[32]

INDIA MUST CONTROL BUDGETS BETTER

India's fiscal policies have been disastrous. Government spending is uncontrollable because the spenders have no check. Legislative control over the executive is in name only. The government obtains whatever money it desires because it controls parliament.

In this all-important area of managing the nation's finances, the US system has shown the best results. The reason for that is simple.

It separates those who want to dole out funds from those who have
the power to tax; and those who spend, from those who are supposed
to check spending. In America, legislative control over purse strings
is for real.

In a 2005 IMF study entitled 'Who Controls the Budget: the
Legislature or the Executive?', the question was studied for twenty-
eight different countries. The measure of 'legislatures' budgetary
authority' gave America the highest score of ten; the UK received only
one. Similarly, in the area of 'legislature's political control', America
received the highest score of fourteen, while parliamentary regimes
received a score of only 5.5. Although India was not included in the
study, if the same questionnaire was applied, India would derive a
score of only two.

The paper reported that in parliamentary systems, the 'political
powers enjoyed by the executive are accompanied by strong *budgetary*
powers. This is in sharp contrast with presidential systems, which
have strongly separated powers and powerful legislatures.' The IMF
study outlined some of the ways in which America exercises budgetary
control: 'there are multiple committees and subcommittees in both
chambers of Congress (which result from separate and independent
electoral systems). These committees are very influential on budget
processes, the size of the annual budget and the allocation of spending.
An independent non-partisan Congressional Budget Office provides
a powerful counterweight to the president's Office of Budget
Management, which prepares the initial draft budget. This budget must
be submitted to the legislature by the president eight months before
the beginning of the new fiscal year – much further in advance than
any other country.'[33]

INDIA NEEDS RESPONSIBLE GOVERNMENT, NOT IN NAME ONLY

Fundamentally, the Indian system cannot possibly be responsible, for
it breaks two basic tenets of the parliamentary form. First, in India
power is not held by people's representatives but by party oligarchs.
Second, supremacy is not held by parliament but by the government.

Proposals are sent to parliament not for debate and approval, but to be rubber-stamped. In such conditions how can members of parliament possibly hold a government accountable?

In fact, the whole notion of responsibility in the Indian system is absurd. Responsibility here means a government can be removed; in the presidential system it means a government is held accountable. The absurdity is that the Indian system expects a government to be removed by those who are in power due to that very government. It expects politicians to remove themselves from power. There is more. There is also an assumption that people's dissatisfaction with their government will translate into immediate action by their representatives in parliament. That those representatives would push at once for a change in government. And that this would happen when the head of government holds the power to dissolve the very House of those representatives. And that somehow this will make the next government more responsible.

The truth is that a parliamentary government is thrown out of office not because of something it has done, but because another faction has managed to gain control over more seats in parliament. The argument that the new coalition better reflects the general will of the people is specious. People elect their representatives to fulfil an agenda, not to find another one. Also, how does this ensure that the new agenda will be executed more responsibly?

The US system keeps governments accountable by not giving them carte blanche in the first place. It places institutional checks on each branch to prevent it from acting irresponsibly. It assigns precise responsibilities to both Central and state governments, so that accountability can be clearly placed. It makes each branch independent, so that none can shirk responsibility for its assigned functions. It gives executive responsibilities to individuals – the president and the governors – rather than councils, so that no one can pass blame. Then, it authorizes the legislature to scrutinize the executive. This scrutiny is not limited to just asking questions; Congress can disapprove programmes or cut funding. It can hold public investigations of officials or departments. Then to top it all, the US system has an electoral check every two years. If Congress misbehaves, the entire House of Representation and a third of the Senate can be thrown out. And if the president does, he can be hobbled or compelled to move along with people's wishes. People take that decision directly, not through their failed representatives.

Still, in this area of responsibility, the presidential system has been criticized for two reasons. One, the president cannot be voted out of office; and two, he and Congress can blame each other. Linz argues that 'there is no way to hold accountable a president who cannot be presented for reelection ... When reelection is possible, the incumbent president ... can try to escape blame by shifting it to the Congress. A prime minister with a majority cannot play such a game. The division of powers can, therefore, provide an alibi for failure.'[34]

The question really is which system is more prone to irresponsible behaviour. The aim of a system of government cannot only be to punish culprits; it must first prevent wrongdoing. Is an executive with supremacy over other branches, which is the case in India, more likely to misbehave, or the one which has no control over other branches? Another fallacy lies in equating the two offices. India's prime minister is an entirely different institution than the American president. The former holds responsibility for both executive and legislative functions, the latter, only for the executive. The separation of powers ensures that the president and the Congress checks each other.

As for penal action against reckless behaviour, the American system dispenses it daily as well as every two years through mid-term elections. Its institutions check all governmental actions – executive and legislative – on an ongoing basis. Congress has real powers to stop a president from taking a course of action, as well as to impeach him. The president can veto Congress's legislative actions. In addition, the US system puts the entire government through an electoral check every two years.

In a truly democratic society, it cannot be argued that people's judgement is inferior to that of their elected representatives. The parliamentary system is absurd in making that argument when it allows members of parliament to select the nation's chief executive.

Fairness in responsibility also works in reverse. Is it fair to a government or a branch to be thrown out of office before getting a chance to fulfil its election promises? Is it fair to ask a government to show performance in less than two years? The American system allows a president and Congress, both popularly elected at the same time, a minimum of two years in office to show progress. After all, the people in their wisdom have put them in office based on certain expectations. What right do people's representatives have to stop these individuals, chosen directly by the people, from functioning for even such a minimal time as two years?

The feature that is the most effective at enforcing responsibility in the US system is congressional oversight. These powers are not expressly stated in the Constitution of the United States. But they are implied, in particular by a clause which authorizes Congress 'to make all laws which shall be necessary and proper for carrying into execution' the powers vested 'in any department or officer'. This intertwines the responsibilities of the legislative and the executive. Congress, to fulfil its legislative function responsibly, must seek executive advice. And the executive must furnish information and consult the Congress.

The US Congress has powers to investigate executive departments and officials. The Supreme Court legitimized these powers in a 1927 ruling. Attempts by the executive to restrict Congress's authority are routinely fought back. Gag orders issued by presidents have been overturned, and whistle-blower laws have been passed to protect those who disclose wrongdoings. Oversight occurs in America through a variety of activities. Congress holds appropriation hearings on budget requests from executive departments, authorization hearings for existing programmes, regular hearings to examine an executive department's implementation of specific programmes, and, the most publicized, investigations into major scandals or administrative misbehaviour. Congress even has the authority to investigate a president in case of an impeachment. In its 225-year history, two presidents (Andrew Johnson and Bill Clinton) have in fact been impeached by the House of Representatives, although both were acquitted by the Senate. One president (Richard Nixon) resigned in the face of imminent impeachment.

INDIA'S BUREAUCRACY MUST BE MERIT-BASED

India desperately needs better administrators. The most impractical feature of India's parliamentary system is the practice of appointing legislators as ministers. Legislators are elected by the people to devise solutions to social problems, not to become administrators themselves. Also, when career politicians are placed in charge of career administrators, it defeats the purposes of both. When politicians masquerade as managers, it not only reduces their own ability to perform their primary tasks of lawmaking and oversight, it makes the entire administration partisan. Besides, how can one oversee oneself? It is also a fact that politicians are usually not knowledgeable about the area of their ministry nor are they experienced managers.

The performance of career bureaucrats suffers too. They must not only train their boss also but go along with his politics. The powers granted to the politicians makes patronage, not performance, the fastest path to advancement. Bureaucrats become sycophants. With no scrutiny from any other branch of government, the two become cohorts in corruption.

The US system controls the bureaucracy better because officials have two political masters. The top administrative officials are appointed by the president, but only after Senate's approval. Separation of powers requires that officials of the administration are accountable to both the executive and the legislative. This compels them to disclose information fully. Since legislators cannot also be ministers, the politics of the day or of a region have very little influence on administration. This reduces patronage of government officials, makes the bureaucracy merit-based, and keeps it honest. Fred Riggs, a professor of political science, writes that 'the presence of non-partisan, merit-based and functionist careerists in the American government has contributed significantly to its survival'.[35]

Merit is the basis of government employment in America also because it is decreed by law. In order to end the 'spoils' system by which government jobs were doled out to political supporters, Congress passed a law in 1883 creating a merit-based federal civil service. It established open and competitive exams for government jobs. Today 85 to 90 per cent of federal employees are appointed on the basis of these exams.[36]

The upshot is that government employees in the US are usually building a career. Since as 'functionists' they are dedicated to specific government departments, they become experts in their field. As careerists, they are 'emphatically non-partisan to avoid being rotated out of office when a new party came to power', Riggs noted. And since the system is designed to find or make specialists, it employs at all levels instead of just entry level, and through practical tests instead of just academic performance. Quotas are assigned, but only to assure recruitment from all states. This avoids elitism. Riggs notes, that in America 'had the British system (itself derived from the Chinese Confucian prototype, via the Indian Civil Service) prevailed, an elite class of career generalists would have become so powerful that it could have unbalanced the separation of powers principle'.

INDIA NEEDS STABLE GOVERNMENTS

There is no telling when an Indian government will fall or a new one will start functioning. Forming coalitions is a dirty deal-making exercise in private, no matter the public affirmations of ideology or principle. As a result governments can take forever to form and can fall within days (Chapter 8).

Since 1947, India has had fourteen prime ministers who have formed a total of twenty-two governments. In the same period, the UK has had fifteen prime ministers and twenty-two governments, while the US has had twelve presidents and seventeen administrations.

On an average, an Indian government has remained in office for only three years, finishing not even 60 per cent of the five-year term. A US president, on the other hand, completes on average nearly 95 per cent of his four-year term, and this is after accounting for deaths or assassinations.

Parliamentary governments are notorious for their instability. This is evident all over the world. Japan has had thirty-one prime ministers since 1947. Israel has had eighteen since 1948. A prime minister may have to form different governments. Italy, for instance, has had sixty-one governments since 1946 under about thirty-five different prime ministers. Worse, a nation under this system can be without government for months. And many have. In an article entitled 'Rudderless', *The Economist* reported in November 2010: 'European coalition governments are frequently born late and fragile. The Netherlands currently holds the region's record for the longest time to form a government (208 days). And Belgium is still without a functioning cabinet since its last coalition collapsed five months ago. Moreover, once formed, these much-anticipated governments do not always last long. In 2007-08 Belgium took over six months to produce a government, only to see it collapse three months later.'[37]

The United States, though, can never be without a functioning government. And this applies to all three branches. The moment one president's term ends, the next one takes over. In the legislature, a new House of Representatives is elected every two years. The new Speaker is elected in the very first session. Two-thirds of the Senators are always present. The terms of all elective offices are fixed, to the extent that the precise date and time are mentioned in the Constitution. In case of the president's death, resignation or removal from office, the vice-president takes over. In case neither is alive or qualified, there is a prescribed line of succession: Speaker of the House, president *pro tempore* of the Senate, Secretary of State, and so on. The justices of the Supreme Court are appointed for life. Hence, all three branches never stop functioning.

For stability, a fixed term in office for each branch of government is an essential feature. The separation of powers works only when each institution's term is unchangeable, by itself or by any other power. Fred Riggs considers a regime presidential 'only if the effective head of government is elected for a fixed term'.[38] This is so because benefits of separation of powers flow only when neither the executive nor the legislature can dissolve the other.

Some, however, criticize that fixed terms make the presidential system rigid, less able to adjust to changing circumstances. Bagehot charged that an American government had 'no elastic element, everything is rigid, specified, dated'. 'Whether it suits you or not, whether it works well or works ill, whether it is what you want or not, by law you must keep it,' he said. Under parliamentary system he argued 'people can choose a ruler for the occasion ... replace the pilot of the calm by the pilot of the storm'.[39] Similarly, Linz says that in the presidential system the political process is 'broken into discontinuous, rigidly determined periods without the possibility of continuous readjustments'. He argues that this makes the system 'less predictable and often weaker than that of a prime minister, who can always reinforce his authority and democratic legitimacy by asking for a vote of confidence'.[40]

The first question is whether a nation should rely more on its system of government or on an official? In America, the system works regardless of who is sitting in any single seat of power. The quality of leadership matters, of course, but the system is capable of delivering good governance with or without good leaders. As for quality of leaders, the president comes to office after winning a nationwide election, whereas a prime minister only runs, if at all, in a few districts within a state. The president has much wider support, and far better leadership and administrative abilities.

Then there is the question whether it is practical or advisable to change leaders for one exigency or for failure to pass one law. It only hinders good governance in all other areas, and invites politicking in bringing government down. To even consider Bagehot's extreme example of wartime change in leadership: is it better to always be prepared for a sudden war, or to rely on a change in leadership when it comes? Let's not forget that the chief protector of Churchill during the Second World War was a peacetime American leader, President Roosevelt.

The 'continuous readjustments' of the parliamentary system that Linz prefers, in fact, represent the most troublesome aspect of this system. For it only means continuous political scheming to retain or gain power. It is not the people's issues that require 'readjustment' in coalitions, it is politics. As far as the people's wishes are concerned, they can only be of two types: those that come before the elections and those that come after. Obviously, a government came to power because it promised to meet the former. So, no readjustment is needed. As for demands that come after the elections, a problem arises only when they are raised by a minority which is not represented in the ruling coalition. By the basic principle of the parliamentary system, those demands should just wait until the next election. But this is exactly where the politicking starts. More and more enticements are offered in order to fragment the existing coalition.

The US system, on the other hand, accommodates minority views on an ongoing basis, and without destabilizing governments.

INDIA MUST CONTROL ITS POLITICAL PARTIES, NOW

Instead of having policies that bring a political party to power, in India the pursuit of power brings a party its policies. Since their primary purpose is to win seats in parliament, these policies are inherently unfair. They are designed to appeal to a vote bank, not to reason. Once in power, a party would rarely require the opposition's support or face scrutiny. Constituencies are small, so a populist promise or an inflammatory claim can swing enough votes to win. Then, when the system gives power to political parties, it makes party bosses unfettered leaders. It is remarkable that India's Constitution requires political parties to function but does nothing to regulate them. As a result almost all parties have become personal fiefdoms, and the nation a political oligarchy.

David Mayhew describes the key difference between the British and American systems thus: 'Political parties can be powerful instruments, but in the United States they seem to play more of a role as "policy factions" than as, in the British case, governing instruments.'[41] In America's 'complicated, multi-component setting, British-style governing by party majorities does not have much of a chance', he said.

Governance by majority rule is, in fact, unfair to everyone. It is obviously unfair to the huge minority which is not represented. But it is also unfair to the majority itself, for it is expected to understand and solve the problems of those it doesn't represent. 'Government by the people,' Verney pointed out, 'means that no group, however large, may claim to speak on behalf of the entire populace. In order that action may be taken, the will of the majority shall normally prevail, but it does not follow that the minority, by virtue of being a minority, is wrong.'[42]

Reasonable policies that appeal to the widest sections of society take centre stage in the US system. Political parties build coalitions based on issues rather than on social classes or castes or religion.

Then there are structural factors that make parties in the US less hegemonic. Parties in America are 'open' because of their decentralized structure. Since they have to select candidates through open primaries, they become responsive. Before candidates can acquire a party label they campaign on their own, making elections much more centred on the candidate than on the party. The candidates' competence, instead of a party boss, decides who represents the party in general elections. As a result, parties are open to all those who want to run. They seek out capable candidates and view them as assets to be nurtured, not owned.

Not that state level parties don't exist in America; they do. But they are far less influential in national politics than in India. This is due to another fundamental feature of the system: a multiplicity of directly elected officials. There are many offices to win. The state governments have so many directly elected representatives – governors, state legislators, mayors, city councilmen, etc. – that the national parties always have a chance of winning some of them. 'Some states have had a single dominant party,' Riggs pointed out, 'but because these state governments exist within the framework of the American federal system, their hegemonic parties cannot monopolize power but must share it with national and local authorities, often of a different party.'[43]

What makes parties in America centripetal instead of centrifugal – uniting instead dividing – are a couple of other structural features. In the US elections are held by the single member district (SMD) system, whereby the candidate who gets the most votes wins. This, combined with the fact that voting is not compulsory, stacks the odds against fringe candidates. The voters' right to abstain makes the supporters of candidates who are unlikely to win less interested in voting. Similarly, SMD produces a single-winner representative of the majority, instead of multiple representatives from smaller parties. Major political parties benefit because people vote for the candidates most likely to win. This helps establish a two-party system.

INDIA'S SYSTEM MUST UNITE, NOT CAUSE FRAGMENTATION

In India, parties succumb to centrifugal tendencies because the Indian system rewards the creation of new parties. First of all, in parliament itself, the coalition structure of government encourages political leaders to create their own outfits. This way they obtain more powers in return for their support in parliament. Then in states, the delinking of national and state elections also created a huge incentive for fragmentation. Supporters of a local issue or from a small caste could bring a small-time leader to power. Once a party gets some traction in state elections, it can also win a few seats in parliament. As a result, India now has more than 900 recognized parties, and a nation deeply divided.

What also causes fragmentation in India is the fact that while society is clamouring for representation in government, there are not enough representatives, per capita. The Indian system offers far fewer directly elected representatives to each citizen than does the US system. With so few seats to go around, dissatisfied sections splinter from main parties to try their hand on their own.

But the structural factor that causes the worst kind of fragmentation is that all elections are small. Small constituencies make it possible for elections to be won by buying a few votes or inflaming small groups of people. In this regard, SMD works in just the opposite way than it does in America. A candidate can win an election by getting only a small percentage of votes.

Last but not the least, Indian parties fragment because of the nature of parties themselves. In India parties are highly centralized undemocratic organizations. Party officials and its candidates in elections are all selected by diktat. No party selects candidates through primary elections, as is done in America. As a result, disgruntled members routinely form their own outfits.

The parliamentary system's structure and functioning would cause fragmentation in any nation, especially one as diverse as India. T.J.M. Wilson declared the same about America: 'If a parliamentary system … were installed in a nation as heterogeneous as the United States, we might get more party cohesion only at the price of multiplying the number of parties, so that although the parties might be more cohesive, public policy would be less so.'[44]

INDIA'S SYSTEM MUST PRODUCE BETTER LEADERS

India's method of selecting party candidates behind closed doors is the root of the problem. Not only does this rob party members of the right to pick their leaders, it ensures the picking of lousy candidates, weakening the parties in turn. Those who are selected don't really know whether they have the support of the people, those who are rejected don't know why, and the people get a candidate thrust upon them. Infighting is the norm as is bossism and corruption. But the worst outcome is that the system usually throws up leaders who are good deal makers but poor characters.

The problem is not the Indian voter. For good reasons he almost always votes for the party, not the candidate. He knows that under the Indian system his vote will show results not if his favourite candidate wins, but only if his party does. So he pays little attention to the candidates' qualifications or character. In America the electorate pays more attention to the quality of candidates and their record, because each legislator or executive official has an independent authority. A vote cast is not wasted even if a candidate's party doesn't gain a majority. It is remarkable that more than 40 per cent of Americans classify themselves as 'independents', not identifying themselves with either of the two major parties.

Another factor behind the poor quality of leaders in India is that the number of elected representatives is very small. The US system offers many more elective offices and, therefore, yields a much better crop of political leaders. 'Under a parliamentary system power is held by a relatively small number of officials,' Ceaser writes. 'In the United States, by contrast, the existence of an independent legislature provides an institution that can satisfy the desire for political honour for a much larger number of people. The United States is the world's second largest democracy, and the number of people yearning for a place in the sun is accordingly much greater than in Britain.'[45]

For a nation of roughly 300 million people, the United States offers 535 representatives in the national legislature alone (435 in the House of Representatives, 100 in the Senate). Then, it has fifty state legislatures, and a whole slew of executive positions, from the president down to a small-town mayor, which are also elected. India, a nation of 1. 2 billion, provides less than 800 seats in parliament (a maximum of 552 seats in the Lok Sabha, and 250 in the Rajya Sabha), and only twenty-nine state legislatures. It offers no additional national or state executive positions to be elected. The Indian system offers so few slots, and with such little transparency, that those who want to serve their nation are denied an open chance to compete.

Yet, small constituencies remain the big problem. The type of leaders the Indian system thus produces consists of local politicians, knowledgeable only of local issues. These are not leaders who can win across a wide variety of social segments, or organize major campaigns, or forcefully articulate a vision. Occasionally, a local leader may show such promise, but the skills that bring most of them to power can hardly be called leadership.

This dearth of national leaders of quality harms India the most when it comes to the office of the prime minister. A feckless prime minister cannot bring about a national vision. He cannot give direction to the nation's agenda. He cannot establish priorities. He cannot keep discipline in his Cabinet. But, above all, he cannot move people to action. In America, the president does all of the above and more. His political philosophy, character and experience are showcased in a long, gruelling election. The candidate who has the best combination of these factors normally wins. He is not only the head of government, but also the head of state.

Candidates for any office in America have to declare their political beliefs and aims *before* they obtain their party's nomination. As a first step, they have to run in a primary election in which the party faithful normally vote. A debate with the opposing candidates and the media ensues. Each candidate's record is compared with his pronouncements. Did he vote in favour of that or a similar government programme in the past? All forms of campaigning tools are used to expose or promote a candidate. Live debates are held on TV. All of this is done even before the candidate has been nominated by a party. In the 2012 presidential election in America, the Republican Party organized more than twenty live debates among twelve candidates before picking the party's nominee through primary elections.

Direct election makes all the difference when it comes to selecting leaders of quality. Bagehot once admitted that 'generally speaking, in an electioneering country … the election of candidates to elect candidates is a farce'.[46] Selecting the nation's topmost leader indirectly is not just absurd, it is utterly impractical. A leader so selected always has doubts about his legitimacy. This diminishes his ability to influence people and move them to action. In the parliamentary system the people never know why someone was selected as prime minister. Usually he is not selected because of his vision and ability, but because he was the most acceptable to party bosses. Routinely, prime ministers are pulled out of a bag. A bureaucrat or state-level politician whose name had never previously been heard by the nation is suddenly made prime minister.

But direct election is not the only reason an American president in general is a better leader than an Indian prime minister. In the United States, one doesn't have to be a career politician to become president. One of the beauties of that system is that anyone with ideas and ability has a shot at becoming the leader of the nation. People from all walks of life regularly come forward, and accomplished individuals with real-life experiences are chosen to lead. Most American presidents have had a different career before entering politics. Of the past ten presidents, only half were career politicians. The other half included a military commander, a farmer, an actor and a couple of businessmen. Not that these individuals are unaware of politics. Invariably, they come to the limelight because of their performance in high public offices. Among the ten most recent presidents, three were senators, four were governors and three were vice-presidents before attaining the highest office.

NOTES

1   Thoreau, Henry David, 'On the Duty of Civil Disobedience', first published 1849; downloaded September 2012 from http://www.ibiblio.org/ebooks/Thoreau/index.html. (Gandhi called Thoreau one of the greatest and most moral men America has produced. Gandhi, M.K., 'For Passive Resisters', *Indian Opinion*, 26 October 1907, downloaded 26 September 2012 from http://en.wikipedia.org/wiki/Civil_Disobedience_(Thoreau))

2   Lijphart, A. (1992), *Parliamentary Versus Presidential Government*, New York: Oxford University Press, Introduction.

3   Bagehot, W. (2007), *The English Constitution*, Charleston, SC, USA: BiblioBazaar, p. 40.

4   Inaugural Address, 20 January 1981; downloaded September 2012 from http://www.reaganfoundation.org/reagan-quotes-detail.aspx?tx=2072

5   Downloaded March 2014 from http://www.brainyquote.com/
    quotes/quotes/r/ronaldreag109937.htm

6   Goldwin, Robert. A., and Art Kaufman (eds) (1986), *Separation
    of Powers: Does It Still Work?*, Washington DC, USA: American
    Enterprise Institute for Public Policy Research (henceforth *SOP*),
    p. 181.

7   Verney, D. V. (1959), *The Analysis of Political Systems*, Chicago, IL,
    USA: The Free Press, p. 41.

8   Goldwin, *SOP*, pp. 171–72.

9   Verney, op. cit., p. 210.

10 Bagehot, op. cit., p. 229.

11 Gitelson, Alan R., Robert L. Dudley and Melvin J. Dubnick,
    (2008), *American Government*, Boston, MA, USA: Houghton Mifflin
    Company, p. 203.

12 Noorani, A.G. (2010), *Constitutional Questions & Citizens' Rights*,
    New Delhi: Oxford University Press, Preface, Ethics of Ministers
    and MPs.

13 Verney, op. cit., pp. 116–22.

14 Lijphart, op. cit., p. 13.

15 Ibid., p. 11.

16 Goldwin, *SOP*, p. 49.

17 Ibid., *SOP*, pp. 68–70.

18 Verney, op. cit., p. 55.

19 *The Times of India*, 30 July 2009.

20 Goldwin, *SOP*, p. 134.

21 Ibid., pp. 138–39.

22 Ibid., p. 139.

23 Bagehot, op. cit., p. 63.

24 Linz, J.J. (1994), *The Failure of Presidential Democracy*, Vol. 1,
    Baltimore, MD, USA: The Johns Hopkins University Press, p. 7.

25 *The Economist*, November 2010.

26 Mayhew, D. R. (1991), *Divided We Govern*, New Haven, CT, USA:
    Yale University Press (henceforth *DWG*), p. 80.

27 Ibid., p. 199.

28 *The Economist*, 18 February 2010.

29 Mayhew, *DWG*, p. 119.
30 Gitelson et al., op. cit., p. 291.
31 Mayhew, *DWG*, pp. 129–35.
32 *The Economist,* 8, September 2010.
33 Lienert, Ian, 'Who Controls the Budget: The Legislature or the Executive?', IMF Working Paper, 2005, downloaded September 2012 from http://www.imf.org/external/pubs/ft/wp/2005/wp05115.pdf
34 Linz, op. cit., p. 13.
35 Riggs, F.W. (1994). Draft for the text published as 'Conceptual Homogenization of a Heterogenous field: presidentialism in comparative perspective', in Mattei and Ali Kazancigil (eds.), *Comparing Nations: Concepts, Strategies, Substance.* Blackwell, 1994, pp. 72-152. Accessed from http://correctphilippines. org//problems-of- presidentialism/
36 'American Government' at ushistory.org; http://www.ushistory.org/gov/8c.asp, accessed 26 March 2014.
37 *The Economist,* 11 November 2010. In December 2011 government was formed in Belgium after a gap of 589 days, a new record.
38 Riggs, op. cit., p. 80.
39 Bagehot, op. cit., p. 68.
40 Linz, op. cit., p. 8.
41 Mayhew, *DWG*, p. 199.
42 Verney, op. cit., p. 102.
43 Riggs, op. cit., p. 136.
44 Goldwin, *SOP*, p. 34.
45 Ibid., p. 185.
46 Bagehot, op. cit., p. 64.

12

Repelling Authoritarianism

The general depiction of America's president as the most powerful man on the planet has created an erroneous impression. The US system vests the executive power in a single individual not to bestow him with all authority, but to assign him all responsibility.

The prime directive in framing the US Constitution was to ensure that powers had no chance of finding a focal point; that they remained divided in the hands of many. In more than 200 years, an American president has never been so much as accused of autocratic behaviour. There are reasons, however, why this erroneous impression took hold in India, chief among them a lack of familiarity with the American system.

The notion that the presidential system could lapse into dictatorship took root first during Indira Gandhi's Emergency in the mid-1970s. It was widely believed that she wanted to adopt the presidential form of government to further her own autocratic reign. A few members of her coterie had suggested a directly elected chief executive, in a paper entitled 'A Fresh Look at Our Constitution'. But other than this one feature, the suggested system was downright un-American. For instance, it noted that 'unlike the USA the legislature will not be too independent of the executive'.

In any case, Indira Gandhi opted to stick with the parliamentary system because it was most suited to autocracy. The Swaran Singh Committee appointed by her to look into the matter quickly decided that an American-style system was unsuitable. A.R. Antulay, the author of a paper titled 'A fresh look at our Constitution – Some suggestions' and a member of the Swaran Singh Committee, admitted as much. In an interview with Granville Austin in 1994, Antulay said: 'Indira Gandhi wanted to be a dictator, which is why in October 1976, she wanted a presidential system. But you can't be a dictator in a presidential system.'[1]

The fallacy that the presidential system has autocratic tendencies, however, still prevails. Even as he wrote recently that India should consider adopting the presidential system, well-known columnist Kuldip Nayar worried: 'No doubt, there is a danger that the President might turn into a dictator.'[2] Similarly, A.G. Noorani, a constitutional expert, argued against the presidential form because 'in India, it would pave the way for a legitimized autocracy'.[3]

The presidential system's reputation in India is sullied because its name became associated with an autocrat. But it is important to remember that it was the parliamentary system that allowed Indira Gandhi to become a dictator. The US system has never, in its 225-year history, seen a president even attempt autocratic rule.

PRESIDENTIAL STRUCTURE MAKES SINGLE RULER IMPOSSIBLE

How exactly does the American structure make it impossible for the president to become a dictator? First, there is the federal structure. The state governments are genuinely sovereign. They cannot be controlled, even by the combined forces of Congress and the president. Second, the executive, legislative and judiciary are not just separate in powers but in institutions. Each institution derives its legitimacy directly from the people, not from another branch. Third, each institution is balanced with others. In the legislature, the balance is between the House and the Senate, and then with the president. In the judiciary it is with the executive and legislature, and with the states. The executive is balanced with the Senate with regard to treaties and appointments. Lastly, the people hold direct sway over them all. They elect the legislative and the executive branches separately.

There are so many power centres in the US system that a president, no matter how popular, cannot possibly control an entire government. He is not a tyrant in waiting. On the contrary, he is 'the guardian of the people ... against legislative tyranny', as Gouverneur Morris said in America's Constitutional Convention.

PRESIDENT IS NOT PRIME MINISTER

Another error is in seeing the position of the president as analogous to that of the prime minister. The president is not the centre of all governmental powers. His position was devised to balance the legislature. He can pass no laws. He cannot amend the Constitution. He cannot declare war. He cannot borrow money, nor does he have the power to tax the people. All of these powers are given exclusively to Congress. In the US, Congress authorizes the president to do what he does. And it can revoke those authorities. Congress approves his budget. It can refuse to give him money for programmes, or disallow previously approved funding. Even the authorities specifically given to the president, he must share with the Senate. This body of Congress must ratify all treaties that the president makes with other governments. The president cannot appoint judges, unless they are confirmed by the Senate. He cannot even appoint members of his own Cabinet unless the Senate approves.

This works because in the United States the legislature is truly independent. He cannot choose who gets elected to the House of Representatives or to the Senate. Then, the president has no control over Congress's leadership; especially so if they happen to be from the opposite party. He must work with whomever the House and the Senate select as their leaders. Also, the president of the United States cannot dissolve the legislature. The legislature, however, can impeach the president.

That is not all. The president has no control over state governments. In America no power – neither the president nor Congress – can dissolve a state government. Each state is independent and decides on its own whether or not to participate in a president's programme. A state government can seek favours from a president, but since in the Senate all states have equal representation, favouritism has no chance.

Just how drastically different the office of the president is from that of the prime minister can be understood by examining the big-picture rationale for the former's existence. The principal purpose of the presidency is to provide a national government, not just a chief executive. For a government to be truly national in character, it must flow directly from the entire nation. In India, the office of the prime minister doesn't meet this essential requirement. Then, for a national government to be truly independent, it must be supported by the people directly. The office of the prime minister doesn't serve that purpose either. Further, for an independent national government to be genuinely strong, it must have an executive who is independent of the legislative. This is the main reason the office of the president is a separate institution in the United States. And finally, for a strong and independent national government to have the right mix of energy and responsibility, its chief executive must be a single individual. These are the reasons the office of the president exists. Not to become, as is the case with the prime minister, the focal point of all executive and legislative powers of the nation.

The president is an integral part of the American structure, but not its master. He is the most visible government official, since he is both head of state and head of government. But that doesn't mean he can conduct the affairs of government by himself.

WINNER DOESN'T TAKE ALL

Still, some contend that the presidential system allows the winners to take all. They imply that in this system there is either a threat of arbitrary rule by the victors of a presidential election, or a danger of undemocratic behaviour by the vanquished. Nothing could be farther from the truth. Pluralism is built into its very structure. It compels governments to build coalitions on issues rather than on politics (Chapter 10).

316 WHY INDIA NEEDS THE PRESIDENTIAL SYSTEM

By contrast, the Indian system provides far fewer representatives and much less influence to the minority view. Evidence has shown that *this* really is the winner-takes-all system. Since the very beginning of the republic, Indian governments have ruled arbitrarily, or not at all. The concentration of powers is so extreme that it brought democracy to a complete halt during the Emergency.

Those who make the winner-takes-all charge against the presidential system cite two reasons. One, that it doesn't share the executive power; and two, that it doesn't guarantee the loser of a presidential election a place in government. But in India, unless a prime minister forms a coalition, the minority views have no chance of being heard. In the US system, the entire executive power is shared with the legislature, not just with a few partners in a coalition. Sharing of powers in a parliamentary system occurs only when there isn't a clear majority winner, but in the US system it is routine. It is inherent to the system because of its separation of institutions and their powers.

As for the loser of a presidential election, the US system offers many opportunities. He can continue in his earlier role. For instance, the loser of the 2008 presidential election, Senator John McCain, continues as a senator to this day. He can run for president again, or for any other office. Often the loser has succeeded in a later election. And his stature almost always improves as a result of running in a presidential election. If his views found some traction with the people, his running for president serves to advance his agenda significantly, as Al Gore did with his environmental activism.

It is the parliamentary system that really offers no place to the vanquished. As the British constitutional scholar Sir Sidney Low wrote: 'We do not attempt to mitigate the disaster inflicted on the defeated party at a general election by giving its members any real share either in the executive government or in the making of laws.'[4]

PRESIDENT DOESN'T HAVE SOLE CONTROL OF MILITARY

The Constitution of the United States divides control over the military between the two elective branches. The president is the chief commander of America's armed forces, but Congress must approve military actions. The Constitution gives the powers 'to declare war', 'to raise and support an army', 'to maintain a navy', and 'to provide for a militia' to the legislature. The president is authorized to be the 'commander-in-chief' but only when the armed forces are 'called into the actual service of the United States'.

To bring this about, the entire defence structure of American government was created through legislation. Congress created the War Department and the Navy Department in the early years of the republic. And when in the aftermath of the Second World War the departments needed to be reorganized, it was Congress that did so after much deliberation. The National Security Act of 1947 set up a unified military command known as the National Military Establishment (changed to the Department of Defence in 1949). It also created the Central Intelligence Agency, the National Security Council, National Security Resources Board, United States Air Force (formerly the Army Air Forces) and the Joint Chiefs of Staff.

The Act placed the military establishment under the control of a single secretary of defence, who is appointed jointly by the president and the Senate. The secretary of defence is the principal defence policy advisor to the president. Under the president's direction, he controls the Department of Defence (also known as the Pentagon), but he also reports to Congress.

Congress's independence is the key to maintaining dual control over the armed forces. Presidents routinely engage in a tug of war with the legislature to gain more control, but Congress keeps them in check through restrictive laws, control of funding, and oversight. There have been periods when presidents took over the power to make war, but only when Congress allowed it to happen considering the circumstances. When presidents overreach, Congress pushes back. The latest such legislative action was the War Powers Resolution of 1973. It provided that the president could send troops into hostile territory for a period of up to sixty days. If Congress doesn't approve within that time, the troops must be withdrawn. The 1973 Act also requires that the president must consult with Congress 'in every possible instance' before placing US service personnel in harm's way. Then, Congress has the power to deny funds for military actions. For instance, in 1974 Congress passed a bill requiring the president to reduce military assistance to any government that violated human rights. Congress hasn't actually cut funding for US troops, but it compels the president to reconsider.

Where the American legislature is especially effective in exercising control over the military is through its powers of oversight. Members of Congress routinely question key defence officials while considering the Pentagon's budget requests. The secretary of defence, the director of the CIA, other agency chiefs, as well as generals, often appear before congressional committees to answer questions. They can also be required to prepare detailed reports of their activities. In the 1996 Defence Appropriations Act, for instance, Congress mandated so many reports that it took the Pentagon 111 pages just to list them.[5] Congress can also use its investigative powers to influence defence policy. In 1987, for example, it investigated President Reagan's National Security Council staff for alleged violations of a congressional prohibition on providing military assistance to rebels in Nicaragua.

HEAD OF STATE BUT NOT SYMBOL OF PATRIOTISM

One reason the myth of an all-powerful president has spread is that he is both the head of government and head of state. Even though his functions as head of state are purely symbolic (like that of any other country), this gives the office a special aura.

Having a head of state different from a head of government doesn't make sense in a democracy. It may be a necessity in a monarchical democracy, like that of Britain, but it weakens the force of government in a country like India. Commenting on the practice of separating the two offices, Verney noted: 'There seems no apparent reason, at first glance, for dividing it in Republics.'[6] In fact, combining the two has substantial and practical advantages. It enhances the American president's credibility in his dealings with foreign countries. And it provides him special affinity with his people in times of celebration or in moments of crisis. This makes an American president much more effective than an Indian prime minister or president.

The other very important advantage of combining the head of state and head of government into a transitory official is that patriotism is not focused on an individual. People find more permanent symbols to represent their unity and love for their nation. Riggs describes their significance: 'Impersonal symbols play an exceptionally important role in America, contributing to a sense of national unity or patriotism that the president, in person, cannot sustain. Americans pledge allegiance to the flag ... sing the national anthem, visit patriotic monuments and the Statue of Liberty. Above all, they honor the constitution and take oaths to support it.'[7]

PRESIDENT CAN BE REMOVED FROM OFFICE

In one important respect, the American presidential system is more true to the parliamentary principle of an executive removable by the legislative than is the Indian system. In the US, a president can actually be removed from office for misconduct through impeachment by the Congress. In India, there are no provisions to remove a prime minister as long as his party holds a majority in parliament. The president of India can be impeached, but he is only a symbolic head of the executive.

Removing a president involves two steps. First, the House of Representatives votes on formal charges, and then the Senate conducts a trial. If the Senate returns a guilty verdict, the president is removed from office.

Nine presidents have been considered for impeachment by the House of Representatives. Of those, the cases of two – Andrew Johnson in 1868 and Bill Clinton in 1999 – went as far as the Senate. President Andrew Johnson had infuriated many with his conciliatory policies toward the South in the aftermath of American Civil War. However, his trial in the Senate ended in an acquittal by a single vote.

President Clinton, who was charged with lewd behaviour in office, also survived in the Senate, by twelve votes. But the threat of impeachment has caused one president to resign. Embroiled in the Watergate scandal, President Richard Nixon left office to avoid impeachment soon after a House committee decided to conduct a full House vote.

SAFEGUARDS AGAINST MONEY CONTROLLING THE GOVERNMENT

The American Constitution foresaw money control as a crucial issue and instituted provisions to address it. First, it is the structure; when power is divided between national and state governments, and then among many different institutions of each, grabbing control becomes impossible. Second, there is an almost complete absence of 'black money' in the US system. Unlike India, the American economy doesn't operate on cash transactions. All revenue and expenditure items have to enter the banking system at some point, which makes it very difficult to conceal them. The American principle of limited government has avoided government's intervention in areas of private enterprise. Thus, there is no 'licence raj' creating unfair opportunities for buying governmental favours. The real estate industry – the chief source of black money in India – works on an entirely different basis in the US. Almost all real estate transactions involve borrowing from regulated banks or other institutions. Hiding their value works for neither side. Campaign or political contributions are extremely difficult to make in secret in such a system.

Then, there are campaign finance laws that make wilful violations a criminal offence. Here again, the independence of Congress has allowed it to pass effective laws restricting the influence of money in presidential elections. In 1975, Congress passed the Federal Election Campaign Act (FECA), and created the Federal Election Commission (FEC), to track the financing of federal elections. And once again, it was the separation of powers that made it possible to keep the FEC bipartisan and under the control of both the executive and the legislature. The commission is made up of six members, who are appointed by the president but have to be confirmed by the Senate. FEC doesn't attempt to control the overall size of campaign expenditures, but it tries to limit the imbalances between candidates. It monitors the flow of funds and sets limits for contributions. It provides public financing to presidential candidates if they agree to limit spending. Similar reforms were instituted by a bipartisan Campaign Finance Act in 2002.

The American presidential elections are lengthy campaigns in which huge sums of money are spent, but that is a reflection of the American people's spirit of participation. For instance, in the 2008 presidential election, of the roughly $745 million in campaign contributions received by Barack Obama, $657 million was made by individual donors.[8] His campaign was so well funded by the people that Obama became the first presidential candidate to deny public financing so that he could avoid spending limits. Limiting the expenditure on campaigns has not found favour in America in general because a large percentage of its people consider it a restriction on freedom of speech.

'The reality is that money is a necessary, but not a sufficient, factor in a successful bid for many political offices,' reports Gitelson about conditions in the US. He lists many other factors that influence elections: partisanship, national tides, presidential coat-tails, issues, candidates' personalities and skills, scandals, incumbency, etc.[9]

When all is said and done, there is an overarching reason why money doesn't 'own' an American government: self-preservation. As Riggs wrote, 'Wealthy and powerful individuals, corporations and associations recognize the advantages they enjoy as a result of the open party system ... Their interests lie with the system rather than with either political party.'

NOTES

1 Austin, G. (1999), *Working a Democratic Constitution: A History of the Indian Experience*, New Delhi: Oxford University Press (henceforth *WDC*), p. 382, note 40.

2 *Deccan Herald*, 17 May 2012.

3   *Frontline*, February 2010.

4   Low, S., (1915), *Governance of England*, New York: G.P. Putnam's Sons, p. 117.

5   Gitelson, Alan R., Robert L. Dudley and Melvin J. Dubnick, (2008), *American Government*, Boston, MA, USA: Houghton Mifflin Company, p. 277.

6   Verney, D.V. (1959), *The Analysis of Political Systems*, Chicago, IL, USA: The Free Press, p. 25.

7   Riggs, F.W. (1994). Draft for the text published as 'Conceptual Homogenization of a Heterogenous field: presidentialism in comparative perspective', in Mattei and Ali Kazancigil (eds.), *Comparing Nations: Concepts, Strategies, Substance*. Blackwell, 1994, pp. 72-152. Accessed from http://correctphilippines. org//problems-of- presidentialism/

8   From Federal Election Commission; accessed September 2012; http://www. fec.gov/data/CandidateSummary. do?format=html&election_yr=2008

9   Gitelson et al., op. cit., p. 200.

13

The Dissipation of Prejudices

In India any talk about the presidential system suffers from three great prejudices. The aura surrounding India's founding fathers, particularly Jawaharlal Nehru and B.R. Ambedkar, is huge, as is the belief that the parliamentary system was their consensual choice. Second, due to Indira Gandhi's tampering, the presidential system has come to be known as an authoritarian tool. Third, the belief that the parliamentary system is more responsible. The debate is still framed along Ambedkar's lines that the choice is between stability and accountability.

Over the years, many Indian thinkers have advocated switching to the presidential form of government. However, they failed to address the misconceptions that shroud both systems of governance. Slowly but surely, however, these biases are now dissipating.

AMBEDKAR DISOWNED THE PARLIAMENTARY SYSTEM

It may come as a surprise to many that B.R. Ambedkar was the first to disown the parliamentary system. In an astonishing admission in 1953, only three years after the adoption of India's Constitution, Ambedkar blurted out in the Rajya Sabha: 'Sir, my friends tell me that I have made the Constitution. But I am quite prepared to say that I shall be the first person to burn it out. I do not want it. It does not suit anybody…'[1]

Ambedkar was advocating that the Constitution be changed to give governors the powers of oversight. This in spite of the fact that he had written to the Constituent Assembly arguing for a reversal of the decision to have directly elected governors. Then, he had written to the Assembly that 'the co-existence of a Governor elected by the people and a Chief Minister responsible to the Legislature might lead to friction'.[2] But now he told the Rajya Sabha: 'We have inherited the idea that the Governor must have no power at all, that he must be a rubber stamp. If a minister, however scoundrelly he may be, if he puts up a proposal before the Governor, he has to ditto it. That is the kind of conception about democracy which we have developed in this country.'

'But you defended it,' said a member.

Ambedkar snapped back: 'We lawyers defend many things... People always keep on saying to me: "Oh, you are the maker of the Constitution." My answer is I was a hack. What I was asked to do, I did much against my will.'

A member asked: 'Why did you serve your masters then like that?'

'...you had drafted this Constitution,' said another.

Ambedkar wasn't backing down: 'You want to accuse me for your blemishes? – typically, I might add.'

As the House was brought to order, K.S. Hegde, who would later become a Supreme Court justice, expressed shock: 'It came with ill grace from Dr Ambedkar when he said that his heart was not in the Constitution, that he was merely perpetuating a fraud, to put it in the mildest form.'[3]

INSIDERS CHANGE THEIR MIND

Another stalwart of India's Constituent Assembly, and in fact one of the chief proponents of the parliamentary system, K.M. Munshi, also changed his mind. Munshi, who was considered closest to both Nehru and Patel, was the first insider to start deriding the parliamentary system publicly.

Within a decade and a half of functioning under the new system, he said, 'If I had to make a choice again, I would vote for the presidential form of government so that, whenever the politicians fail the country there is at least one strong organ of the State capable of tiding over the crisis.'[4]

. Years before he became president of India, R. Venkataraman, yet another member of the Constituent Assembly, wrote a letter to his Congress party's top committee, reporting 'grave doubts in the minds of many thinkers ... regarding the future of our parliamentary democracy'. Worried about the instability of parliamentary governments, he wanted the party to constitute a committee to study 'whether the present cabinet form of government ... be replaced by an executive directly elected by the people for a fixed term'.[5] Such a committee was never formed.

In his letter, Venkataraman, who had been a senior minister in Union and state governments and a UN delegate, explained why the American system was better suited for India. 'In a presidential system,' he wrote, 'the sad spectacle of party members forming several permutations and combinations for ousting the party chief will be eliminated. ... With the grave threat of aggression on our borders, it behooves us to give unto ourselves an executive which will be stable and not depend on the vagaries of groups and dissidents. Such an executive must derive its strength and authority from the people of the country and should not be removable except on the expiry of the term or by impeachment. The presidential system offers the best solution ...'

In a lecture in 1999, after his term as president, he said that in India 'governments were engaged more in their survival rather than in service of the people'. His diagnosis of the problem was that India's 'multi-party system was found incompatible with the Westminster type of democracy based on a two-party system'. But his remedy now was not as drastic. He called for either a 'derecognition of more than two political parties', or a 'national government consisting of the parties in the House'.[6]

Another member of India's power elite, B.K. Nehru, also wished publicly that his nation would adopt the presidential system. A cousin of Jawaharlal Nehru, Brij Kumar, was India's ambassador to the US for nearly a decade. In an article he explained why the presidential system would work better for India: 'A governor in the states and a President at the Centre, elected by universal adult suffrage (to give him the necessary authority) for a fixed term of years (which would free his energies from continuously arranging for his continued survival) would be able to formulate a set of consistent policies and would have time enough to carry them through ... Furthermore, the ineligibility of legislators to occupy ministerial office would automatically stop the intrigue for that purpose which is often their most absorbing occupation.'[7]

INDIRA GANDHI AND THE PROPOSED PRESIDENTIAL SYSTEM

In the early 1970s when his niece, Indira Gandhi, came to power with an overwhelming majority, Nehru thought it was an opportune time. Instead, the sycophants around Gandhi proposed a system that was presidential in name only. It was designed to make her a dictator. Ironically, the proposal wasn't considered necessary, because she found the existing parliamentary system suitably authoritarian.

The attempt by Indira Gandhi's clique to abuse the presidential system provoked Nani Palkhivala, an eminent constitutional scholar, to come forward and set the matter right.

'It is erroneous to think that the presidential system, necessarily involves a higher concentration of power,' Palkhivala wrote. 'In fact, the Prime Minister of India today under our Westminster parliamentary model has wider powers than the President of the US.' He cited four advantages in adopting the presidential form:

First, it enables the President to have a cabinet of outstanding competence and integrity, since the choice is not restricted to Parliament. A wise President can substitute excellence for the deadwood which passes for government today. Secondly, since the cabinet ministers are not elected, they are not motivated to adopt cheap populist measures which are so costly to the country in the long run....Thirdly, the presidential system permits the cabinet ministers to be absorbed in the job of governing the country, instead of wasting their time and potential in endless politicking. Fourthly, it would stop defections and desertions on the part of legislators, which are in most cases motivated purely by thirst for power and hunger for office.[8]

In conclusion Palkhivala noted that 'Prima facie and in normal times, I would have thought that there are more advantages in the presidential system than its opponents concede.'

In the face of severe opposition, Indira Gandhi's men stopped pushing their fake version of the presidential system. But a member of her inner circle, Vasant Sathe, continued to advocate one particular feature of the system: the direct election of the nation's chief executive.

In his 1984 book *Towards a Social Revolution*, Sathe proposed a directly elected executive who was 'answerable to Parliament in matters of policy,' but 'shall not be liable to be removed by Parliament except by way of impeachment.'[9]

Sathe's idea found little support. The main reason was that he was considered one of Indira Gandhi's 'puppets' (among others, by journalist Romesh Thapar). Even his book was dedicated to Indira Gandhi, and to his parents. So, Sathe couldn't dispel the suspicion that his proposal was really designed to benefit Indira Gandhi. Also Sathe mistakenly thought that it could be implemented without changing the basic structure of the Constitution.[10]

He wrote to Rajiv Gandhi, then a general secretary of the Congress party, to consider converting the existing Parliament into a Constituent Assembly to bring about these changes.[11] This proposal too received little support from the opposition parties.

In 1989 he made his final appeal in the form of another book, *Two Swords in One Scabbard: A Case for Presidential Form of Parliamentary Democracy*. He now proposed a *single* national authority, elected directly by the people. Pointing to the long-standing issue of whether the president or the prime minister had supremacy, Sathe wrote: 'This matter can no longer be left to chance or personal qualities or equation between two individuals. It must be constitutionally resolved ...'[12]

The idea of a directly elected prime minister intrigued Indira Gandhi, but she knew that wouldn't pass for the presidential system. In an interview in the early 1980s, she noted that 'in a country of 700 million people, the prime minister gets elected by a small electorate comprising six lakhs or so. A prime minister, so elected, may not be aware of the problems of the country as a whole ... If he or she is elected by the entire country then the person would have ... to concern himself or herself with every problem of every area, of every section of the people.' About switching to the presidential system, however, Indira Gandhi said, 'It cannot be dealt with on the basis of taking on just one aspect.'[13]

OPPOSITION SHOWS INTEREST IN THE PRESIDENTIAL SYSTEM

The first time non-Congress leaders showed any willingness to look at the presidential system was in the late 1980s. Two major opposition leaders, Ramakrishna Hegde and L.K. Advani, let it be known that they were open to an examination of this system's suitability.

Hegde, as chief minister of Karnataka, was attracted to this system mainly because of its true federalism. He had opposed it earlier because its proposal 'appeared to be with a view to concentrating more and more power in one individual's hands'. Now he was willing to accept the presidential system as long as it brought 'decentralization of power and the establishment of a real federation of states'.[14] Hegde also noted that the 'direct election of the President could project leaders who represent the entire country, unlike the Prime Minister representing just one constituency or enjoying the confidence of just a single party'. Also, he noted 'a directly elected chief executive would transcend regional, communal and caste divisions'.[15]

Advani, as president of the main opposition party, was much more cautious. In his January 1987 address to the BJP National Council he suggested setting up a commission to examine 'the suitability of the presidential system'. But he quickly made it clear that he had 'not advocated the presidential system' but only 'de-frozen the party's resolute opposition to the idea'. A few days later he made similar remarks at a session billed as *Should We Change the System*, which he attended along with Sathe and Hegde. He said that he was willing to consider this system, if it would 'strengthen the concept of one nation and contain centrifugal forces', and help create a 'highly decentralized unitary state'.[16]

Within days of the *Should We Change* session, many of India's leading thinkers came out openly in favour of a drastic change in the nation's system. In a joint statement published in the *Hindustan Times*, twenty eminent Indians pleaded 'that the critical situation facing the nation needs to be urgently debated across the country ... totally untrammeled by political partisanship'. The signatories to the joint statement included big names, such as B.K. Nehru; Inder Gujral, who would later become prime minister; Krishan Kant, a future vice-president; Inder Malhotra and Khushwant Singh, two of India's leading journalists; J.R.D. Tata, the nation's most respected industrialist; Aruna Asaf Ali, a Bharat Ratna; and P.P. Kumaramangalam, a former chief of staff of Indian armed forces.[17]

The statement highlighted areas in desperate need of reform. Instability was the top concern. 'The Prime Minister or the chief minister loses power if they lose their legislative majority ... this makes these majorities the targets of manipulations,' it said. The signatories were also deeply concerned about bad laws: 'The Prime Minister/chief minister ... can bring in measures unacceptable to the legislature and to the public at large, as the Opposition is in a minority and cannot prevail.' Also, the direct election of the chief executive was something they wanted to be considered seriously.

Advani's commission to study the presidential system, however, never materialized. This was not surprising, given that he had declared that 'I have not advocated the presidential system ... the fact is that I have shown my resolute opposition.' In closing, he added that the 'system which obtains in West Germany which my party has been canvassing for ... perhaps the adoption of that system will be the best for the country.'

Advani was concerned that the presidential system would foster 'an ethnic federal structure' in the country. In the US system, each state could have its own Constitution. He disagreed with those who 'seem to think that there would be no harm if a state like Jammu and Kashmir is allowed to have its own Constitution'.[18] Apparently, Advani had one more reservation. In a conversation with the author in 2011 he said: 'I used to be enamoured of the presidential system, but I began to doubt it will work in India because people vote here on the basis of caste.'

The fact is that only an American-type federation fulfils Advani's stated requirements. It creates a decentralized structure in which local governments have autonomy, yet the national government is supreme. It offers all states, ethnically dominated or not, a degree of independence without jeopardizing the integrity of the nation. It offers no provisions for states' secession or for changing states' boundaries without their approval. The states have the best of all worlds: a complete say in domestic matters, a fair say in national policies and the benefits of size. They have everything to gain by continuing to be a part of a strong federation.

With respect to Advani's remark about Indians voting along caste or similar lines, Hegde, his co-speaker at the 'Should We Change' session, had already given the answer. The presidential system's nationwide elections would 'transcend regional, communal and caste divisions', he had said.

Advani's interest in the presidential system was casual and brief, but the passing comment about his party considering the German system was downright cavalier. The current German Constitution has been in operation only since 1949, not much older than the Indian one. Nor is Germany a diverse and large nation like India. Needless to say, Advani's examination of the German and the American systems went no further than his terse 1987 statements.

SCHOLAR'S GLANCE: NOORANI'S MISDIAGNOSIS

The only scholarly study ever undertaken in India on the relative merits of the two systems was the one conducted in the late 1980s by A.G. Noorani, an eminent constitutional lawyer. He was asked by a New Delhi–based think tank, The Centre for Policy Research, to examine whether India should consider switching to the presidential system. The results were published in a 1989 book, *The Presidential System: The Indian Debate*. Noorani concluded that in India's current political environment the presidential system would be hazardous. His main concern was the state of political parties. He found them too fragmented and unprincipled, and failed to see how this would allow proper functioning of the presidential system.

Instead of switching to the presidential system, Noorani suggested that the existing system be revitalized. To this end he made three suggestions: 1) get rid of the reliance on conventions, by codifying the rights of the president and governors; 2) institute a constructive vote of no-confidence, by requiring that the successor is named in the motion itself; and 3) reform the party system.[19]

Noorani argued that since the disease – that the party system was unprincipled and prone to fragmentation – was political, it couldn't be fixed by the system. He worried that while it only makes the parliamentary executive unstable, 'it will render the presidential executive altogether impotent ... A volatile party which can throw out its leader overnight can also create a ruinous deadlock between the legislature and the executive and stability bought at the price of accountability is sure to undermine democracy ... The hazards of the presidential system are grave and outweigh the gains,' Noorani concluded 'especially in a society where ... the cult of bhakti in politics is widely prevalent.'[20]

More than two decades later, Noorani still holds the same reservations about the presidential system. Most recently, in the Sixtieth Republic Day issue of *Frontline* magazine he wrote: 'It is absurd to suggest that the presidential system accorded better with our national character such as it is. The defector or bitter partisan who topples a government in the parliamentary system will bring the government itself to a grinding halt as Newt Gingrich did in the United States.'[21]

Noorani is right in rejecting the idea that national character should determine the choice of the system. Because it is the system that builds the national character, not vice versa. To think otherwise, that Indians are genetically corrupt or unwise, is simply inaccurate and racist. The Indian polity is overly divided because the parliamentary system fosters fragmentation in the nation's legislature; it lacks credible leaders because the current system is incapable of producing them; its leaders resort to unconstitutional means because the system doesn't offer constitutional ways of avoiding deadlocks; its people don't participate in governance because the system doesn't provide enough representation; and so on (Chapters 8 and 11).

Noorani also fails to grasp the importance of oversight in government when he talks about deadlock in a presidential system. Without genuine oversight, government cannot be responsible. And without separate, independent and empowered executive and legislative institutions, true oversight is not possible. If the idea is to grant the executive all that it desires, why have a *system* of government in the first place?

Now, for oversight to be meaningful it must have teeth. It must be able to say no to the executive and stand its ground. A recent American case in point is raised by Noorani himself, that of Newt Gingrich. Speaker Gingrich's famous shutdown of the American government was brought about by the legislature's power of oversight. A long-time member of the House of Representatives, Gingrich became its leader after he spearheaded an unprecedented victory for his party in the 1994 mid-term elections. In 1992 President Bill Clinton had come to power, with only 42 per cent of the popular vote, and in his first two years in office he had terrified Americans with his liberal populist agenda. Gingrich and his colleagues promised, in a contract with America, a ten-point legislative programme based on conservative principles, and won big. One of those promises was the passing of a

Fiscal Responsibility Act compelling governments to balance their budgets. Two years later, in another unprecedented victory, Gingrich and his party retained control of both chambers of the US Congress. This was the first time since 1928 that the Republican majority had been re-elected. Faced with stonewalling from President Clinton against promises made in the contract, Gingrich led the House to deny funds for some government functions. The fight between the two branches led to the first balanced-budget deal in 1997 and the first four consecutive balanced budgets since the 1920s. Credit for which was, of course, claimed by both sides.

What would have happened if this famous Clinton–Gingrich fight occurred under the parliamentary system? This exact question was examined by Manuel and Cammisa in their 1999 book *Checks and Balances: How a Parliamentary System Could Change American Politics*. They concluded: 'It is possible under a parliamentary system that Prime Minister Clinton could be voted out of office and replaced by Prime Minister Gingrich, only to have his party returned to power two years later. In that case, policies easily passed by the Republican majority could just as easily be swept away by a Democratic majority, resulting in rapid and significant policy swings.' In addition there would be two further 'costs', the authors said: 1) 'the government would be less stable'; and 2) 'the minority out of power would not be in a position to act as a check ... on the majority in power'.[22]

Incidentally, under the presidential system this balancing of the two widely different agendas led to unprecedented growth in America's economy. As well as to the passing of some significant social programmes, like welfare reform.

CONSTITUTION'S OFFICIAL REVIEW ACKNOWLEDGES PRESIDENTIAL TENETS

No official effort has ever been made to study or consider the adoption of the presidential system. The Swaran Singh Committee appointed by Indira Gandhi during the Emergency considered this system only informally. The only official review of India's Constitution was undertaken by the National Commission to Review the Working of the Constitution (NCRWC), appointed by Prime Minister Vajpayee in 2000. Although the commission was restricted to work 'within the framework of parliamentary democracy', in view of the dire circumstances of the nation it asked that this system's fundamental tenets be re-examined.

'It is a sad fact,' the NCRWC reported, 'that needlessly harsh, lugubrious, unimaginative and indifferent administration has pushed the poor to the wall.' And that 'the people of India are more divided amongst themselves than at the time of the country's independence'. The commission declared that 'if remedies are not found and implemented speedily there might remain very little of value to salvage'.[23]

This bleak picture had one silver lining. The commission argued that perhaps the stability versus accountability view of India's system of government should be reconsidered. 'In the parliamentary system, if there is conflict between accountability on the one hand and stability on the other,' the commission stated, 'the latter must yield. But accountability and stability need not necessarily and always be mutually conflicting.' It declared that in today's global context 'a reasonable degree of stability' and 'strong governance' both are important [24]

Some of the commission's suggestions have been implemented over the years, but the overall report was never placed before parliament. This only worked to confirm one of its own grim conclusions: 'There is a pervasive and cynical disbelief that anything will change at all.'

PRESIDENTIAL SYSTEM IS 'BUTTER, NOT MARGARINE'

In 2007 a dashing new entrant in India's polity, Shashi Tharoor, attempted to revitalize the debate about the country's system of government. Tharoor had just resigned as an undersecretary general at the United Nations, after losing a close election to Ban Ki-moon for the topmost post. As he entered India's politics, with his new global view, he could see how bad the situation really was. In a series of articles in *The Times of India*, Tharoor presented a forceful case in favour of switching to the presidential system.

'We must have a system of government,' Tharoor wrote, 'whose leaders can focus on governance rather than on staying in power.' In the presidential system, Tharoor liked the idea of a directly elected chief executive the most. 'Any politician with aspirations to rule India as president will have to win the support of people beyond his home turf ... in that may lie the presidential system's ultimate vindication,' he said.[25]

Tharoor reported that even the British recommended that India should consider the US system. 'When former British Prime Minister Clement Attlee suggested the US presidential system as a model to Indian leaders,' he wrote, 'they rejected it with great emphasis.' 'I had the feeling that they thought I was offering them margarine instead of butter,' Attlee recalled.

DISTINGUISHED VETERAN GIVES HIS STAMP OF APPROVAL

In May 2012, the eighty-nine-year-old Kuldip Nayar, India's best-known political commentator, added his voice to the opinion that India's current system is a total failure.

'By shutting eyes to the realities, the facts cannot be denied or wished away,' Nayar wrote, 'the parliamentary system in India has succeeded in sustaining democracy but has failed to deliver the goods.' He said: 'People should seriously consider the option to switch over to the presidential form of government. This too is democratic and transparent like in America and France. In this way, we will get the most acceptable face in the country because people from different parts of India would be voting directly for one person for a fixed tenure, say five years. He or she in turn would have all the attention and time to rule the country, not dependent on coalition or regional parties ... In the process, the nation would feel more coherent and united.' Nayar concluded by saying that 'in democracy, it is important that people have faith in the system because otherwise the very basis of the state comes to be questioned.'[26]

NOTES

1   Shourie, A. (2009), *Worshipping False Gods: Ambedkar, and the Facts Which Have Been Erased*, New Delhi: Rupa & Co., p. 386.
2   *Constituent Assembly Debates (CAD)*, May 1949.
3   Shourie, op. cit., p. 387.
4   Cited in Noorani, A. G. (1989), *The Presidential System: The Indian Debate*, New Delhi: Sage Publications India Pvt. Ltd (henceforth *PS*), p. 29.
5   Letter dated 27 May 1965, Noorani, *PS*, pp. 29–31.
6   Lecture at India International Centre, New Delhi on 16 October 1999. Accessed from http://www. indiastar. com/Venkataraman1. html
7   Noorani, *PS*, p. 32.
8   'The Presidential System', *Hindustan Times,* 7 January 1981; Palkhivala, N.A. (2009), *We, The People*, New Delhi: UBS Publishers, pp. 242–46.
9   Sathe, V. (1984), *Towards a Social Revolution*, New Delhi: Stosius, Advent Books, pp. 44–48.
10 Noorani, *PS*, p. 36.
11 Sathe, V. (1989), *Two Swords in One Scabbard: A Case for Presidential Form of Parliamentary Democracy*, New Delhi: NIB Publisher (henceforth *TSOS*), p. 59.
12 Sathe, *TSOS*, Introduction.
13 Sathe, *TSOS*, pp. 123–24.
14 Ibid., p. 136.
15 *The Times of India,* 18 January 1987, cited in Noorani, *PS*, p. 39.
16 Sathe, *TSOS*, p. 142
17 29 January 1987; cited in Noorani, *PS*, p. 144.
18 Sathe, *TSOS*, pp. 137–41.
19 Noorani, *PS*, p. 99.
20 Ibid., pp. 95–102.
21 *Frontline*, February 2010.
22 Manuel, Paul C. and Anne Marie Cammisa (1999), *Checks & Balances? How a Parliamentary System Could Change American Politics,* Boulder, CO, USA: Westview Press/Perseus Books, pp. 140–41.

23   Kashyap, S.C. (2004), *Constitution Making Since 1950*, Delhi: Universal Law Publishing Co., Vol. 6, p. 305.
24   Ibid., p. 300.
25   *The Times of India*, 16 and 23 December 2007, 24 February 2008.
26   'Presidential System?', *Deccan Herald*, 17 May 2012.

14

Presidential System: The Answer
to India's Problems

India cannot progress as she must with her current system. Not just because it has already been recognized as rotten by the Indians themselves, but because it is inherently incapable of delivering the ingredients essential for a society to rise: high hopes, strong character and fair prospects. Like any other people, Indians can move mountains if only their governments helped rather than hindered their efforts. But with each passing day, India's system of government is destroying her people's moral fibre and killing their initiative.

THE REALITY OF THE INDIAN SYSTEM

Today, India is a brazen oligarchy, pure and simple. The unvarnished truth is that the Indian parliamentary system is now under the total control of a small group of leaders, the bosses of political parties. The reality of the Indian system is starkly different from its theory (see illustrations). In practice, all political power is in the hands of party high commands, who appoint and control all government officials and make all policy decisions.

'They control everything,' says A.G. Noorani about the bosses of India's political parties, in an article in the *Hindustan Times* in 2005. He was discussing the 'obscenity ... unique to India', that people didn't select 'their own candidate rather than have one selected for them by the party's leadership in New Delhi'. 'Few care to reflect on its baleful impact on the working of India's Constitution and on the

338

parliamentary system it establishes,' Noorani wrote. 'The practice perverts both.'[1]

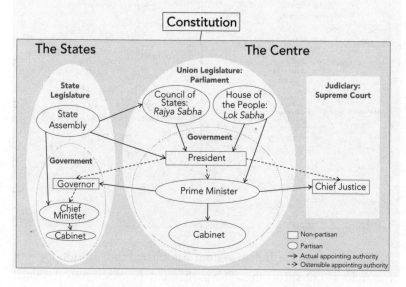

India's Parliamentary System: In Theory

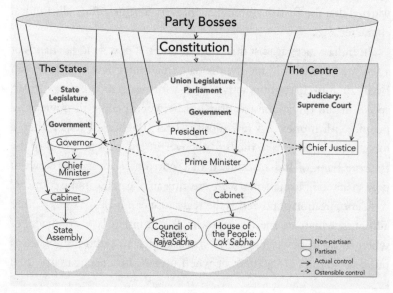

India's Parliamentary System: In Practice

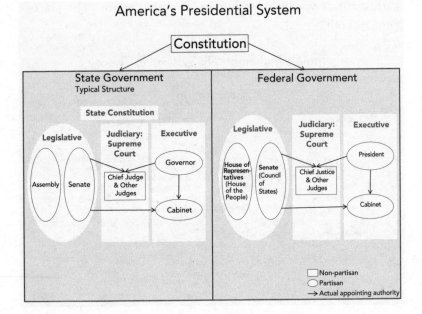

The fact that the Indian system has turned into an out-and-out oligarchy is not surprising. The parliamentary system was designed by oligarchs, for oligarchs (Chapter 2). In 1904 Sir Sidney Low had warned that the British system had 'preserved much of its oligarchical character'.[2]

In India, voices against this concentration of powers in the hands of a few are becoming louder by the day. In an interview in 2011, Kiran Bedi, an anti-corruption activist and a former senior police officer, spoke of 'an oligarchic relationship between people in power and people with money'.[3] A few months later, Raghuram Rajan, then a top economic advisor to the Indian government, now governor of the Reserve Bank of India, admitted that 'corrupt relationships between politicians and businessmen were creating an oligarchy' in the country.[4]

Centralization of powers is the real cause behind all of India's other ailments, which are mere symptoms. When unfair laws are made, or when those in power engage in corruption with impunity, or when public resources are wasted, or when investigative agencies are used for political purposes, or when no attention is paid to the quality of governance, they all point to the rot at the core of this system. It is the concentration of powers in the hands of a few.

The truth is that neither of the two rationales given for the parliamentary system – efficiency and responsibility in government – is justified by hard facts. The Indian system has failed because efficiency without effectiveness is no virtue, and responsibility without oversight is not possible. Without a genuine separation of institutions and powers, it is impossible to achieve these qualities in governance.

When each failing of the Indian system is analysed, almost always the remedy calls for the adoption of the presidential system. In a recent article entitled 'India's Biggest Failing', Tavleen Singh, a political commentator wrote that 'the first thing that comes to mind is the failure of our criminal justice system'. Her search for solution led to the conclusion that 'the biggest problem was that there were too few judges'.[5] Since under the Indian system elected officials are not responsible for the justice system, this is bound to happen. The presidential system fixes this problem by making *both* elected branches accountable for the quantity and quality of judges.

Similarly, when some leading thinkers recently examined why India wasn't living up to her true potential – in *Reimagining India*, a book compiled by the famous consulting firm McKinsey & Company – most solutions were readily possible in an American-type system. Commentator Fareed Zakaria wrote that India would meet its potential only when there was 'a bottom-up process of protest and politics'.[6] A highly participatory democracy is one of the hallmarks of the American system. Ruchir Sharma, investment banker, argued that the solution for India is further decentralization – a trait the presidential system is known for. Anand Mahindra, an Indian industrialist, suggested that the best way for India's economic growth is 'to encourage different parts of the country to go their own way'[7] – a type of federalism that the US system is built upon. And the man who coined the phrase 'India grows at night', Gurcharan Das, author and former head of a consumer product company, cautioned that 'succeeding despite the state may be heroic, but it is not sustainable'. For India to also grow during the day, he called for a 'strong liberal state with three core elements: the authority to take quick and decisive action, a transparent rule of law to ensure that such action is legitimate and accountability to the people'.[8] Once again, a list of benefits – strong government, quick executive action, legislative oversight, and direct elections – the American system is known to deliver.

The Indian system's failings are many because it has innumerable absurdities. The whole system is based on a reliance on people's representatives, yet its legislature has no control. It expects representatives to speak for those who didn't have a direct say in their selection. Such is the case with the topmost representative, the prime minister himself. This system expects representatives to dissolve their own House. It has a committee of the House, the Cabinet, with powers to dissolve the House that created it. It has a Council of States whose members don't have to belong to the state they represent. It can appoint a leader of the nation who has never won a direct election. It has legislators but they don't legislate. However, it has an executive who makes laws. The topmost official in this system follows a subordinate's commands, as is the case with the president. It has a head of state who does what he is told. Political parties are required to function, but are not regulated. It has men running governments from behind the scenes, but they are not accountable to people's representatives. It has a long written Constitution but the powers of government's topmost officials are left to convention. It doesn't specify the precise method of appointing the chief officials of the judiciary. It has an institution created under the Constitution but that institution can amend the Constitution out of all recognition. It has a basic structure but it is not specified. Executive power is vested in an official, but only ostensibly. The real executive is accountable to people's representatives, but, again, only ostensibly. In fact, he is accountable to his party bosses. The list just goes on.

Douglas Verney once said that 'the hallmark of parliamentary government is its ingenuity'.[9] The Indian system is certainly clever.

But with each passing day this crafty system is doing our nation irreparable harm.

PRESIDENTIAL SYSTEM AND INGREDIENTS FOR GREATNESS

The American presidential system cultivates the traits – hope, character and opportunity – that lead to progress. It has done so for more than two hundred years. This system is really the secret behind America's unprecedented success.

Delivers Hope

A political system must help establish national aims that are worthy and noble. This is likely to happen only if the system produces national leaders who are visionaries. This is the biggest benefit of one of the presidential system's chief features, the direct election of a single man as president by people from across the entire country. Nationwide campaigns create a vision, from the bottom up and from across the whole country. Competing visions are debated throughout the nation. Issues – small and big, national and local, domestic and foreign – percolate into priorities. A national agenda emerges.

The Indian structure doesn't allow a national vision to emerge. No national vision can arise when all leaders are local, small-time politicians. Nor can it arise when it is not even clear what constitutes a government. A government's agenda can take shape only when a government takes shape, and that usually happens *after* elections. A national agenda, if it can be termed as such, is a top-down programme of items found acceptable to the party bosses. Also, a national vision cannot emerge under the parliamentary system because it speaks in multiple voices. There is usually no single voice to articulate and move the people; no one man to claim responsibility.

A people without hope in their national vision, or faith in the stability of their government, or confidence in the quality of their leaders, don't make a healthy polity. They don't rally behind their government, nor do they take interest in issues. They don't participate in debates or governance. They vote only to express frustration. They usually vote *against* something – corruption or poor performance – but rarely *for* anything.

Builds Character

Another essential ingredient for greatness is the strength of people's character. The system of government has a huge impact on people's morality because it touches every aspect of their lives, from material well-being to their spiritual development. When the system is fair, fairness develops in the society. But when the system is unfair, people become bitter and corrupt.

The American system is built on the belief that the system of government does have an effect on morality. It is founded on man's 'sense of right', as Jefferson once said.[10] This sense of fairness is evident in many of its features. A US government can be stopped from interfering with people's lives if an action is not authorized under the Constitution. It provides people with direct representatives at every level and in every branch of government. It empowers representatives of one branch to actually stop another branch from taking an action. It gives real powers to those in the minority to stop the majority from running amok. In this system those who want to spend are not given unfettered powers to levy taxes. Those who make laws cannot also execute or judge them. Those who administer laws or spend money must answer openly and publicly, or they can be prosecuted.

The US system doesn't allow politics to interfere with day-to-day administration. This is so because unlike the Indian system, in America a majority doesn't hold all executive and legislative powers; it doesn't 'rule'.

The Indian system of government is inherently unfair. Supremacy – parliamentary or of any other kind – is basically an inequitable concept. The supremacy of parliament in the Indian system places one institution at an unfair advantage over others, like state governments or the judiciary, which are equally accountable to the people. Even worse, parliamentary sovereignty establishes people's representatives above the people themselves. Since there is only one institution, the people are left with no recourse. Similarly unjust is the fusion of executive and legislative powers. When the same people hold both powers, there is no one to stop the passing of unfair laws or to scrutinize governmental actions.

Provides Equal Opportunity

The concept of majority rule, on which the Indian system is based, is fundamentally unjust. By definition, it means politics of exclusion. A faction 'rules' while the others must bide their time.

For a diverse nation like India, the inequity involved in a majority-takes-all system is especially harmful. It worsens the sectarian and other divisions in society, because it offers no mechanism for the minority views to have a say in governance. Unless a minority is large enough that a government can be formed only with its support, it will he locked out of any share of powers. The US system, on the other hand, is designed to include minority voices in governance.

The Indian system also does not allow political participation. In India, the electorate only votes; it has almost no venues to participate in governance. This has created a huge gap between political haves and have-nots. Politics has become an almost exclusive domain of politically connected families and dynasties.

In contrast, the US system provides citizens with many more opportunities to participate in the selection of government authorities and the creation of government policies. There are many more representatives per capita, and they are all directly elected. But the biggest difference is the decentralization of politics. A recent survey found that in a two-year election cycle, 46 per cent of the American public attended a public hearing or meeting, 45 per cent contacted an elected official, 34 per cent contributed time or money to a campaign, and 27 per cent participated in a police-sponsored community watch.[11]

WHY NOT THE AMERICAN SYSTEM

There is very little doubt that if India adopted the US system, it would radically improve governance in India. The benefits are countless. However, the point is often raised that there must be other good systems. People often talk about the French or the Swiss or even the German systems of government.

The question really is, why not the American? It is a system proven over the centuries. It is built on solid arguments. And it has helped America become an exceptional performer in almost every field. There isn't an area of human excellence, from arts to sciences, and from sports to academics, in which the American people are not among the world's best. Isn't the system that built the strongest nation on earth worthy of emulation?

Those who resist are driven either by politics or prejudice. People with socialist or communist leanings would never adopt anything American. Similarly, national pride could cause people to resist adopting anything foreign.

Often an argument is given that Americans themselves are not pleased with their system. There is no doubt that there are many Americans who feel that their system of government is dysfunctional or unfair. Former US president Woodrow Wilson's criticisms of his country's system are often cited in this regard. Wilson wrote his views in his 1884 book *Congressional Government* when he was only a twenty-eight-year-old doctoral student. But as soon as he left academia his views changed. By 1908 when he published his second book *Constitutional Government* he had discarded almost all his earlier criticisms. In this work Wilson examined the American system with "an eye to practice, not the theory," [p. 1] and concluded that it was "a model before all the world." [p. 172]

In his recent book *A More Perfect Constitution*, Larry Sabato, director of University of Virginia's Center for Politics and a winner of the Thomas Jefferson Award, considered twenty-three proposals to 'revitalize' America's Constitution. None proposed changing the founders' fundamental structure. 'The heart of their Constitution (individual liberty, the separation of powers, and federalism) is untouched in these pages,' Sabato wrote.[12]

Another resounding endorsement of the vision of the founders of the United States has just been published. After analysing what's troubling the world's democracies lately, the authors of *The Economist's* series of articles entitled 'Getting Democracy Right', reached the following conclusion: 'The key to a healthier democracy, in short, is a narrower state – an idea that dates back to the American revolution.'[13] The analysis validated two additional American features: its containment of majoritarianism, 'the notion that winning an election entitles the majority to do whatever it pleases'; and its emphasis on local governance, 'local democracy frequently represented democracy at its best'.

As for other systems, none has been tested over as long a period as the American. None other has built a global superpower. The soviets tested their system for more than seven decades, but failed. The Chinese are rapidly adopting the American economic principles; the democratic ones are sure to follow. The French are already on their fifth republican Constitution. They adopted their current hybrid system in 1958 because, as Beyme reported, 'De Gaulle was realistic enough to see that in the current system he would have a considerably stronger position than he could have had in the presidential system.'[14] The German Constitution is only about sixty years old, and the nation is nowhere near as large or diverse as India. The current Swiss Constitution was adopted only recently, in 1999.

Those who are convinced about the value of the US usually have another caveat. 'Let's adopt the American system, but with modifications for Indian conditions,' they say.

As reasonable as that argument is, this question begs to he answered: what are those so-called Indian conditions. If they are about the nature or the character of the Indian people, it would be best to ignore them. Because as we have seen, the nation's political system builds character, not the other way around. But there is a more important reason to not let the current state of the Indian national character be the determining factor. There isn't a single constitutional principle of the US system that is based on the people's character. Every single principle is based on reason, and the laws of managing powers.

There might be other important Indian conditions that should be considered before making a wholesale change in the nation's system. They would have to do with how far India can go with federalism or with communal rights. But the principles of the US system in these areas are so cogently argued that any modification would have to be carefully thought through.

Most presidential systems fail because a nation copied only a few aspects of the US system. As Fred Riggs wrote, 'The failures of presidentialism outside the US were due to deep structural problems with the institutional design rather than with ecological pressures caused by the world system, poverty, culture, religion, geographic constraints, demographic forces, etc.'[15]

HOW TO ADOPT

In fairness to the Indian people, such a total overhaul of the nation's system should only be done by calling another Constituent Assembly. Like the Americans did, each state should select eminent representatives suitable for the task.

The modification of the existing Constitution is faced with two fundamental problems. One, it would have to depend upon the existing parliament. With the oligarchs in charge, and the poor quality of our current representatives, it is highly doubtful that such an exercise would be fruitful. Two, amending the current Constitution would run up against the doctrine of basic structure. When in his book, *The Parliamentary System*, Arun Shourie analysed what the adoption of some of the American principles in India's Constitution would entail, he noted that they would change its basic structure as outlined by some Supreme Court jurists. But as he said, 'the courts will indeed have to assess whether they violate the basic structure, or they are instead the one way to salvage that structure'.[16] The rigidity or reverence shown towards constitutions is unwise. They are documents made by men just like us, not super humans. As Jefferson said, 'some men look at constitutions with sanctimonious reverence and deem them ... too sacred to be touched'. He declared that 'each generation has the right to choose for itself the form of government it believes the most promotive of its own happiness'.[17]

My friends, the moment for our generation to decide our own destiny has come.

NOTES

1   Noorani, A.G. (2010), *Constitutional Questions & Citizens' Rights*, New Delhi: Oxford University Press, p. lxii.

2   Low, S. (1915), *Governance of England*, New York: G.P. Putnam's Sons, p.186.

3   Reuters Video, 11 November 2011.

4   Reuters, 10 August 2012.

5   *The Indian Express*, 26 January 2014.

6   Chandler, Clay and Adil Zainulbhai (eds), *Reimagining India*, New York: McKinsey & Company, Simon & Schuster, 2013, p. 9.

7   Ibid., p. 18.

8   Ibid., p. 23.

9   Verney, D.V. (1959), *The Analysis of Political Systems*, Chicago, IL, USA: The Free Press, p.86.

10   Padover, S.K. (1939), *Thomas Jefferson on Democracy*, New York: Mentor Book, New American Library, Hawthorn Books, p. 66.

11   1999, Council for Excellence in Government, cited in Gitelson, Alan R., Robert L. Dudley, and Melvin J. Dubnick (2008), *American Government*, Boston, MA, USA: Houghton Mifflin Company, p.149.

12   Sabato, Larry (2007), *A More Perfect Constitution*, New York: Walker & Company, p. 6.

13   *The Economist*, 28 February 2014.

14   Beyme, K.V. (1987), *America as a Model*, New York: St. Martin's Press, p. 54.

15   Riggs, F. W. (1994), 'Problems of Presidentialism and the American Exception', in Dogan, Mattei and Ali Kazancigil, (eds.) *Comparing Nations: Concepts, Strategies, Substance*. Blackwell, 1994, pp. 72–152.

16   Shourie, A. (2007), *The Parliamentary System: What We Have Made of It, What We Can Make of It*, New Delhi: ASA Publications, Rupa & Co, p. 192.

17   Padover, op. cit., p. 67.

Select Bibliography

Ambedkar, B.R. (1947), *States and Minorities*, Bombay: Thacker and Co.

Ambedkar, B.R. (1979), *Writings and Speeches*, Volume 1 and Volume 9, Bombay: Government of Maharashtra.

Austin, G. (1966), *The Indian Constitution: Cornerstone of a Nation*, New Delhi: Oxford University Press.

Austin, G. (1999). *Working a Democratic Constitution: A History of the Indian Experience*, New Delhi: Oxford University Press.

Azad, A.K. (1988), *India Wins Freedom (Complete Version)*, New Delhi: Orient Blackswan.

Bagehot, W. (2007, first published 1867), *The English Constitution*, Charleston, SC, USA: BiblioBazaar.

Beeman, R. (2009), *Plain, Honest Men,* New York: Random House.

Beer, S. H. (1982), *Britain Against Itself,* London: Faber and Faber Limited.

Beyme, K. V. (1987), *America as a Model,* New York: St Martin's Press.

Borden, M. (1965, original articles published 1787–88). *Anti-Federalist Papers*, retrieved 2012, from Constitution.org: http://www.constitution.org/afp.htm

Campbell, T. (2004), *Separation of Powers in Practice*, Stanford, CA, USA: Stanford University Press.

Carey, George W., and James McClellan (eds), (2001), *The Federalist (The Gideon Edition),* Indianapolis: Liberty Fund.

Chakrabarty, Bidyut and Rajendra K. Pandey (2008), *Indian Government and Politics*, New Delhi: Sage Publications.

Chandler, Clay and Adil Zainulbhai (eds), *Reimagining India*, New York: McKinsey & Company, Simon & Schuster, 2013.

Chandra, Bipan, M. Mukherjee and A. Mukherjee (2008), *India Since Independence*, New Delhi: Penguin Books.

Chatterjee, D.K. (1984), *Gandhi and Constitution Making in India*, New Delhi: Associated Publishing House.

Collins, Larry and Dominique Lapierre (1975), *Freedom At Midnight*, New York: Simon & Schuster.

Constituent Assembly Debates, Vols. 1–12, (1985), New Delhi: Lok Sabha Secretariat.

Farrand, M. (1911), *The Records of the Federal Convention of 1787*, retrieved 2012, from The Online Library of Liberty: http://oll.libertyfund.org/title/1057

Gitelson, Alan R., Robert L. Dudley and Melvin J. Dubnick, (2008), *American Government*, Boston, MA, USA: Houghton Mifflin Company.

Godbole, M. (2011), *India's Parliamentary Democracy on Trial*, New Delhi: Rupa & Co.

Goldwin, Robert. A. and William A. Schambra (eds) (1981*). How Capitalistic is the Constitution?*, Washington DC: American Enterprise Institute for Public Policy Research.

Goldwin, Robert A. and Art Kaufman (eds) (1986): *Separation of Powers Does It Still Work?*, Washington DC, USA: American Enterprise Institute for Public Policy Research.

Hardin, C.M. (1974), *Presidential Power and Accountability,* Chicago, IL, USA: The University of Chicago Press.

Jefferson, T. (1904), *The Works of Thomas Jefferson*, Putnam's Sons (libertyfund.org).

Jennings, I.W. (1961, first published 1941*), The British Constitution*, London: Cambridge University Press.

Kaiser, F.M. (2006), *Congressional Oversight,* Washington DC: The Library of Congress.

Kashyap, S.C. (2004), *Constitution Making Since 1950*, Delhi: Universal Law Publishing Co.

Khosla, M. (2012), *The Indian Constitution*, New Delhi: Oxford University Press.

Lijphart, A. (ed.) (1992), *Parliamentary Versus Presidential Government*, New York: Oxford University Press.

Linz, J.J. (1994), *The Failure of Presidential Democracy*, Vol. 1., Baltimore, MD, USA: The Johns Hopkins University Press.

Locke, J. (1952, first published 1690), *The Second Treatise of Government*, edited and with an introduction by Thomas P. Peardon, New York: The Liberal Arts Press, The Bobbs-Merrill Company.

Low, S. (1915, first published 1904), *Governance of England*, New York: G.P. Putnam's Sons.

Madison, J., Alexander Hamulton and John Jay (1787–88). *The Federalist Papers*, retrieved 13 February 2011, from The Avalon Project, Yale Law School: http://avalon.law.yale.edu/subject_menus/fed.asp

Madison, J. (1900), *The Writings of James Madison, comprising his Public Papers and his Private Correspondence, including his numerous letters and documents now for the first time printed*, ed., Gaillard Hunt, New York: G.P. Putnam's Sons. Accessed from http://oll.libertyfund.org/title/1937/118854/2400578 on 8 March 2014.

Madison, J. (1787), *Vices of the Political System of the United States*, retrieved 2010, from TeachingAmericanHistory.org: http://teachingamericanhistory.org/library/document/vices-of-the-political-system/

Mann, Thomas E. and Norman J. Ornstein (2012), *It's Even Worse Than It Looks*, New York: Basic Books, Perseus Group.

Manuel, Paul C. and Anne M. Cammisa, (1999), *Checks & Balances? How a Parliamentary System Could Change American Politics*, Boulder, CO, USA: Westview Press/Perseus Books.

Mayhew, D.R. (2011), *Partisan Balance: Why Political Parties Don't Kill the U.S. Constitutional System*, Princeton, NJ, USA: Princeton University Press.

Mayhew, D.R. (1991), *Divided We Govern*, New Haven, CT, USA: Yale University Press.

Munshi, K.M. (1997, first published 1963), *The President Under the Indian Constitution*, Mumbai: Bharatiya Vidya Bhavan.

Nayar, K. (1973), *Supersession of Judges*, New Delhi: Indian Book Company.

Nayar, K. (1977), *The Judgement: Inside Story of the Emergency in India*, New Delhi: Vikas Publishing House Pvt. Ltd.

Nehru, J. (1982, first published 1946), *The Discovery of India*, New Delhi: Jawaharlal Nehru Memorial Fund.

Noorani, A.G. (2010, first published 2006), *Constitutional Questions & Citizens' Rights*, New Delhi: Oxford University Press.

Noorani, A.G. (1989), *The Presidential System: The Indian Debate*, New Delhi: Sage Publications India Pvt. Ltd.

Padover, S.K. (1939), *Thomas Jefferson on Democracy*, New York: Mentor Book, New American Library, Hawthorn Books.

Palkhivala, N.A. (1974), *Our Constitution, Defaced and Defiled*, New Delhi: Macmillan Company of India.

Palkhivala, N.A. (2008, first published 1984), *We, the Nation: The Lost Decades*, New Delhi: UBS Publishers.

Palkhivala, N.A. (2009, first published 1984), *We, The People*, New Delhi: UBS Publishers.

Pandit, H.N. (1974), *The PM's President: A New Concept on Trial*, New Delhi: S. Chand & Co.

parliament.uk/living-heritage. (2011), Retrieved 5 October 2011, from parliament.uk: parliament.uk

Prasad, R. (2010, first published 1946), *India Divided*, New Delhi: Penguin Books India Pvt. Ltd.

Rao, B.S. (2006, first published 1967), *The Framing of India's Constitution*, Vols. 1–6, Delhi: Universal Law Publishing.

Riggs, F.W. (1994). Draft for the text published as 'Conceptual Homogenization of a Heterogenous field: presidentialism in comparative perspective', in Mattei and Ali Kazancigil (eds.), *Comparing Nations: Concepts, Strategies, Substance*. Blackwell, (1994), Accessed from http://correctphilippines. org//problems-of- presidentialism/

Russell, B. (1961), *The Basic Writings of Bertrand Russell*, New York: Simon & Schuster.

Sabato, Larry (2007), *A More Perfect Constitution*, New York: Walker & Company.

Sachau, E.C., (ed.) (1888), *Alberuni's India*, Vol. 1, London: Trubner & Co.

Sathe, V. (1984), *Towards a Social Revolution*, New Delhi: Stosius, Advent Books.

Sathe, V. (1989), *Two Swords in One Scabbard: A Case for Presidential Form of Parliamentary Democracy*, New Delhi: NIB Publisher.

Shourie, A. (2007), *The Parliamentary System: What We Have Made of It, What We Can Make of It*, New Delhi: ASA Publications, Rupa & Co.

Shourie, A. (2009, first published 1997), *Worshipping False Gods: Ambedkar, and the Facts Which Have Been Erased*, New Delhi: Rupa & Co.

Thach, C.C. (2007, first published 1923), *The Creation of the Presidency, 1775-1789*, Indianapolis, IN, USA: Amagi Books, Liberty Fund.

Verney, D.V. (1959), *The Analysis of Political Systems*, Chicago, IL, USA: The Free Press.

Wilson, W. (1973, first published 1885), *Congressional Government*, Cleveland, OH, USA: The World Publishing Company.

Wilson, W. (2004, first published 1908), *Constitutional Government in the United States*, New Brunswick, NJ, USA: Transaction Publishers.

Index

WHY INDIA NEEDS THE PRESIDENTIAL SYSTEM